Biography Today

*Profiles
of People
of Interest
to Young
Readers*

Authors

Volume 18

Cherie D. Abbey
Managing Editor

615 Griswold Street • Detroit, Michigan 48226

Cherie D. Abbey, *Managing Editor*

Joan Axelrod-Contrada, Sheila Fitzgerald, Margaret Haerens, Eve Nagler, Diane Telgen, and Thomas Wiloch, *Sketch Writers*

Allison A. Beckett, Mary Butler, and Linda Strand, *Research Staff*

* * *

Peter E. Ruffner, *Publisher*
Frederick G. Ruffner, Jr., *Chairman*
Matthew P. Barbour, *Senior Vice President*
Kay Gill, *Vice President — Directories*

* * *

Elizabeth Barbour, *Research and Permissions Coordinator*
David P. Bianco, *Marketing Director*
Kevin Hayes, *Operations Manager*
Barry Puckett, *Librarian*
Cherry Stockdale, *Permissions Assistant*

Shirley Amore, Kevin Glover, Martha Johns,
Kirk Kauffman, and Angelesia Thorington, *Administrative Staff*

This book is printed on acid-free paper meeting the ANSI Z39.48 Standard. The infinity symbol that appears above indicates that the paper in this book meets that standard.

Printed in the United States

Contents

Preface 5

Bill Amend 1962- 9
American Cartoonist and Creator of the Comic Strip *FoxTrot*

Joseph Bruchac 1942- 24
American Writer and Storyteller of Native American Heritage

Gennifer Choldenko 1957- 43
American Author of Children's Books, Creator of *Al Capone Does My Shirts*

Shannon Hale 1974- 54
American Fantasy Writer, Author of *Princess Academy*

Carl Hiaasen 1953- 66
American Reporter, Novelist, and Author of the Young Adult Novels *Hoot* and *Flush*

Will Hobbs 1947- 80
American Young Adult Novelist, Author of *Downriver, Far North,* and *Jason's Gold*

Kathryn Lasky 1944- 94
American Writer for Children and Young Adults, Prolific Author of Historical Novels and Nonfiction Works

Arnold Lobel 1933-1987 113
American Author and Illustrator; Creator of the "Frog and Toad" Series, *Fables,* and Other Beloved Books for Children

Janet McDonald 1953- 129
American Novelist for Young Adults, Winner of the 2003 Coretta Scott King/John Steptoe Award for New Talent

Deborah Wiles 1953- 145
   American Children's Writer, Author of *Freedom Summer* and
   Each Little Bird That Sings

Photo and Illustration Credits 157

Cumulative Index 159
   (Includes Names, Occupations, Nationalities, and
   Ethnic and Minority Origins)

The Biography Today Library 205

Preface

Welcome to the 18th volume of the **Biography Today Author Series**. We are publishing this series in response to suggestions from our readers, who want more coverage of more people in *Biography Today*. Several volumes, covering **Artists, Authors, Business Leaders, Performing Artists, Scientists and Inventors, Sports Figures,** and **World Leaders,** have appeared thus far in the Subject Series. Each of these hardcover volumes is 200 pages in length and covers approximately 10 individuals of interest to readers ages 9 and above. The length and format of the entries are like those found in the regular issues of *Biography Today*, but there is **no duplication** between the regular series and the special subject volumes.

The Plan of the Work

As with the regular issues of *Biography Today*, this special subject volume on **Authors** was especially created to appeal to young readers in a format they can enjoy reading and readily understand. Each volume contains alphabetically arranged sketches. Each entry provides at least one picture of the individual profiled, and bold-faced rubrics lead the reader to information on birth, youth, early memories, education, first jobs, marriage and family, career highlights, memorable experiences, hobbies, and honors and awards. Each of the entries ends with a list of easily accessible sources designed to lead the student to further reading on the individual and a current address. Obituary entries are also included, written to provide a perspective on the individual's entire career. Obituaries are clearly marked in both the table of contents and at the beginning of the entry.

Biographies are prepared by Omnigraphics editors after extensive research, utilizing the most current materials available. Those sources that are generally available to students appear in the list of further reading at the end of the sketch.

Indexes

Cumulative indexes are an important component of *Biography Today*. Each issue of the *Biography Today* Subject Series includes a **Cumulative General Index**, which comprises all individuals profiled in *Biography Today* since the series began in 1992. The names appear in bold faced type, followed by the issue in which they appeared. The Cumulative General Index also contains the occupations, nationalities, and ethnic and minority origins of individuals profiled. In addition, we compile three other indexes: Names Index, Places of Birth Index, and Birthday Index. These three indexes are featured on our web site, www.biographytoday.com. All *Biography Today* indexes are cumulative, including all individuals profiled in both the General Series and the Subject Series.

Our Advisors

This series was reviewed by an Advisory Board comprised of librarians, children's literature specialists, and reading instructors to ensure that the concept of this publication — to provide a readable and accessible biographical magazine for young readers — was on target. They evaluated the title as it developed, and their suggestions have proved invaluable. Any errors, however, are ours alone. We'd like to list the Advisory Board members, and to thank them for their efforts.

Gail Beaver
Adjunct Lecturer
University of Michigan
Ann Arbor, MI

Cindy Cares
Youth Services Librarian
Southfield Public Library
Southfield, MI

Carol A. Doll
School of Information Science and Policy
University of Albany, SUNY
Albany, NY

Kathleen Hayes-Parvin
Language Arts Teacher
Birney Middle School
Southfield, MI

Karen Imarisio
Assistant Head of Adult Services
Bloomfield Twp. Public Library
Bloomfield Hills, MI

Rosemary Orlando
Director
St. Clair Shores Public Library
St. Clair Shores, MI

Our Advisory Board stressed to us that we should not shy away from controversial or unconventional people in our profiles, and we have tried to follow their advice. The Advisory Board also mentioned that the sketches might be useful in reluctant reader and adult literacy programs, and we would value any comments librarians might have about the suitability of our magazine for those purposes.

Your Comments Are Welcome

Our goal is to be accurate and up-to-date, to give young readers information they can learn from and enjoy. Now we want to know what you think. Take a look at this issue of *Biography Today*, on approval. Write or call me with your comments. We want to provide an excellent source of biographical information for young people. Let us know how you think we're doing.

Cherie Abbey
Managing Editor, *Biography Today*
Omnigraphics, Inc.
615 Griswold Street
Detroit, MI 48226

editor@biographytoday.com
www.biographytoday.com

Bill Amend 1962-

American Cartoonist
Creator of the Comic Strip *FoxTrot*

BIRTH

Bill Amend (rhymes with Raymond) was born in 1962 in Northampton, Massachusetts. His father is a doctor, and his mother is a travel agent. The oldest of four children, Amend has two brothers and a sister.

YOUTH

Amend spent his early years in New England, and some of his childhood memories have been recreated in his popular

9

comic strip *FoxTrot*. "A lot of the chaos that goes on in *FoxTrot* is somewhat a depiction of the chaos that went on in my own household as a kid," he said. Amend has called the three years he lived in Newton, Massachusetts, his "Jason Fox" era. That's when he was around the same age at the nerdy 10-year-old Jason in *FoxTrot* and had a similar passion for math and science. Like Jason, Amend had a pet named Quincy—but in his case it was a hamster. He later named Jason's iguana after his childhood pet.

In elementary school, Amend wanted to become a member of the secret service, the law enforcement agency that protects the president, the vice president, and other high government officials. But Amend didn't want to be a typical agent—he wanted to be just like James West from his favorite TV show, "The Wild, Wild West."

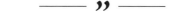

> *Amend began drawing cartoons for fun when he was nine. "I liked to draw frogs and dinosaurs which may partly explain why I have an iguana in my strip,"*
> *he explained.*

Amend began drawing cartoons for fun when he was nine. "I liked to draw frogs and dinosaurs which may partly explain why I have an iguana in my strip," he explained. When he was in fourth or fifth grade, he and a friend created a comic book starring a super hero. He often spent his allowance on purchases of comic books and *Mad* magazine.

When Amend was 12, his family moved from the East Coast to California, settling in the San Francisco Bay area.

EDUCATION

Burlingame High School

Amend attended Burlingame High School in Burlingame, California. He was an excellent student in high school, earning an "A" average. He was also president of the math club and played tuba in the school band. After many years of being a Boy Scout, he earned the rank of Eagle Scout, the highest rank in Boy Scouts. During his teen years, Amend created his own movies on Super-8 film. His longest film project was called "Trek Wars," and it was full of homemade explosions. For a while, he thought about pursuing a career as a filmmaker. "I had aspirations to be the next George Lucas or Steven Spielberg," he said, referring to the famous movie directors.

Meanwhile, Amend kept drawing cartoons, and many were published in school publications. One cartoon strip that wasn't very successful was

The FoxTrot *kids: Paige, Jason, and Peter.*

about a dog. "The idea was that this little dog would be brutally killed in every strip," Amend recalled. "The first strip featured this cute little puppy dog being thrown into a pit of lions by an old lady. It ran one day. I was politely informed that they didn't need my services any more."

The teenaged Amend also tried to sell his cartoons. When he was a sophomore or junior in high school, he made a trip to the Lee Mendelson Film Productions headquarters in Burlingame. The Mendelson company produced the animated movies of the *Peanuts* comic strip. "I remember gathering up my courage and loading up all kinds of cartoons I had drawn," Amend said. "I assumed that was where they made the Charlie Brown Christmas movie and all that. I went in there with all my cartoons, ready to sell myself. There was a secretary behind the desk, smoking a cigarette, and then no one else. I said, 'Where are all the animators hard at work?' She said, "Oh no, honey. That's all done in Los Angeles.'"

Amend became a big fan of the comic strip *Doonesbury* while he was in high school. He was also inspired by several strips that were retired: *The Far Side, Calvin and Hobbes,* and *Bloom County,* which was later revived. "There are not really any strips out there that still excite me as much as those four did," he said.

FoxTrot *by Bill Amend.*

Amherst College

Amend returned to his New England roots to attend Amherst College in Amherst, Massachusetts.

He majored in physics. "My major was probably not the most direct route to success in the cartooning business," he admitted, "but it did help me with Jason's character because he's such a little math and science wizard." Except for a basic drawing class in his senior year, he never studied art. "Some say it shows," he joked.

Amend worked for the *Amherst Student* while in college, creating editorial cartoons and writing opinion pieces. He became the opinion editor of the paper, and often worked through the night to get the bi-weekly newspaper ready for publication. He eventually left the staff. "During my junior year, the *Student* was announcing editorial positions for the next term," Amend recalled. "When a friend and I didn't get the promotions we thought we deserved, we quit in a huff and started our own paper." That newspaper, called *Sidelines,* was an entertainment weekly about movies, film, and popular culture. For the next year and a half, Amend wrote, edited, and contributed cartoons to the paper.

Amend graduated with honors from Amherst in 1984 with a Bachelor of Arts (BA) degree in physics. "Amherst exposed me to a whole array of disci-

plines and interests," he said. Amend sprinkles references to the college in *FoxTrot*, including names of his former teachers. Careful readers of the strip will notice that Peter, the 16-year-old son in the strip, always wears a cap with an "A" on it.

CAREER HIGHLIGHTS

Early Rejections

After college, Amend moved back to California to pursue his dream of being a cartoonist. He created a comic strip called *Bango Ridge*, which featured talking animals in the jungle. He sent it to several syndicates, the companies that sell comic strips to newspapers, but none of them would take him on. "I never got a 'no,'" Amend recalled. "I got a bunch of, 'Well, it's not so bad, keep sending us stuff.'"

Meanwhile, Amend worked for a while for animation and film companies in San Francisco. His brief career as an assistant animator hit a low point when he accidentally erased and then re-drew the work of a lead animator. "There was a period in my life for about a year when I was essentially unemployed and living with my parents," he admitted.

Amend said that his parents were supportive during this "pathetic" time of unemployment. "I'd get subtle hints every now and then," he recalled. "I

13

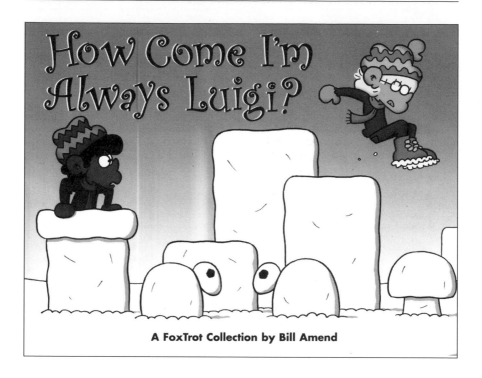

A FoxTrot Collection by Bill Amend

remember watching some TV about the space shuttle and my parents were in the room, and I said, 'It would be pretty cool to work for NASA.' I remember my dad saying, 'Aeronautical engineering, Bill. In case that cartooning thing doesn't work out.'"

Creating *FoxTrot*

Amend kept sending samples to the comic-strip syndicates, and he took some encouragement from the rejection letters that the syndicates kept sending him. "I got the sense from the letters that my writing and humor [were] good and that my artwork was fairly decent and that the main problem was the concept of my strip," he said.

Amend decided to create a family strip with characters that would display the tensions and humor of modern American life. "I looked at the funny pages, and most of the strips out there seemed to be very safe, very tame, and almost rooted in a bygone era," he said. "There didn't seem to be anything at the time that I connected with as a young adult in America. My sense of family life was that there was a lot more chaos and politics and silliness and fewer trips to the golf course and running into the mailman."

Amend's inspiration resulted in *FoxTrot*, a comic strip that showcases the lives of the Fox family: Roger and Andy Fox and their three children, Peter, Paige, and Jason. They live in a suburb that is never named. "I grew up in New England and Northern California, and I think bits of that come through," Amend said, "but it's nowhere specific."

After two years of submitting and resubmitting the strip to the comic syndicates, he finally got a contract from Universal Press Syndicate. *FoxTrot* debuted in newspapers across the country on April 10, 1988, when Amend was 25 years old. It didn't take long for the strip to win a devoted following, including Lucy Shelton Caswell, professor and curator of the Ohio State Cartoon Research Library. "Bill has created believable characters," Caswell told *Editor and Publisher*. "He does gags, but *FoxTrot* is not just a gag-a-day-strip. It's character driven."

The *Foxtrot* Characters

The characters in *FoxTrot* all have their own distinctive personalities. Roger, the balding father, is a pleasant, dreamy man who works for a nameless corporation. He is no match for his demanding children, although he tries to encourage family togetherness with outdoor trips. "Roger is sort of an overworked, confused dad who hasn't figured how to keep up with his kids," Amend said. "He stands there bravely as waves of life go past."

Amend had a tough time getting started in his career. "There was a period in my life for about a year when I was essentially unemployed and living with my parents."

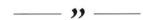

Andy (short for Andrea), the mother, works at home as a columnist for a local newspaper. She is the one who keeps the kids in line, and is wise to many of their tricks. Amend calls her the "sanest" member of the family. Andy is always trying to get her children to play less violent video games and eat more healthy food—although most of what she cooks sounds pretty disgusting.

Peter, 16, a high-school junior, loves sports and music, but he's not very talented in either field. He is a member of his high school baseball team, but is always on the bench. He tries to bulk up by eating a lot, but can't seem to gain weight. Despite these flaws, Peter is "an egomaniac who thinks very highly of himself," said Amend. Peter's girlfriend, Denise, has no problem putting him in his place. The plain-talking Denise is blind, which is a rare handicap to be portrayed in a comic strip. Denise was a

FoxTrot *by Bill Amend.*

recurring character early on, but she has been seen much less frequently in recent years.

Paige, 14, is a high-school freshman. She loves fashion, shopping, and talking on the telephone. She is boy-crazy and spends hours with her girl-friends mooning about boys. She is always complaining about the other members of the family, especially Jason, who loves to make her look fool-ish. She puts up with a lot of aggravation from her younger brother, Jason, who likes to torment her.

At age 10, Jason is the undisputed *FoxTrot* star. He is a math whiz, a computer geek, and a physics nerd. He is up on every new trend in computers, video games, movies, and television. He likes to hang out with his friend, the equally nerdy Marcus. While very intelligent, Jason lacks common sense, which often gets him into trouble. The Fox household has seen more than one of Jason's experiments go awry. "Jason prays for homework and hard tests and freaks out if he 'only' gets an A++ on tests," Amend says. Jason loves to show off how smart he is, which drives his sister crazy.

Jason provides the outlet for Amend's interest in technology. When the strip started, "[Jason] let me talk about modems and computer and high-tech gadgets," Amend said. "At the time, this was not particularly main-stream. Now Jason very much represents the younger computer genera-tion. I accidentally captured that in a way readers enjoy." Amend has called

all the characters in *FoxTrot* an extension of himself, with Jason being the closest.

Jason has a pet iguana named Quincy, named after Amend's childhood pet. Amend has described the iguana as a "kind of prop. He makes appearances from time, to time, largely in some situation resulting in a scream from Paige." In one memorable series of strips, Paige is beside herself when Quincy chews up her autographed photograph of a rock group. Andy had promised to look after the photo while Paige was in school. Then, in a typical *FoxTrot* twist, Paige uses her mother's guilty feelings to get Andy to wait on her hand and foot—until new autographed photos arrive.

How *FoxTrot* Has Changed Over the Years

During the first five years of *FoxTrot*, Amend wrote the strip mostly from the children's point of view. Then he got married and started having children of his own. "I see the parents' side of things a little more readily than I used to," he said. But he still relates to his younger readers. "I'm blessed, I guess, with a sort of immature sensibility," he explained. "I tell my wife, 'I have to play these video games. It's research.' Or, 'I have to go see Godzilla at the matinee show today. Research.'"

The characters have also changed over time, especially Jason and Paige. "In the first five years, there was a lot more fighting between Jason and Paige,"

Amend said. "Then I thought, 'This is turning into a Tom and Jerry [cat and mouse cartoon characters who always fight], so I mellowed their relationship a bit. I'm trying to keep the strip fresh, interesting to read and interesting to do."

When Amend started the strip, he thought his readers would be mostly young, college-educated adults. But as it turned out, his most enthusiastic fans are kids around 12 years old. "I ask myself how could they possibly get these jokes?" Amend said. "But they seem to, and I like the fact that there seem to be some smart kids out there."

> ————— " —————
>
> *"There is a moment in just about every week where I stare at my blank piece of paper and think that the well has at last run dry and it's all over for me. And then somehow, through a mix of panic and caffeine I get seven decent ideas out to live to see another week."*
>
> ————— " —————

FoxTrot has many adult fans who like the math problems and scientific terms that often turn up in the strip, including Peter Beyersdorf, a California physics teacher. "People don't notice, but in the background of his comics there are little math references and physics references," Beyersdorf told the *San Francisco Chronicle*. "If you just read the text, you'll miss out on a lot. Look at the pictures that are posted on the refrigerator. The kids' drawings. The pictures in the background on the walls. Whenever someone's reading a newspaper, you'll look on the back and there will be an article: 'Cartoonist parties after Oscars.'"

Not all parents are *FoxTrot* fans, however. Once the strip became popular, Amend began to get some letters asking him why the characters in the strip had to argue so much and use insulting language. One letter asked why the *FoxTrot* kids couldn't be better role models. Amend said that "got me where it hurts. I genuinely like children. I was a camp counselor. I taught kids. I'm a parent." At first Amend thought the criticism was unfair, since his characters are, after all, cartoon figures. But then he remembered that as a kid, he had tried to dive down the stairs like a Fantastic Four cartoon character. So in recent years, he's tried to choose his language a little more carefully, although the Foxes still have plenty of arguments. To do otherwise, Amend said, would make the family unrecognizable and not nearly as funny. "If you want kids to take away a positive message, you have to be honest with them," he said.

FoxTrot's popularity has grown steadily over the years, as more and more newspapers have signed on to carry the strip. In 1999, *FoxTrot* passed the 1,000-newspaper mark, which is considered the "gold standard" in comic-strip syndication. Very few strips ever reach that level of success. When told of the news, Amend said he was very flattered. "I was excited for 15 minutes and then went back to work," he recalled. "It's a nice round number, but it doesn't change what I do. I do the same thing now as when I was in 50 papers, although the checks are bigger."

Coming Up with Fresh Ideas

Creating a daily comic strip can be very challenging, Amend has said. "There is a moment in just about every week where I stare at my blank piece of paper and think that the well has at last run dry and it's all over for me," he explained. "And then somehow, through a mix of panic and caffeine I get seven decent ideas out to live to see another week. I think what helps me most is through luck and design, I've put together a cast of characters that lets me cover a very wide range of subjects. So I can write computer jokes and golf jokes and academic jokes, etc., and having that range gives me a lot of options when ideas seem scarce."

19

FoxTrot *by Bill Amend.*

Children often send Amend suggestions for storylines, but he prefers to come up with the ideas himself. "Every now and then I'll get an e-mail of some kid saying, 'I think you should add a new character named Billy who skateboards and he's not good in English but he's really good at math.' Signed Billy Johnson. Those are fun."

Amend uses pencils and markers to create his strips. In recent years, he's started to scan the images onto his Macintosh computer and use the software program Photoshop to position and shade them. This lets him work on the art and dialogue until right before his deadline, which is two weeks before a strip is published in the newspaper. Amend does all the work on the strips by himself, in addition to maintaining his web sites, working on his book collections, and answering e-mail requests. He didn't get any time off from *FoxTrot* until 1995, when Universal Press Syndicate began to allow its veteran cartoonists four weeks off a year. "I don't get holidays or sick days off, or any of the normal breaks from work regular folks enjoy," Amend said. "My suspicion is Universal's vacation policy has kept me out of the loony bin."

Advice for Young Cartoonists

Amend gets many letters from children who want to know how they can become cartoonists. "I recommend that the aspiring cartoonist obtain the

best possible education he/she can in as broad a range of subjects as possible," Amend wrote on the FAQ (Frequently Asked Questions) section of the *FoxTrot* web site, http://www.foxtrot.com. "Too many young cartoonists forget that what makes a comic strip work is much more than the ability to draw funny pictures. What sustains a strip, what makes it worth reading day after day, is the mind behind it."

MARRIAGE AND FAMILY

Amend and his wife live in Kansas City, Missouri, with their two children and the family dog, a German Shepherd. Amend became familiar with Kansas City while making business trips to the Kansas City headquarters of Universal Press Syndicate. He and his wife liked the area and the relatively inexpensive home prices. "It's an awfully nice place, and we didn't have to commit to staying," he said. "We came out here with the intention of staying just a few years." The family has grown very attached to the area and has settled in. Amend's studio is right at home, above the garage. "It would be tough to leave at this point," he said.

Amend's school-aged children have gotten old enough to read and appreciate the humor of *FoxTrot*. His son has even imitated some of Jason's behavior. "He's been scolded for things I have Jason doing in the strip," Amend said. "It's sort of flattering and sort of weird."

HOBBIES AND OTHER INTERESTS

Like his cartoon creation Jason Fox, Amend loves computers and likes to keep up with the latest equipment and software. He is a fan of Apple Computer's Macintosh, and has included references and jokes about the iMac, which he calls iFruit, in *FoxTrot*. He maintains two web sites, http://www.foxtrot.com and http://homepage.mac.com/billamend, which include games for *FoxTrot* fans.

SELECTED WORKS

All the following are collections of *FoxTrot*.

FoxTrot, 1989
Pass the Loot, 1990
FoxTrot: The Works, 1990 (anthology)
Black Bart Says Draw, 1991
Eight Yards, Down and Out, 1992
FoxTrot En Masse, 1992 (anthology)
Bury My Heart at Fun-Fun Mountain, 1993
Say Hello to Cactus Flats, 1993
Enormously FoxTrot, 1994 (anthology)
May the Force Be With Us, Please, 1994
Take Us to Your Mall, 1995
Wildly FoxTrot, 1995 (anthology)
The Return of the Lone Iguana, 1996
At Least This Place Sells T-Shirts, 1996
FoxTrot Beyond a Doubt, 1997 (anthology)
Come Closer, Roger, There's a Mosquito on Your Nose, 1997
Welcome to Jasorassic Park, 1998
Camp Fox Trot, 1998 (anthology)
I'm Flying, Jack ... I Mean Roger, 1999
Think iFruity, 2000
Assorted FoxTrot, 2000 (anthology)
Death By Field Trip, 2001
Encyclopedias Brown and White, 2001
His Code Name Was the Fox, 2002
FoxTrot: Assembled With Care, 2002 (anthology)
Your Momma Thinks Square Roots Are Vegetables, 2003
Who's Up for Some Bonding?, 2003
Am I a Mutant, or What!, 2004
FoxTrot Maximus, 2004 (anthology)
My Hot Dog Went Out, Can I Have Another?, 2005

Orlando Bloom Has Ruined Everything, 2005
How Come I'm Always Luigi?, 2006

FURTHER READING

Books

Authors and Artists for Young Adults, Vol. 52, 2003
Contemporary Authors, Vol. 221, 2004

Periodicals

Akron Beacon Journal, Dec. 7, 1997, p.D1
Current Biography Yearbook, 2003
Dallas Morning News, June 8, 1998, p.C4
Editor & Publisher, Sep. 9, 1995; Apr. 17, 1999, p52; July 14, 2003, p.29
Kansas City Star, May 31, 2004, p.D1
News and Observer, Jan. 1, 1996, p.C1
San Francisco Chronicle, Dec. 8, 2004, p.E1
St. Petersburg Times, Aug. 25, 2003, p.D3

Online Articles

http://www.amherst.edu/~astudent/1999-2000/issue005/features/06.shtml
    (Amherst Student Online, "Amend '84 Does Funny Business," 1999)
http://www.macworld.com/2001/06/bc/buzzamend/index.php?pf=1
    (Macworld.com, "Pro File: Drawn to the Mac, Q&A with Bill Amend,"
    June 1, 2001)
http://www.ucomics.com/foxtrot/bio.phtml
    (ucomics.com, "Meet Bill Amend," no date)
http://www.wired.com/news/culture/0,1284,31981,00.html
    (Wired News, "Of Physics and the Funny Papers," Nov. 1, 1999)

Online Databases

Biography Resource Center Online, 2006, articles from *Authors and Artists for Young Adults,* 2003 and *Contemporary Authors Online,* 2004

WORLD WIDE WEB SITES

http://www.foxtrot.com
http://homepage.mac.com/billamend

Joseph Bruchac 1942-

American Author
Writer and Storyteller of Native American Heritage

BIRTH

Joseph Bruchac III (pronounced BROO-shack) was born on
October 16, 1942, in Saratoga Springs, New York, to Joseph
Bruchac, Jr., a taxidermist, and Marion Flora Bowman Bruchac.
He has two younger sisters, Mary Ann and Margaret.
Bruchac's family background includes Slovak and English
roots, but it is his Native American heritage, on his mother's
side, that has become the cornerstone of his life.

YOUTH

Bruchac grew up in the home of his maternal grandparents, Jesse Bowman and Marion Dunham Bowman. His grandmother was a very educated woman: she graduated from law school, but never practiced law. His grandfather did not finish grade school and could barely read and write. Jesse Bowman was "a dark-skinned, very Indian-looking man," Bruchac said, but he always denied his Abenaki Indian ancestry, insisting that he was French. "I know now that he did this because of the prejudice against Indians that his family and many other Native families in the Northeast had experienced," Bruchac wrote in his memoir, *Bowman's Store: A Journey to Myself.*

Bruchac's grandparents ran a general store and gas station, called Bowman's Store, in the small, rural town of Greenfield Center, New York. He lived in his grandparents' house next to the store with his parents and baby sister Mary Ann. When he was almost two years old, his parents moved out, taking Mary Ann with them. Bruchac was supposed to stay with his grandparents for only a short time, but remained with them throughout his childhood. "Though my parents' home was less than half a mile away from Bowman's Store, I never spent a single night under their roof," Bruchac said.

In his memoir, Bruchac never explained why he stayed with his grandparents or why he didn't go to live with his parents. But he did share this story: "Because I grew up with my grandparents I did not see a great deal of my parents when I was a child. Mary Ann would spend Saturday night with us sometimes when my parents went out together, but it was never the other way around. I never spent the night at my parents' house. When I was 11 years old, they built a new house, 50 yards from the old one that Grampa and Grama had given to them, on the 80 acres of property that we always called 'The Farm.' In that house there was a bedroom for me. They called it 'Sonny's room.' It was always empty."

As a young boy, Bruchac spent so much time with his grandfather that people called him "Jess's Shadow." A favorite activity was gardening. While

---

> "
>
> *"Because I grew up with my grandparents I did not see a great deal of my parents when I was a child. [My sister] Mary Ann would spend Saturday night with us sometimes when my parents went out together, but it was never the other way around. I never spent the night at my parents' house."*
>
> "

learning how to plant corn and other vegetables, Bruchac soaked up his grandfather's stories about nature and animals. He "really planted the seed in me that would continue as an adult, wanting to be close to nature, and wanting to know more about that heritage that I knew was there, but that I hadn't been given directly," Bruchac said.

Bruchac did not have many friends. "Because we lived in the country, I didn't play much with other children," he remembered. "I was buried in my grandmother's books half the time and outside with my grandfather in the woods and fields the other half." Bruchac started to write creatively in the second grade. "I wrote poems to my teacher," he recalled. "One day, when she read one to the class, some of the bigger boys got jealous. They beat me up after school . . . but I kept on writing. And I was always reading, especially classic children's stories about animals."

> ———— " ————
>
> *"Because we lived in the country, I didn't play much with other children. I was buried in my grandmother's books half the time and outside with my grandfather in the woods and fields the other half."*
>
> ———— " ————

Bruchac liked helping his grandparents run their store. He worked the cash register, stocked shelves, and pumped gas. In the fall and winter, neighborhood people often gathered around the wood stove in the store, swapping stories. Bruchac loved to listen to them. "Hearing those stories about the things people in town did and said, sometimes [playing] a song or a fiddle tune from the Adirondack woods — for 'Grampa' Jesse had been a logger — stirred my imagination," he said. "It made me want to tell stories, too."

EDUCATION

High School

Bruchac attended Saratoga Springs High School in Sarasota Springs, New York. By his junior year, he had shot up in height to almost six foot, two inches. High school coaches encouraged him to become more athletic. Bruchac joined the track-and-field team and learned to throw the shot put and discus, and he also played right tackle for the football team. But it was as a wrestler that he really shone. To get on the wrestling team, the 200-pound Bruchac had to beat the school's starting heavyweight, who was 80 pounds heavier. He did. It was the first of many wrestle-off victories that

Bruchac achieved through high school. In his senior year, he won the Western Conference Tournament of New York State, as his grandfather cheered him on. Bruchac went on to win many wrestling trophies in college. "But no trophy or award that I've been given means more to me than the small metal figure of a wrestler, arms held out as if ready to begin again a match that would reward an old man's pride and prove that a small boy's dreams really can come true," he wrote in his memoir.

In addition to his athletic achievements, Bruchac was also a good student, especially in English, social studies, and science. Along with many other New York State high school students, he competed for a merit scholarship to a state college. Students took a standardized test and the highest scorers were awarded a Regents Scholarship. Bruchac was one of the winners.

BOWMAN'S STORE
◇ A JOURNEY TO MYSELF ◇

JOSEPH BRUCHAC

In his memoir, Bruchac reveals stories about his early life, especially about his life with his grandparents. On the cover, he is shown with his grandfather.

Cornell University

Bruchac attended Cornell University in Ithaca, New York. He joined Cornell's wrestling team and was a varsity heavyweight wrestler for four years, before a neck injury ended his career two weeks before the national wrestling tournament.

When he first got to Cornell, Bruchac was enrolled in the School of Agriculture. He wanted to pursue a career as a naturalist or park ranger. But he was also interested in writing and signed up for a creative writing class. After three weeks of trying his hand at poetry, the instructor told him that he would never write a good poem. "From that point on, I literally ate, slept, and dreamed poetry," he remembered. Bruchac eventually improved enough to have several of his poems published in *The Trojan Horse*, Cornell's literary magazine. He began to think about becoming a professional writer. "I wanted to write about the natural world—and the more I wrote, the more the writing led me into a quest for my own Native ancestry," Bruchac said.

In his third year at Cornell, Bruchac transferred to the School of Arts and Sciences, which meant he would have to spend an extra year at college to fulfill a new major. At about the same time he was changing majors, he met Carol Worthen. They were married in a chapel on the Cornell campus, and worked to pay for their own expenses while Bruchac was still in school. He graduated from Cornell in 1965, with a Bachelor of Arts (BA) degree in English literature.

Graduate School

For graduate school, Bruchac won a creative writing fellowship to Syracuse University in Syracuse, New York. The Onondaga Indian Reservation was only a few miles away, and he often went to visit the reservation elders. The stories and poems he wrote during this period reflect his search to understand his Native roots. Bruchac graduated from Syracuse in 1966 with a Master of Arts (MA) degree in literature and creative writing. He later returned to school, earning a doctorate (PhD) in 1975 in comparative literature from the Union Institute of Ohio Graduate School.

FIRST JOBS

Volunteer in Africa

After graduating from Syracuse, Bruchac and his wife joined a volunteer teachers' program called Teachers for West Africa. He taught English and literature at Keta Secondary School in Ghana from 1966 to 1969. He learned "a great deal about traditional community," he said. "I'll never forget the warmth and beauty and depth of Ewe culture [the daily lives and customs of Native Ghanians]. But Africa also taught me about myself and my own country. For one, it gave me the perspective to see the Abenaki Indian heritage that had been set aside by generations before me."

While in Africa, Bruchac was inspired by the Nigerian novelist Chinua Achebe. "I taught his books when I was a volunteer in Ghana," Bruchac said, "and I have tried to follow his example—portraying my own Native people honestly, using stories as a source of inspiration, countering the bad images other writers have created in the past."

When Bruchac and his wife and infant son, James, returned from Ghana in 1969, they moved into the house where his grandparents had raised him.

His grandmother had died by then, and his grandfather died about six months later. Bruchac took a job at Skidmore College in Saratoga Springs, teaching African and black literatures and creative writing. In 1974, he became the coordinator of Skidmore's University Without Walls program at Great Meadow Correctional Facility, a maximum-security prison in Comstock, New York. Bruchac inspired many prisoners to express themselves through creative writing. "I would see this light come on in their eyes," he recalled. "They're all human beings. Every human being has a story to tell." Nick Di Spoldo, a former prisoner who became a published writer with Bruchac's help, wrote in *America* magazine that Bruchac gave "fresh motivation to countless men and women, developing and nurturing tender talents and fragile egos, with the sincerity of a saint."

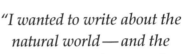

"I wanted to write about the natural world — and the more I wrote, the more the writing led me into a quest for my own Native ancestry," Bruchac said.

In 1975 Bruchac was awarded a grant from the National Endowment of the Arts, which he used to expand his prison program. He started publishing the *Prison Project Newsletter*, which became a showcase of aspiring prison writers. He also traveled to prisons throughout the country, often paying his own way, to establish writing workshops and train instructors.

Meanwhile, in 1970, Bruchac and his wife established the Greenfield Review Press. Its first book, a collection of poems written by prisoners in California, was published a year later. Since then, Greenfield Press has printed some of Bruchac's work, as well as books from writers of many cultures, including African, African American, Arab American, Asian American, American Indian, Caribbean, and Chicano. The company continues to be a small, family-run organization.

CAREER HIGHLIGHTS

Bruchac is a prolific author who has written over 70 books. His poems, articles, and stories have appeared in over 500 publications, and he's won many awards for his work. He's written for various audiences, including elementary and middle-school children, teenagers, and adults. His writing covers a wide range of styles, including folk tales, legends, nonfiction, and fiction. He has also edited several anthologies of poetry and fiction. Bruchac's work typically covers Native American themes and history, portraying the importance of respect for family, the environment, and animals.

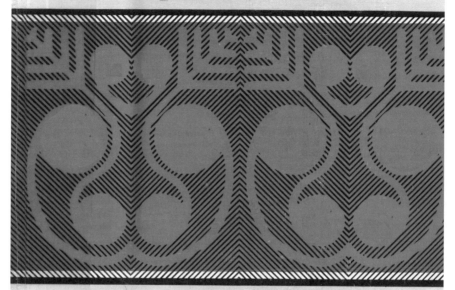

Turkey Brother and Other Tales, *a collection of folk tales, was Bruchac's first book for children.*

He has also aimed to "gently correct," as one reviewer noted, the stereotypes of Native Americans and their culture that are depicted in many books and films.

Bruchac started his career as a poet, contributing to many adult poetry magazines. His first book, *Indian Mountain and Other Poems,* was published in 1971. Four other volumes of poetry soon followed. He also edited several poetry anthologies, including the award-winning *Breaking Silence: An Anthology of Contemporary Asian American Poets* (1983).

Becoming a Writer for Children

By 1972, Bruchac was the father of two young sons, and he often told them stories of Native folklore. "I think the process of storytelling and the process of writing can be deeply connected," he said. "I'd try to type the stories as I listened to myself tell them." The result, *Turkey Brother and Other Tales: Iroquois Folk Stories*, published in 1975, was his first book for children. The title story is about two brothers who return to their homeland. The turtle is the star of three stories, which tell how he uses his brain to overcome his slow pace. Another story tells the legend of how the bear got a short tail. These tales "emphasize the Indian principle of kindness to animals," Marily Richards noted in a review in *School Library Journal*. "The stories are well paced and make their point without condescension or moralizing."

Bruchac discovered that he enjoyed being a children's author, and the majority of his work since then has been for kids. "[Children] really, deeply appreciate what you do," he said. "They're not just reading you because you're the latest bestseller and everybody else is buying the book." He liked being able to entertain and educate children.

> **"**
>
> *"[Children] really, deeply appreciate what you do,"* Bruchac said about writing for kids. *"They're not just reading you because you're the latest bestseller and everybody else is buying the book."*
>
> **"**

Collections of Shorter Works — Folktales, Poems, Short Stories, and More

Since his first collection of folk tales, Bruchac has published collections of various types of shorter works. He followed up the success of *Turkey Brother* with several other collections of Native American folk stories. Some of his folktale collections feature stories from his own Abenaki heritage. These include *The Wind Eagle and Other Abenaki Stories* (1985) and *The Faithful Hunter: More Abenaki Stories* (1988). In an interview with children for the Scholastic website, Bruchac explained that the Abenaki are part of the larger group of Algonquin native peoples of the northeastern part of the United States and Canada. "Today, many Abenakis live, dress, and work just like other Americans," he said. "However, quite a few of us still practice traditional crafts, gather food from the forest, have festivals together, and retell our old stories." He has also written folktales from other native groups, including the acclaimed *The Boy Who Lived with the Bears and Other Iroquois Stories* (1995).

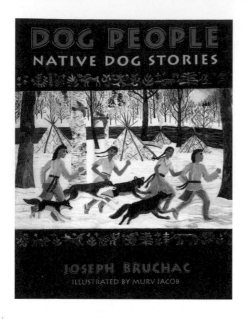

"Bruchac's style is clean and spare," Janice Del Negro wrote in *Booklist*. "His direct, immediate language makes the book accessible to a wide range of children."

In addition to Bruchac's earlier poetry for adults, he has also written poetry for children. One of his best-known collections is *Thirteen Moons on Turtle's Back: A Native American Year of Moons* (1992), which he co-authored with Jonathan London. The book opens with an Abenaki grandfather explaining to his grandson that each of the 13 full moons that appear in a year has a name and a story, and the 13 scales on a turtle's back are the secret to those stories. The poems that follow are based on the moon myths of several Indian tribes and follow the seasons of the year. Some of Bruchac's poetry books include Native American songs. He has also written a collection of plays based on Indian tales called *Pushing Up the Sky: Seven Native American Plays for Children* (2000).

Bruchac has also written several collections of short stories with Native themes. In Native American cultures, children were expected to participate in traditional rites and passages in order to become adults. These traditions included both practical and mystical activities, which Bruchac described in two books of short stories. One collection, *Flying with the Eagle, Racing the Great Bear: Stories from Native North America* (1993), has 16 stories about boys who must pass into manhood. The companion book, *The Girl Who Married the Moon: Tales from Native North America* (1994), which Bruchac co-authored with Gayle Ross, is a collection of 16 growing-up stories about girls. Ross noted in the book's introduction that the role of women in Native American cultures is "perhaps the most falsely portrayed" of all the stereotypes about Indians. "These tales bring a perspective that is little known outside the communities they represent," Karen Hutt wrote in *Booklist*. In his 17-story collection called *Turtle Meat and Other Stories* (1992), written for older teen readers and adults, Bruchac depicted the relationships between Native Americans and their non-Indian neighbors in upstate New York. In another short story collection, *Dog People: Native Dog Stories* (1995), he explored the special relationship between Abenaki Indian children and their dogs. The five stories in this book are set in northern New England 10,000 years ago and show how dogs were not just considered useful animals, but were treated as important members of the family.

The *Keepers* Series

Among Bruchac's best-known works are the four *Keepers* books he co-authored with Michael J. Caduto, an environmental educator. The books are primarily written for educators who want to help children understand their relationship with the environment. It was Caduto's idea to use the stories of Native peoples as teaching tools, and he asked Bruchac to collaborate with him. Bruchac hesitated at first "because I want to make sure, if traditional materials are going to appear in a public format, that they appear in a way that is respectful and proper," he said. "But as I got to know Michael better, I realized he had a sincere interest." Each book has several Native American stories, written by Bruchac, that make a point about the natural world. After each story is a discussion section, crafted by Caputo, and a list of activities for children to try.

The first book, *Keepers of the Earth: Native American Stories and Environmental Activities for Children* (1989), was rejected by 24 publishers before the Colorado-based Fulcrum Publishing Company took it on. The book became a best seller for the small company. *Keepers of the Earth* "is a wonderful tool for teachers who want to remind our children of our cultural heritage and our need to care for our environment," Marya Jansen-Gruber noted in *Children's Literature*.

After that first book, Bruchac and Caduto followed with three additional titles in the series: *Keepers of the Animals: Native American Stories and Wildlife Activities for Children* (1990); *Keepers of Life: Discovering Plants through Native American Stories and Earth Activities for Children* (1994); and *Keepers of the Night: Native American Stories and Nocturnal Activities for Children* (1994).

33

Novels

Bruchac has written several historical novels for young adults; his first novel, *Dawn Land,* was published in 1993. It takes place about 10,000 years ago, when the Abenaki and Iroquois tribes lived in the Adirondack Mountain area. The main character is Young Hunter, an Abenaki warrior, who learns in his dreams that a race of giants, called the Ancient Ones, are coming to destroy his people. He embarks on a journey to find them. In the process, he must rely on his own strength of mind and character, as well as the wisdom passed on by his elders. The book, which is primarily for teenagers and young adults, was very well-reviewed. A sequel, *Long River* (1995), continues Young Hunter's story.

In the introduction to *Dawn Land*, Bruchac addressed the criticism that his portrait of ancient Native life is too idealistic and romantic. In an interview with the journal *MELUS*, he explained, "One thing I try to point out, for example, is that Native patterns of what is called subsistence might be seen as romantic by some observers. You know, showing respect to the animals and praying to their spirits. Some people might say, 'Oh no. They didn't really do that. They weren't intelligent enough to understand ecology.' When in fact, you're really talking about people who have a very practical relationship, because of the necessity of survival, with their environment. And that practical relationship required them to show respect, and not to over-hunt or over-fish or do things that would make it untenable for their children or their children's children to live. I call it practical spirituality."

> "[Native Americans] have a very practical relationship, because of the necessity of survival, with their environment. And that practical relationship required them to show respect, and not to over-hunt or over-fish or do things that would make it untenable for their children or their children's children to live. I call it practical spirituality."

Several of Bruchac's historical novels are set in the more recent past, including *The Arrow Over the Door* (1998), which tells, in alternating narratives, the stories of an Abenaki boy and a Quaker boy during the American Revolutionary War. *Sacajawea: The Story of Bird Woman and the Lewis and Clark Expedition* (2000) is based on the story of the young Indian who helped guide Meriwether Lewis and William Clark on their famous 1804 to 1806 exploration of the Missouri River. Bruchac, who has traveled along many parts of the expedition trail, read the journals of the participants before crafting his novel. "Sacajawea is one of the great stories of America," he said. "The fact that a young woman only in her teens with a small baby to care for could prove to be so good natured, resourceful, and intelligent under some of the worst conditions imaginable, is truly inspiring."

In *The Winter People* (2002), a novel set during the French and Indian War, the story is told by a 14-year-old boy who sees his house destroyed and his mother and sisters taken away. *The Winter People* was called "gripping" by GraceAnne A. DeCandido in *Booklist*. "Historical fiction doesn't get much better than this," DeCandido wrote. Another example of this genre is *Pocahontas* (2003), in which Bruchac tells the tale of the young Indian woman who helped the early English settlers in America. The book has alternating chapters "written" by Pocahontas and by Captain John Smith, the English man she befriended.

Bruchac's most recent historical novel is called *Code Talker: A Novel About the Navajo Marines of World War Two* (2005). It tells the story of Ned Begay, a 16-year-old Navajo Indian. Growing up, he had been forbidden from using his Navajo language in school. But when he enlists in the U.S. Marines during World War II, Ned is trained to use his Native language to radio secret battlefield information and commands. The Navajo language is so complex that the military uses it for a top-secret code. The novel, which is told as a remembrance by the elderly Begay to his grandchildren, is based on true stories of Navajo code breakers that were kept secret until 1969.

Bruchac has also written modern-day, realistic novels about Native American children who are trying to deal with the turmoil in their lives. In *Eagle Song* (1997), Danny Bigtree, a fourth grader from a Mohawk reservation, moves to Brooklyn, New York, and has a hard time adjusting to his new life. In *The Heart of a Chief* (1998), Chris, a 11-year-old sixth grader, lives on a Penacook Indian reservation but goes to a school that has a non-Indian majority. Chris has his hands full dealing with his father's alcoholism, his tribe's debate over whether to permit casino gambling on the reservation, and his school's debate over the use of an Indian name for a sports team. The conflicts in these books "came directly from my experience of working with Native children," Bruchac said, "hearing their questions, listening to their concerns, and sometimes feeling their pain."

In *Skeleton Man* (2001), Bruchac takes an Abenaki ghost story and weaves it into a book of modern fiction with a scary bent. The main character is Molly, a young woman who likes the ancient tale of a monster who eats himself and his relatives—until her parents disappear and it seems like the spooky story has become real. The novel has been compared to the *Goosebump* tales of R.L. Stine and the horror stories of Stephen King. Two other novels in the same scary vein are *The Dark Pond* (2004) and *Whisper in the Dark* (2005).

Books for Younger Readers

Bruchac, along with a series of talented illustrators, has created many picture books. Several are retold Indian folk tales aimed at younger readers, including three books co-authored with his son, James Bruchac: *How Chipmunk Got His Stripes* (2001), *Turtle's Race with Beaver: A Traditional Seneca Story* (2003); and *Raccoon's Last Race: A Traditional Abenaki Story* (2004).

Bruchac has also written a series of picture-book biographies, including *Jim Thorpe's Bright Path* (2004), about the legendary Native American athlete who was a gold-medal winner at the 1912 Olympic Games, as well as a professional baseball and football player. Another book in this genre is *Crazy Horse's Vision* (2000), the story of the famous Lakota Indian chief. As a boy, the chief was called Curly, because of his curly hair. His name was changed to Crazy Horse after the wild horse he mounted couldn't throw him off. After a battle that killed Chief Conquering Bear, Crazy Horse went on a vision quest. Seeking a vision that would guide him, Crazy Horse had a vision that changed his life forever.

One of Bruchac's most famous picture book biographies is the award-winning *A Boy Called Slow: The True Story of Sitting Bull* (1995). It recounts the boyhood of the man who became one of the great Sioux warriors. He was nicknamed Slow, which he disliked, because of the careful and deliberate way he did everything. "Today's children of any background can empathize with his efforts to outgrow his childhood name and take his place as an adult among his people," Carolyn Polese wrote in *School Library Journal*. "By

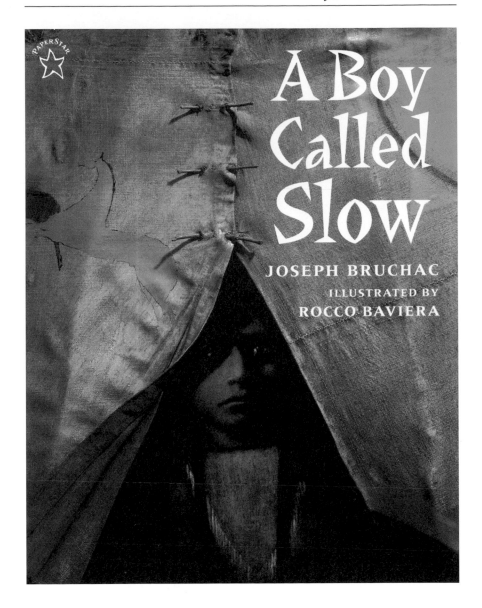

the time Slow earns his new name, young readers will feel they know a real person — the man who was to become Sitting Bull, one of the great Sioux warriors and a hero at the Battle of Little Bighorn," Polese said, referring to the 1876 battle in which the troops of U.S. Army General George Custer were roundly defeated by Sioux and Cheyenne Indians led by Sitting Bull.

As an offshoot of his love of the land, Bruchac wrote *Rachel Carson: Preserving a Sense of Wonder* (2004), a picture tribute to the person whom many people credit with inspiring the environmental movement of the 1960s. Bruchac has also created a picture book of his own life called *Seeing the Circle* (1999). This autobiography tells the story of how Bruchac learned about his Native American background and how he became a writer and storyteller.

Nonfiction Books

Bruchac has also written nonfiction books that cover a wide range of topics and reading levels. In *Trail of Tears* (1999), he recounted how the Cherokees, after fighting to keep their land in the 1800s, were forced to leave and travel 1,200 miles to a new settlement in Oklahoma. Like the Cherokees, the Navajos were forced to relocate, which Bruchac described in *Navajo Long Walk: The Tragic Story of a Proud People's Forced March from Their Homeland* (2002).

> *Once Bruchac develops a fictional character, he or she becomes real to him. "I feel as if that person is making their own decisions and I'm just taking notes! I don't often know what my characters will do until they have done it."*

Bowman's Store: A Journey to Myself (1997), is Bruchac's moving account of growing up with his grandparents in rural, upstate New York, and his discovery of his Native American roots. It is recommended for ages 14 and up, but middle-school readers may enjoy it as well. Bruchac describes another facet of his life, storytelling, in *Tell Me A Tale: A Book about Storytelling* (1997). This book gives tips on how to spin a good tale and has stories for novice storytellers.

Getting Ideas for His Books

Bruchac has gotten some of the inspiration for books in his dreams, as happened with his scary novel *Skeleton Man*. Other ideas have come from suggestions from his editors, who ask him to write about a particular topic or person. Still other ideas have come from children, particularly Native American children, who have asked Bruchac to write about their lives now, as he did in *The Heart of a Chief* and *Eagle Song*. Once Bruchac develops a fictional character, he or she becomes real to him. "I feel as if that person is making their own decisions and I'm just taking notes!" he said. "I don't often know what my characters will do until they have done it."

Advice for Young Writers

Bruchac suggests that aspiring novelists and poets follow the same advice he gives to himself: do a page at a time, and keep at it. "When you write your own story, put everything you know into it," he added. "When you write a poem, keep writing as long as possible. And remember, as my Slovak grandfather, on the European side of my family, always used to say: 'It's easier to cut a board too long and then make it shorter.'"

MARRIAGE AND FAMILY

Bruchac and his wife, Carol, live in Greenfield Center, New York, in the house where he was raised by his grandparents. They have two children, James, born in 1968, and Jesse, born in 1972. The house has been joined to the former general store, where the Bruchac family now runs The Greenfield Review Press.

HOBBIES AND OTHER INTERESTS

In addition to being a writer, Bruchac is a professional storyteller. This career started years ago, when he was invited to an elementary school to read from his first children's book, *Turkey Brother*. "I got up in front of a group of kids with a book in my hand," he recalled. "[Then] I just put the book down and said, 'Let me *tell* you these stories." He has been enchanting people of all ages ever since, often visiting schools, colleges, museums, education conferences, and arts workshops, among other places, to spin his tales of Native American life and love of the land. Bruchac also performs music, some of which he's written himself. He plays the guitar, the Native American flute, and the Native American drum. He is part of a music group called the Dawn Land Singers that includes his sister, Marge, and his sons, James and Jesse.

SELECTED WRITINGS

Collections of Folktales, Poetry, Plays, and Short Stories

Turkey Brother and Other Tales: Iroquois Folk Stories, 1975
Stone Giants and Flying Heads: Adventure Stories of the Iroquois, 1979
The Wind Eagle and Other Abenaki Stories, 1985
The Faithful Hunter: More Abenaki Stories, 1988
Native American Stories, 1991
Turtle Meat and Other Stories, 1992
Thirteen Moons on Turtle's Back: A Native American Year of Moons, 1992
    (with Jonathan London)

The First Strawberries: A Cherokee Story, 1993

Flying With the Eagle, Racing the Great Bear: Stories from Native North America, 1993

The Girl Who Married the Moon: Tales from Native North America, 1994 (with Gayle Ross)

The Boy Who Lived with the Bears and Other Iroquois Stories, 1995

Dog People: Native Dog Stories, 1995

Between Earth and Sky: Legends of Native American Sacred Places, 1996

Four Ancestors: Stories, Songs and Poems from Native North America, 1996

The Earth Under Sky Bear's Feet: Native American Poems of the Land, 1998

Pushing Up the Sky: Seven Native American Plays for Children, 2000

Keeper Series (all co-authored with Michael J. Caduto)

Keepers of the Earth: Native American Stories and Environmental Activities for Children, 1989

Keeper of the Animals: Native American Stories and Wildlife Activities for Children, 1990

Keepers of Life: Discovering Plants Through Native American Stories and Earth Activities for Children, 1994

Keepers of the Light: Native American Stories and Nocturnal Activities for Children, 1994

Novels

Dawn Land, 1993

Long River, 1995

Eagle Song, 1997

The Arrow Over the Door, 1998

The Heart of a Chief, 1998

Sacajawea: The Story of Bird Woman and the Lewis and Clark Expedition, 2000

The Journal of Jesse Smoke, a Cherokee Boy, 2001

Skeleton Man, 2001

The Winter People, 2002

Pocahontas, 2003

The Warriors, 2003

The Dark Pond, 2004

Whisper in the Dark, 2005

Code Talker: A Novel About the Navajo Marines of World War Two, 2005

Books for Younger Readers

A Boy Called Slow: The True Story of Sitting Bull, 1995

Seeing the Circle, 1999

Crazy Horse's Vision, 2000
Squanto's Journey: The Story of the First Thanksgiving, 2000
How Chipmunk Got His Stripes, 2001 (with James Bruchac)
Turtle's Race with Beaver: A Traditional Seneca Story, 2003 (with James Bruchac)
Raccoon's Last Race: A Traditional Abenaki Story, 2004 (with James Bruchac)
Jim Thorpe's Bright Path, 2004
Rachel Carson: Preserving a Sense of Wonder, 2004

Nonfiction Books

Bowman's Store: A Journey to Myself, 1997
Tell Me a Tale: A Book about Storytelling, 1997
Trail of Tears, 1999
Navajo Long Walk: The Tragic Story of a Proud People's Forced March from Their Homeland, 2002

SELECTED HONORS AND AWARDS

American Book Award: 1984, for *Breaking Silence: An Anthology of Asian America Poets*
Hope S. Dean Memorial Award: 1993, for lifetime contribution to children's books
Cherokee Nation Prose Award: 1996, for *The Boy Who Lived with the Bears*
Notable Books for Children (American Library Association): 1996, for *The Boy Who Lived with the Bears* and *A Boy Called Slow;* 2002, for *Skeleton Man*
Paterson Children's Book Award: 1996, for *Dog People*
Best Books (*School Library Journal*): 2001, for *Skeleton Man;* 2002, for *The Winter People*
Best Children's Books of the Year (Bank Street College): 2001, for *Squanto's Journey;* 2002, for *Skeleton Man;* 2003, for *The Winter People;* 2004, for *Hidden Roots*
Notable Social Studies Trade Books for Young People (National Council for the Social Studies): 2001, for *Squanto's Journey;* 2003, for *The Winter People*
Notable Books for Children (*Smithsonian Magazine*): 2002, for *The Winter People*

FURTHER READING

Books

Authors and Artists for Young Adults, Vol. 19, 1996
Bruchac, Joseph. *Bowman's Store: A Journey to Myself,* 1997
Contemporary Authors New Revision Series, Vol. 137, 2005

Major Authors and Illustrators for Children and Young Adults, 2002
Notable Native Americans, 1995
Rockman, Connie. *Eighth Book of Junior Authors & Illustrators*, 2000
St. James Guide to Children's Writers, 1999

Periodicals

Albany (NY) Times Union, Sep. 25, 1998, p.D1
Detroit News, Sep. 9, 2000, p.C1
Lancaster (PA) New Era, Jan. 4, 2000, p.B5
MELEUS, Fall 1996, p.159
Writer's Digest, June 1995, p.6

Online Articles

http://www.childrenslit.com/f_mai.htm
    (Children's Literature, "Meet Authors and Illustrators: Joseph Bruchac,"
    undated)
http://www.education.wisc.edu/ccbc/authors/bruchac.asp
    (Cooperative Children's Book Center, University of Wisconsin, "An
    Interview with Joseph Bruchac," Oct. 22, 1999)
http://www.eduplace.com/kids/hmr/mtai/bruchac.html
    (Houghton Mifflin, "Meet the Author: Joseph Bruchac," undated)
http://books.scholastic.com/teachers
    (Scholastic, "Joseph Bruchac's Biography," undated)

Online Databases

Biography Resource Center Online, 2006, articles from *Authors and Artists for
    Young Adults*, 1996; *Contemporary Authors Online*, 2005; *Notable Native
    Americans*, 1995; *St. James Guide to Children's Writers*, 1999

ADDRESS

Joseph Bruchac
P.O. Box 308
Greenfield Center, NY 12833

WORLD WIDE WEB SITES

http://www.josephbruchac.com
http://www.ndakinna.com

Gennifer Choldenko 1957-

American Writer of Children's Books
Author of *Al Capone Does My Shirts*

BIRTH

Gennifer Choldenko was born in 1957 in Santa Monica, California. She was the youngest of four children. Her father, a business executive, wrote in his spare time, but his work was never published.

YOUTH

Choldenko grew up with the nickname Snot-Nose and an imaginative sense of humor. At the age of six, she went with her family to visit some friends of her parents. That night, a certain slap-happiness hit her, and she began to make up jokes and stories. Her family referred to those quirky, nonsensical stories as Gennifer Jokes. Before long, Choldenko began writing down her stories. At the age of eight, she wrote her first manuscript, *The Adventures of Genny Rice*, about a grain of rice traveling down the garbage disposal.

When she wasn't making up stories, Choldenko spent much of her time horseback riding. "I was totally horse crazy," she recalled. As a teenager, she braided manes and tails for horse shows. Soon after that, she became a horseback-riding instructor for blind and deaf children.

—————— " ——————

"My father left for work wearing a starched white shirt and shiny black wing tips. But when he got home, he slid his feet into blue canvas slip-ons, donned a funny plaid shirt that buttoned easily over his big belly, and sat down behind an enormous Underwood typewriter. Clearly, this was the treat he'd been waiting for all day."

—————— " ——————

Throughout her childhood, Choldenko grappled with a variety of challenges. Her father died during her teen years. In addition, one of her sisters suffered from autism, a disorder characterized by withdrawal, difficulty communicating and interacting with others, resistance to change, obsessive attachment to things, showing inappropriate emotional responses, and other traits. The Autism Society of America defines it like this: "Autism is a complex developmental disability that typically appears during the first three years of life and is the result of a neurological disorder that affects the normal functioning of the brain, impacting development in the areas of social interaction and communication skills. Both children and adults with autism typically show difficulties in verbal and non-verbal communication, social interactions, and leisure or play activities. . . . It affects each individual differently and at varying degrees."

EDUCATION

In high school, Choldenko excelled in English, the subject most important to her family. After high school, she enrolled at Brandeis University in Massachusetts. By the time she got to Brandeis, she knew she wanted to be a writer. Not surprisingly, her favorite subject was creative writing.

"When I was in college, I used to drive my poor roommate out of her mind because I was always typing well into the night," she admitted. "But that's okay. She got back at me. She took up tap dancing."

Choldenko graduated from Brandeis *cum laude* (with honors), earning a Bachelor of Arts (BA) degree in English. She later attended the Rhode Island School of Design and earned a Bachelor of Fine Arts (BFA) degree in illustration. RISD (pronounced ris-dee), as it's commonly known, is a renowned art school.

BECOMING A WRITER

After college, Choldenko worked as a copywriter for a small advertising agency. At night, she took art courses. Eventually she got a degree in illustration. Two things held her back from launching a career as a fiction writer: her father's disappointments in the field and her own misguided belief that real writers wrote for adults, not children. J.K. Rowling's success with the Harry Potter series helped give new legitimacy to writing for children. Before long, Choldenko lost interest in writing for adults. "It was such a relief when I realized that I was a children's writer," she said.

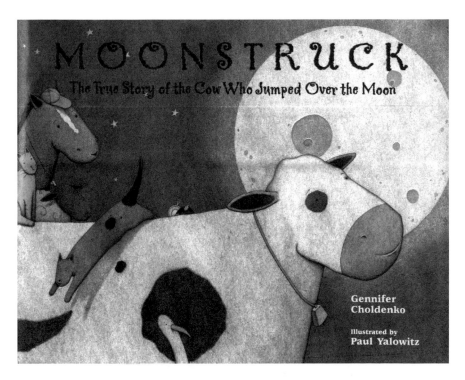

"Suddenly I went from having one book idea I wasn't too keen on to having hundred of book ideas I couldn't wait to write."

Choldenko felt drawn to writing about the challenges of growing up. The ages between 10 and 13 particularly interested her. As she saw it, every character had a different way of leaving childhood behind. But, instead of writing directly about her own experiences, she wanted to create something new. She had no interest in writing autobiographical fiction. "I already know what happened in my childhood; the problem is I don't understand it," she said. "To gain mastery I seem to need to take wild flights of fantasy and make up a whole pack of lies."

———— " ————

"It was such a relief when I realized that I was a children's writer. Suddenly I went from having one book idea I wasn't too keen on to having hundred of book ideas I couldn't wait to write."

———— " ————

CAREER HIGHLIGHTS

Getting Published

Choldenko eventually left a successful career in advertising to work on her fiction. She approached fiction writing like a job, getting dressed up every day and keeping the study door closed so her characters would stay put.

All the hard work finally paid off in 1997 with the publication of her first book, *Moonstruck: The True Story of the Cow Who Jumped Over the Moon.* The book is a spoof on the "Hey Diddle Diddle" nursery rhyme. The premise of this spoof is that, once upon a time, only horses jumped over the moon. They were trained for it. Then, one day, a cow shows up at the training center. At first, she just watches, but then she starts using the training equipment. "Honey, come on, you're a cow!" the narrator, who's a horse, tells her. No one believes the cow will be able to jump over the moon. But she proves them all wrong.

Critics applauded the book as a witty tribute to hard work and perseverance. "In this saucy picture book, the scoop is delivered straight from the horse's mouth—literally," *Publishers Weekly* wrote. *Booklist* hailed *Moonstruck* as "fractured and funny."

Choldenko described *Moonstruck* as the most autobiographical book of her career. "I am the cow no one thought would ever amount to anything," she confided.

Notes From a Liar and Her Dog

Choldenko's first novel, *Notes From a Liar and Her Dog*, was published in 2001. It tells the story of 12-year-old Antonia "Ant" McPherson, who feels like a misfit in her own family. Her mother finds fault with everything she does. Both her sisters have royal-sounding names. Ant's older sister, whom she calls "Her Highness Elizabeth," looks down on her. Her younger sister, Katherine the Great, takes notes on Ant's misbehaviors to get her in trouble.

Ant starts lying because she doesn't want to "waste the truth on people who won't understand." She tells people she was adopted and starts keeping a diary for her "real mom." Only her tiny dog, Pistachio, and her best friend, Harrison, seem to understand her. Then a sympathetic teacher, nicknamed Just Carol ("she always says, 'Just call me Carol'"), takes Ant under her wing. Just Carol gets Ant and Harrison involved in volunteering at the local zoo. Before long, Just Carol begins challenging Ant to start telling the truth.

The prickly character of Ant came to Choldenko when she had just moved into a new house. She has said that the new house felt like it had been "built with a stapler" because cabinet doors fell off when people opened them and the roof leaked in 11 different places. Although the book as a whole is not autobiographical, Choldenko did draw on some old feelings from her childhood. Like Ant, she believed she was really adopted. But, unlike Ant, she was never a liar.

Critics applauded the book for its wit and candor. "Funny, moving, and completely believable, this is a fine first novel," *Booklist* wrote. "Choldenko vividly captures the feelings of a middle child torn between wanting to be noticed and wanting to be invisible," noted *Publisher's Weekly*. "This funny and touching novel portrays the tug of war within this strong heroine and taps into very real emotions."

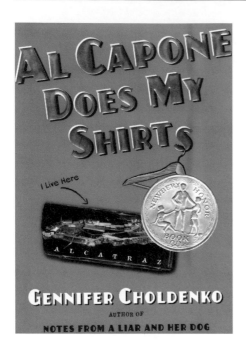

Al Capone Does My Shirts

Choldenko found the inspiration for her next novel, *Al Capone Does My Shirts* (2004), in a newspaper article about kids who grew up at Alcatraz. Located on a rocky island in the bay near San Francisco, California, Alcatraz was a high security prison from 1934 to 1963. Because of its remote location, many employees and their families lived right on the island. Alcatraz housed some of the nation's most famous criminals, including gangster Al Capone.

Soon after reading the article, Choldenko volunteered as a guide on Alcatraz, which is now a national historic site that is part of the U.S. National Park Service. She interviewed people who grew up on the island and read handwritten records of inmates, guards, and kids who lived on Alcatraz. She learned that Al Capone worked in the laundry of the prison.

After a year of research, Choldenko began writing. However, it took several drafts for her to develop the right voice for her main character, 12-year-old Moose Flanagan. "The early drafts of the manuscript sounded like every 1930s book, radio program, or movie I'd ever heard all rolled into one," she said in an interview. "Then one day I realized there were millions and millions of people alive in 1935 — each with his or her own voice. That was a breakthrough. Moose's voice came soon after that."

In developing the storyline for *Al Capone Does My Shirts*, Choldenko drew on her own experiences growing up with a sister who had autism. Having autism, Choldenko felt, was like living in prison. In 1935, autistic children were viewed as mentally retarded or difficult. Autism wasn't recognized as a condition until 1943. Choldenko worked hard to develop a story that would incorporate autism without becoming a "dreary-downer-dealing-with-disease" kind of book.

Al Capone Does My Shirts begins with 12-year old Moose Flanagan moving to Alcatraz so his father can work as a prison guard/electrician at the prison and his autistic sister Natalie can attend a special school in San

Francisco. Depressed about having to leave his friends and winning baseball team behind, Moose complains, "You get to Alcatraz by being the worst of the worst. Unless you're me. I came here because my mother said I had to."

In this strange and isolated setting, Moose meets the warden's scheming and bossy daughter, Piper, who heads up a group of kids on the island that includes Jimmy and his quirky, pesty, tagalong younger sister Theresa. At school on the mainland, Piper hatches a scheme to charge classmates for the privilege of having their clothes washed by the famous Al Capone. Meanwhile, Moose's mother decides to give piano lessons to help make ends meet. It's the Great Depression, a time of great economic hardship, and the family needs money to survive. Moose's mother leaves him in charge of Natalie's care until she is deemed to be ready for her new school. Moose finally comes up with his own scheme for helping his family that involves the famous Al Capone.

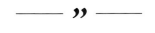

Children's writer Sid Fleischman, author of **The Whipping Boy**, *lavished praise on* **Al Capone Does My Shirts.** *"Choldenko's novel is a marvel. Writing with great tenderness and freshness and style, she unfolds a taut drama of two kids struggling to come of age against an extraordinary background — Alcatraz Island. A major achievement. Applause!"*

In her Author's Note at the end of the book, Choldenko described Al Capone as a man of both horrible ruthlessness and surprising generosity. Although he authorized or performed the slaying of hundreds of people, he also opened a soup kitchen at the beginning of the Great Depression.

Reviewers praised *Al Capone Does My Shirts* for its quick pacing, humor, and skillful use of setting. "Basing her story on the actual experience of those who supported the prison in the '30s — when Al Capone was an inmate — Choldenko's pacing is exquisite, balancing the tense family dynamics alongside the often-humorous and riveting school story of peer pressure and friendship. Fascinating setting as a metaphor for Moose's own imprisonment [enables] some hysterically funny scenes, but a great read no matter where it takes place," trumpeted *Kirkus Reviews.* "With its unique setting and well-developed characters, this warm, engaging coming-of-age story has plenty of appeal, and Choldenko offers some fascinating historical background on Alcatraz Island in an afterword," proclaimed *Booklist*. The novel won this praise from fellow children's writer Sid Fleishchman, who won the Newbery Award for his novel *The Whipping Boy*: "Choldenko's novel is a marvel. Writing with great tenderness and freshness and style, she unfolds a taut drama of two kids struggling to come of age against an extraordinary background — Alcatraz Island. A major achievement. Applause!"

Al Capone Does My Shirts won several important awards; certainly one of the most thrilling was being named a Newbery Honor Book by the American Library Association. The Newbery Honor Book is a runner-up for the Newbery Award, one of the most prestigious awards in children's literature. For Choldenko, the recognition capped off years of hard work. "While I was working on the book, I stood on my tippy toes stretching to do more than I was quite able," she said. "I've never worked so hard on anything, not ever. But I've also never felt so proud of anything I've done before." And recognition from the Newbery committee was the highlight. "When *Al Capone* won the Newbery Honor I really did feel I jumped the moon."

Upcoming Books

Choldenko's new picture book, *How to Make Friends with a Giant*, is scheduled for release in summer 2006. She's also working on *If a Tree Falls at Lunch Period* (working title), slated for spring 2007, and *Louder Lili*, slated for summer 2007.

Advice for Young Writers

Choldenko takes issue with the traditional advice to "Write what you know." Instead, she recommends that young writers write about what they desperately want to understand. "I wrote what I knew, and no one wanted to buy it, which is quite a lucky thing because it wasn't very good," she explained. "Turns out what I know is what everybody else knows, too. When I write about what I don't know, what I don't understand, and what I wish with the deepest part of myself could be . . . my writing gets better."

She also advises young writers to embrace the revision process. When Choldenko revises, she looks at her characters not only as individuals but also as members of a group. "It's like a party," she says. "Sometimes the chemistry works between guests, and everyone mingles, and sometimes it doesn't." After writing one of her final drafts of *Al Capone Does My Shirts*, she decided that her secondary characters hadn't gelled as a group. So she got rid of them. "It was a huge amount of work," she acknowledged. "It nearly killed me. But out of that came the funniest character in the whole novel, Theresa Mattaman."

Finally, Choldenko tells aspiring writers to write no matter how they feel. "I write best at my desk in the morning with two caffeine lattes and three oatmeal cookies within an inch of my hand," she revealed. "I'm stale in the afternoon, and no amount of caffeine or cookies can help, but I write then, too. Just in case."

MAJOR INFLUENCES

Choldenko's father played an important role in her development as a writer. Although he earned a living as a business executive, he spent much of his spare time writing. "My father left for work wearing a starched white shirt and shiny black wing tips," she disclosed in an interview. "But when he got home, he slid his feet into blue canvas slip-ons, donned a funny plaid shirt that buttoned easily over his big belly, and sat down behind an enormous Underwood typewriter. Clearly, this was the treat he'd been waiting for all day."

"I write best at my desk in the morning with two caffeine lattes and three oatmeal cookies within an inch of my hand," Choldenko revealed. "I'm stale in the afternoon, and no amount of caffeine or cookies can help, but I write then, too. Just in case."

But, despite his passion for writing, he was never published. "And so I learned two things from him," Choldenko explained. "One was that writing was a blast, and two was that it would break your heart." As a result, it took her a long time to decide to pursue a career as a writer. Unfortunately, her father died when she was a teenager, so he never got to see her published. "I know he would have been very proud of me," she said.

MARRIAGE AND FAMILY

Choldenko lives in the San Francisco Bay area with her husband, Jacob, and their two children, Ian and Kai. They have a white German Shepherd named Sophie. Because Sophie can pick locks with her long nose and crafty paws, Choldenko says that, if she were a human, she would be a con artist.

HOBBIES AND OTHER INTERESTS

When she is not writing, Choldenko likes to draw animals at the zoo, particularly turtles and crocodiles because they don't move around as much as other animals. She also enjoys jazz music and pizza topped with black olives and red onions.

WRITINGS

Moonstruck: The True Story of the Cow Who Jumped Over the Moon, 1997
Notes From a Liar and Her Dog, 2001
Al Capone Does My Shirts, 2004

HONORS AND AWARDS

National Parenting Center Seal of Approval: 2001, for *Moonstruck: The True Story of the Cow Who Jumped Over the Moon*
Best Books (Center for Children's Books): 2002, for *Notes from a Liar and Her Dog*
Best Book of the Year (*School Library Journal*): 2002, for *Notes from a Liar and Her Dog*
Books That Can Support Character Development (U.S. Department of Education): 2002, for *Notes from a Liar and Her Dog*
Notable Book (American Library Association): 2005, for *Al Capone Does My Shirts*
Best Book of the Year (*Publishers Weekly*): 2005, for *Al Capone Does My Shirts*
Best Book of the Year (*Kirkus Reviews*): 2005, for *Al Capone Does My Shirts*
Favorite Novel of the Year (Children's Bookseller's Award): 2005, for *Al Capone Does My Shirts*
Sid Fleischman Humor Award (Society of Children's Book Writers and Illustrators): 2005, for *Al Capone Does My Shirts*
Notable Social Studies Trade Books for Young People (Children's Book Council — National Council for Social Studies): 2005, for *Al Capone Does My Shirts*

FURTHER READING

Books

Contemporary Authors, Vol. 204, 2003

Periodicals

New York Times, July 31, 2005, p.23
Oregonian, Dec. 20, 2001, p.12

Online Databases

Biography Resource Center Online, 2006, article from *Contemporary Authors Online, 2005*

ADDRESS

Gennifer Choldenko
Penguin Young Readers Group
345 Hudson Street
New York, NY 10014

WORLD WIDE WEB SITES

http://www.choldenko.com
http://www.bloomsbury.com
http://www.nps.gov/alcatraz
http://www.autism-society.org

Shannon Hale 1974-

American Fantasy Writer
Author of *Princess Academy*

BIRTH

Shannon Hale was born on January 26, 1974, in Salt Lake City, Utah. Hale has described her father, Wallace Bryner, as a world-class banjo picker, and her mother, Bonnie Bryner, as someone who encouraged her as a writer. Shannon was the middle daughter in a family of five girls.

YOUTH

Hale was an imaginative and story-loving child from an early age. As soon as she could speak, she made up stories, enlisting her sisters to perform them in mini-plays. She loved reading from her mother's big book of fairy tales.

In the first grade, Hale dictated a story to her teacher and then drew the illustrations. The story involved a nasty witch with long green fingernails. She adored C.S. Lewis's books and sobbed when she realized she couldn't get to Narnia through her parents' closet. In fourth grade, Hale's teacher introduced her to the process of writing down her poems and stories. Up until then, her storytelling was limited to games she made up with her friends and plays enacted at home. Writing down her stories became a new passion. "I'm going to be a writer," she wrote in a fourth grade essay. "I'm going to write books."

——— **"** ———

"[I was] different from the rest of my family (as most people are). I'm the only one in my seven-member family who pursued a creative art. I remember when I was about 17, my mother saying to me, 'Shannon, you're living in a fantasy land!' And I thought, 'How did she know?' I'd thought I was keeping it pretty hidden."

——— **"** ———

At that point, Hale wrote mostly fantasy stories and imitations of Nancy Drew books. Increasingly, she found herself drawn to reading fantasy novels. "When I was a kid, I got bored with books like 'Mandy Moves to a New Town' unless it was 'Mandy Moves Objects with her Mind!'" she said in an interview. "I was thinking, 'Yeah, yeah, girl gets her period and is embarrassed, but doesn't anyone have ESP?'"

By the time she got to high school, Hale stopped telling people she wanted to be a writer. It was like telling them she wanted to be a princess. "It's one of those things people just don't do," she said later. But she began to write in secret. Like many teenagers, Hale felt that the dramatic themes of fantasy novels—such as expulsion from one's homeland—captured her own reality. "If you stuck that in a high school setting it would feel really silly," she told the *Salt Lake Tribune*. "Nevertheless, that's how people feel in high school." She was no exception. "I was very misunderstood and not appreciated," she said.

"I think adolescence is a tough time for everyone," Hale told *Biography Today*. "It's the time when we're really figuring out our identity, separating ourselves from our parents, and finding our own place in the world, making it very easy (and perhaps, essential?) to feel misunderstood and under-

———— **❝** ————

"As a reader, I've never been very interested in the kind of magic where someone waves a wand, leaving me ignorant of why it works or how it is done. As a writer, it was important to me to create a magic system that I believed might be possible and that I could get inside of and understand."

———— **❞** ————

appreciated. I think I was also different from the rest of my family (as most people are). I'm the only one in my seven-member family who pursued a creative art. I remember when I was about 17, my mother saying to me, 'Shannon, you're living in a fantasy land!' And I thought, 'How did she know?' I'd thought I was keeping it pretty hidden."

EDUCATION

Hale graduated from West High School in 1992, then enrolled at the University of Utah. She continued to write in secret, claiming that she had decided to be an English major because she wanted to become a teacher. She also pursued acting. She took 18 months off college to live in Paraguay as an unpaid Mormon missionary, a volunteer representative of the Church of Jesus Christ of Latter-Day Saints. She also spent time studying in Mexico and the United Kingdom. Hale earned her Bachelor of Arts (BA) degree in English from the University of Utah in 1998.

Shortly before finishing college, Hale saw an inexpensive middle-grade reader and said to herself, "Anyone can write these." She found, however, that writing a book like that was harder than it looked. So she forced herself out of the "writer's closet" by applying to graduate school to study creative writing.

The following year, she began a master's degree program at the University of Montana. Graduate school, however, proved less inspiring than she had imagined. She found herself putting fantastical elements into her short stories, much to the disapproval of some of her professors, who favored more serious literary fiction. "Everything I was reading felt the same, because everyone was trying to write *New Yorker* stories," she said. "They all ended with helplessness. Ultimately, everyone fails."

In 2000, Hale earned her Master of Fine Arts (MFA) degree in creative writing from the University of Montana. With her degree completed, she decided to move away from straight literary fiction. She wanted to write the kind of book that had inspired her as a teenager.

BECOMING A FANTASY WRITER

In the summer between her first and second years of graduate school, Hale made a pact with a fellow fantasy lover in the program. They each agreed to write a novel during the summer break. Although neither succeeded, the challenge set Hale on the path toward becoming a published novelist.

In choosing fantasy, however, Hale did not reject realism. She wanted to make imaginary worlds seem believable. Her imagination took her to mythical realms populated by real people rather than the fairies, elves, sorcerers, and dragons. "As a reader, I've never been very interested in the kind of magic where someone waves a wand, leaving me ignorant of why it works or how it is done," she said. "As a writer, it was important to me to create a magic system that I believed might be possible and that I could get inside of and understand."

Financial realities, however, kept her from working full-time as a writer. After completing graduate school, she worked mostly as an instructional designer for an e-learning company. She continued to work on her novel, writing about five pages a day.

CAREER HIGHLIGHTS

The Goose Girl

Hale decided to make her first novel a retelling of a fairy tale. "The old tales, the tales the Grimm Brothers collected, lasted for decades and centuries for a reason," she explained. Those stories captivated readers. Inspired by Robin McKinley's *Beauty: A Retelling of Beauty and the Beast*, Hale decided to use her own favorite fairytale, "The Goose Girl" by the Brothers Grimm, as a springboard for her novel.

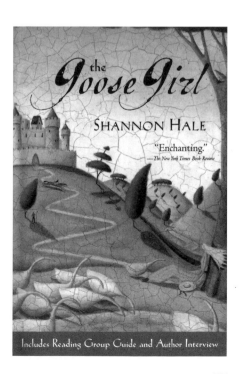

In the four-page version by the Brothers Grimm, a princess is set to wed a prince in a faraway kingdom. A jealous maid, however, steals the princess's identity and tricks the king into thinking she is his son's bride-to-be. The real princess is forced to take a job herding geese. The fairy tale had left Hale wanting to know more. "Why did the princess let her lady in waiting steal her identity?" she wondered. "How did she learn to command the wind? And what about the prince?" Hale worked on fleshing out the story, writing draft after draft while working full-time. During this period, she also got married.

Hale's version of *The Goose Girl* (2003) tells the story of Princess Ani, a young princess who has an amazing ability to communicate with animals but has trouble connecting with her fellow human beings. Ani's mother, the queen, arranges for her daughter to marry a prince in the neighboring kingdom of Bayern. On the way to her new home, Ani's ambitious lady-in-waiting, Selia, steals her identity and tries to kill her. Selia then tries to incite a war between the two kingdoms. Ani, meanwhile, disguises herself as a goose herder and makes her way to the royal palace. But will she have what it takes to reclaim her rightful position?

> "Dare I say it this early in her career? Shannon Hale is already, after only a few books, one of our best writers of fantasy," said noted science fiction writer Orson Scott Card. "She is also one of those rare storytellers who can bring a jaded old reviewer like me to well-earned tears. . . . [Hale's novels are] every bit as good for adults as for children."

Critics praised the book for its well-developed heroine, richly textured writing, and complex plot. "In layer upon layer of detail, a beautiful coming-of-age story emerges, a tale about learning to rescue yourself rather than fall accidentally into happily ever," commented the *New York Times*. "Young readers may recognize parallels with their own lives in even her most magical adventures: the loneliness of feeling peculiar, the devastation of betrayal, the pride of sharing your talents, and the joy of finding people to love and trust." The book also received a glowing response from noted science fiction writer Orson Scott Card. "Dare I say it this early in her career? Shannon Hale is already, after only a few books, one of our best writers of fantasy. She is also one of those rare storytellers who can bring a jaded old reviewer like me to well-earned tears. This is a novel that is every bit as good for adults as for children."

Enna Burning

Hale began working on her second novel before knowing whether or not her first would be published. The new book grew out of the friendship between Ani, the princess, and Enna, the forest girl, in *The Goose Girl.* Hale modeled the friendship on her relationship with her best friend Rosi. After writing about Princess Ani, Hale found Enna a welcome change of pace. "I longed to write someone very different, someone who would seek out problems, dive head first and worry later, someone with astounding self-confidence," Hale said. "Enna, though she had a very small part in *Goose Girl,* stepped forward and demanded attention. I thought she would be fun to write, and she was!"

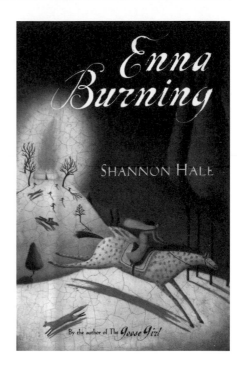

In the middle of working on the new book, Hale got some good news: Bloomsbury wanted to publish *The Goose Girl.* She needed to revise it, though, which meant putting the new book on hold. "There was about a two-month period when I had to abandon Enna in a tent," she recalled. "Poor lady!" Several months later, though, she finished *Enna Burning* and sent it to her editor, who loved it. She delivered her final draft of the book the first week of December 2003, a week before giving birth to her son, Max. The book was published in 2004, the year she left her full-time job.

A darker, more dramatic book than *The Goose Girl, Enna Burning* revolves around the 16-year-old heroine's struggles with fire. One night, Enna sees her brother magically light the hearth. His power, though, makes him moody. After he uses his firepower on the enemy and then dies in a blaze, Enna inherits his magic. She vows to control her new power and use it for good, but the warm glow of the fire turns destructive. Unable to control the urge to burn, Enna uses her power in a battle and burns hundreds of people alive. Her friend's gift of wind-speak is similarly out of control. The two women set off on a journey to discover a remedy for their problems. Enna's gentle, devoted suitor, Finn, finds a place by her side.

Reviewers praised the book, although some commented on its dark and sometimes violent themes. Enna's fire lust, they said, could be compared to a more realistic type of addiction. "Enna's power can be seen as desire, or a drug, or the will to power, or simply as a gift that must be made manifest," wrote *Kirkus Reviews*. "Powerful and romantic." *Booklist,* however, cautioned that "readers will need a high tolerance for grisly violence and leisurely plot development," but praised the book for its rich writing and sharply drawn characters. Similarly, *School Library Journal* maintained "With a richly detailed setting, eloquent descriptions, a complex plot, a large cast of characters, and romance, this high fantasy will be welcomed both by fans of *The Goose Girl* and those who have yet to discover it."

Princess Academy

Hale's third novel, *Princess Academy* (2005), grew out of a conversation Hale had one evening with her husband, Dean. They were sitting at home, having their evening talk, when Dean mentioned an adult fantasy book he was reading. The main character, he said, was a "tutor to the princesses." Although he meant that the tutor lived in a the palace and taught the daughters of the king, Hale's mind flashed to a school where common girls would receive instruction in order to qualify for the job of princess. She ran for her notebook and jotted down the idea. "Whenever I get book ideas, I have those 'rushing forward' moments where my thoughts tumble and race ahead, and I get so excited about the ideas I scarcely jot them down," she explained. "But writing it out is never so electrifying. It is work, like any other profession."

At first, Hale thought the new book would be easier to write than her first two. It would be shorter and for slightly younger readers. "I thought the process of discovering the story might be a little less tortuous," she recalled. "Ha. This book challenged me more than the previous. Length and age were irrelevant." On two separate occasions, she thought she would have to "trash the whole thing." She was having trouble figuring out the main character, and the core of the story did not come easily. But she persisted. She drew on her Scandinavian roots to create a setting for the book, thumbing through medieval Danish cookbooks to research the food of the era. Finally, everything fell into place. "That I was able to find the story, finish it, and be pleased with the end result is, truly, miraculous," she observed.

Princess Academy takes place on a mountain inspired by one Hale had visited in Southern Utah. The main character, 14-year-old Miri, thinks she is being kept from working in the quarry of her beloved Mount Eskel because she is too small. Word comes from the valley that Mount Eskel is to

be the home of the prince's bride-to-be—the next princess. But first all girls must attend a makeshift mountain academy to prepare themselves for the royal life of the lowlanders. Then the prince will choose his wife.

At the Princess Academy, Miri finds herself confronted by bitter competition among the girls. A cruel tutor denies her a visit home. Then the girls are cut off from their village by heavy winter snowstorms. The dangers mount. Will Miri's ability to communicate wordlessly via magical "quarry speech" help save her classmates from harm? And who will the prince choose for his mate?

Some reviewers found the ending of *Princess Academy* somewhat unsatisfying, but most praised the book for its suspenseful story, descriptive writing, and strong heroine. *School Library Journal,* for instance, remarked that "The story is much like the mountains, with plenty of suspenseful moments that peak and fall, building into the next intense event. Each girl's story is brought to a satisfying conclusion, but this is not a fluffy, predictable fairy tale, even though it has wonderful moments of humor. Instead, Hale weaves an intricate, multi-layered story about families, relationships, education, and the place we call home." *Booklist* observed that "Hale nicely interweaves feminist sensibilities in this quest-for-a-prince-charming, historical-fantasy tale. Strong suspense and plot drive the action as the girls outwit would-be kidnappers and explore the boundaries of leadership, competition, and friendship." Writer Orson Scott Card responded to the story, commenting that "I believe it's a book for everybody. Hale knows that 'realistic' doesn't have to mean "unrelentingly ugly.' Hale offers us a world full of grief and fear and loneliness — but also full of love and trust and decency. There are adventures and dangers, and the most compelling, believable, poignant love story I have read in many a year. I was moved to tears and to laughter, and caught up in the grace and beauty."

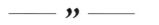

"Whenever I get book ideas, I have those 'rushing forward' moments where my thoughts tumble and race ahead, and I get so excited about the ideas I scarcely jot them down. But writing it out is never so electrifying. It is work, like any other profession."

Of all the comments, though, one stood out in importance: the opinion of the American Library Association's Newbery Award committee. *Princess Academy* was selected as a Newbery Honor Book, a runner-up for the Newbery Award, one of the most prestigious awards in children's literature. The committee observed that "The book is a fresh approach to the traditional princess story with unexpected plot twists and great emotional resonance." When Hale got the call from the Newbery committee, she burst into tears. She thanked the committee, hugged her husband, and cried some more. Then she turned to him and said, "I can't believe it" over and over again.

The characteristically humble Hale used the Newbery Honor as an occasion to encourage other writers. "It's a complete miracle!" she said. "I was the worst writer in the graduate school program at the University of Montana! Don't listen to people who say you won't make it!"

Future Projects

The prolific Hale has several projects in the works. Razo, one of the characters from *Enna Burning,* will be getting a book of his own, tentatively titled *River Secrets,* scheduled for release in fall 2006. Hale's first book for adults, which tells the story of a contemporary woman trying to overcome her addiction to the novel *Pride and Prejudice* by Jane Austen, is due out in mid 2007. Hale also recently finished a draft of another fairy tale retelling, tentatively titled *Diary of a Lady's Maid,* which may come out in fall 2007. Meanwhile, she has been collaborating with her husband on a graphic novel (a book-length comic book) called *Rapunzel's Revenge* set in the Old West and slated for publication in 2008. The heroine of this updated tale teaches herself to use her braids as lassos and whips.

Advice for Young Writers

"I highly recommend focusing on your writing and storytelling and not worrying about the publishing part for as long as you can stand it," Hale has suggested to young writers. "When you do decide that you must publish or perish, the following items do seem to improve your odds: read a lot, write a lot, seek and accept constructive feedback, rewrite a lot, learn as much as you can about publishing, and develop a tough skin. It also wouldn't hurt if your favorite aunt is a top editor in a large New York publishing house or a powerhouse literary agent."

Writers write, she said simply. By that, she means: Just do it! She makes herself write at least 1,000 words a day. If she hasn't made her 5,000-word quota by the end of Friday, then she writes on Saturday, too. She takes Sundays off.

She has encouraged aspiring writers to follow their dreams but understand the difficulties involved in the field. "Don't be afraid of failing," she counseled. "And love the creative process more than you love the idea of being published."

> —— **"** ——
>
> *When asked for advice for young writers, Hale said, "Try not to keep rice crackers by your computer because then you'll be addicted and always want to eat rice crackers every time you write." Then she added wryly, "Not that it's ever happened to me."*
>
> —— **"** ——

One final bit of advice? "Try not to keep rice crackers by your computer because then you'll be addicted and always want to eat rice crackers every time you write," she warned. Then she added wryly, "Not that it's ever happened to me."

MARRIAGE AND FAMILY

In 2000, Hale married her high school friend, Dean, after 11 years of friendship and courtship. She models the romantic themes in her books on her own experiences of seeing boys first as good friends and later as romantic interests. In December 2003, Hale gave birth to their first child, Max. She writes when he naps. The family lives in Salt Lake City, Utah. They currently have no pets, but — after noticing that many writers are photographed with their animals — Hale jokingly chose a plastic pig for her pet.

HOBBIES AND OTHER INTERESTS

Hale enjoys improvisational comedy and has taught Sunday school to inner-city girls. She spends most of her time, though, writing or being with her family. "It's very surreal when I go to conferences and signings and such and meet people who think I'm cool, because actually I'm quite boring, " she admitted.

SELECTED WORKS

The Goose Girl, 2003
Enna Burning, 2004
Princess Academy, 2005

HONORS AND AWARDS

Top Ten Teen Book (American Library Association): 2004, for *The Goose Girl*
Josette Frank Award for Fiction (Bank Street College): 2003, for *The Goose Girl*
Best Children's Books of the Year (Bank Street College): 2004, for *The Goose Girl;* 2006, for *Princess Academy*

100 Titles for Reading and Sharing (New York Public Library): 2004, for
  The Goose Girl; 2006, for *Princess Academy*
Best Book (Association of Booksellers for Children): 2005, for *Enna
  Burning,* science fiction and fantasy category
Book Sense Pick for Fall: 2005, for *Princess Academy*
Notable Children's Book (American Library Association): 2006, for *Princess
  Academy*
Book for the Teen Age (New York Public Library): 2006, for *Princess Academy*

FURTHER READING

Books

Contemporary Authors, Vol. 234, 2005

Periodicals

Deseret Morning News, Aug. 17, 2003; Feb. 5, 2006
Salt Lake Tribune, Sep. 6, 2004, p.C1; Aug.12, 2005, p.G1

Online Databases

Biography Resource Center Online, 2006, article from *Contemporary Authors
  Online,* 2005

Online Articles

http://www.childrenslit.com/f_hale.html
  (Children's Literature, "Shannon Hale," Apr. 4, 2005)
http://kidsreads.com/authors/au-hale-shannon.asp
  (KidsReads.com, "Author: Shannon Hale," Aug. 2005)

ADDRESS

Shannon Hale
Bloomsbury Children's Books USA
104 Fifth Avenue, 7th Floor
New York, NY 10011

WORLD WIDE WEB SITE

http://www.squeetus.com

Carl Hiaasen 1953-

American Journalist and Novelist
Author of the Young Adult Novels *Hoot* and *Flush*

BIRTH

Carl Andrew Hiaasen was born on March 12, 1953, in Plantation, Florida, which is a suburb of Fort Lauderdale. His father,
K. Odel, was a lawyer, and his mother, Patricia, was a homemaker. Hiaasen's grandfather, also named Carl Hiaasen, was a
prominent lawyer and one of the founders of the first law firm
in Fort Lauderdale. Hiaasen has three younger siblings: a
brother, Rob, and two sisters, Judith and Barbara.

YOUTH

Hiaasen grew up in Plantation, Florida, a region that had experienced little commercial and residential development up until that time. As a young child, he was able to enjoy the pristine streams, wetlands, and forests in the area, frequently going fishing with his grandfather, father, and friends. He developed a love of the outdoors and forged his ecological consciousness at a young age.

At age four, Hiaasen learned to read using *Miami Herald* sports stories and Florida maps as primers. He quickly developed a love for it. "I was a manic reader when I was young," he recalled. "That's what got me interested in writing. I burned through the whole Hardy Boy series when I was in fourth grade, and from then on I read all kinds of stuff, from Ian Fleming to J. D. Salinger to sports biographies of Vince Lombardi and Lou Gehrig."

After his father gave him his first typewriter in 1960, Hiaasen taught himself to type and produced a neighborhood sports page. "I knew from a young age that I wanted to be a writer," he said in an interview on his web site. "I got a typewriter when I was six, and I was hooked. I wrote a neighborhood sports paper and handed out the carbons to my friends. Kickball scores, stuff like that."

—— **"** ——

"I knew from a young age that I wanted to be a writer. I got a typewriter when I was six, and I was hooked. I wrote a neighborhood sports paper and handed out the carbons to my friends. Kickball scores, stuff like that."

—— **"** ——

Hiaasen has described himself as the class clown. "I was a year younger than everybody, so I was always the smallest kid in my class, all through high school," he declared. "I had to develop a wit. I became a class clown to disarm [bullies] with words because physically I would just get . . . pounded." He traced his interest in writing to being the class clown and wanting to express himself. "I know I wanted to do this from a very young age and I was lucky in that sense, that I knew early on that I enjoyed writing and getting a reaction," he said. "I think it's some sort of extension of being a class clown—that if you could write something and make somebody laugh, it was a good gig to have. I think there was an element of psychotherapy—it was a legal outlet for some of the ideas I was wanting to express as a kid."

As Hiaasen grew up, commercial and residential developers began to pave over and build on the land around his family's home. Shopping malls, strip malls, condominiums, and housing developments replaced the natural landscape that he loved so much.

The steady march of commercial and residential development and its effect on the environment has been a recurring concern in Hiaasen's life and work. "At the time I grew up, it was the westernmost fringe of civilization in south Florida, literally on the edge of the Everglades," he recalled. "Now, of course, it's unrecognizable." The speed in which Florida's wilderness was developed was shocking to Hiaasen. "There were no laws to protect anything," he remembered. "The next thing you'd know, there would be bulldozers and pavement and one more piece of the real Florida would be gone."

Cow pastures and pristine streams that Hiaasen had fished with his beloved grandfather were ploughed over and made into shopping malls and housing developments. To retaliate, he stole survey markers and created other mischief with his friends. "My friends and I had little guerrilla warfares going with developers," he admitted. "And of course, we lost."

> "At the time I grew up, [my neighborhood] was the westernmost fringe of civilization in south Florida, literally on the edge of the Everglades. Now, of course, it's unrecognizable," Hiaasen said, lamenting how Florida's wilderness has been over-developed. "There were no laws to protect anything. The next thing you'd know, there would be bulldozers and pavement and one more piece of the real Florida would be gone."

These losses took a toll on Hiaasen and his friends. One, in particular, was devastated by the destruction of Florida's natural beauty. Clyde Ingalls, one of Hiaasen's best friends, committed suicide at the age of 17. Hiaasen reported that Ingalls "was angry about a lot of things. But he was particularly angry about the fact that every time we'd go out West, there'd be a new bulldozer doing something to some place we knew." Ingalls later became the inspiration for Clinton "Skink" Tyree, a memorable character that appears in many of his novels for adults.

EDUCATION

Hiaasen attended Plantation High School. He was notorious for publishing an underground newsletter called *More Trash* that reported on teen

Hiaasen has been dedicated to the Florida environment since he was young, and fishing has been one of his long-time hobbies.

culture and depicted teachers and administration in a comical light. Later, he would bring that biting wit and insight into human behavior to his newspaper columns, novels, and young adult fiction.

After graduating from high school, Hiaasen enrolled at Emory University in Atlanta, Georgia. His two years at Emory are the only time that he has lived outside of the state of Florida. He then transferred to the University of Florida at Gainesville. In 1974 he graduated with a Bachelor of Science (BS) degree in journalism.

CAREER HIGHLIGHTS

After graduating from college, Hiaasen began working as a reporter for *Cocoa Today*, a newspaper based in Cocoa, Florida. Two years later, he joined the *Miami Herald* as a general assignment reporter. He also joined the newspaper's weekly magazine and investigations team.

In the early 1980s, Hiaasen and a fellow reporter, Brian Duffy, conducted an investigation of Port Bougainville, the largest condominium and hotel development ever planned in the Florida Keys. They discovered that developers had misrepresented the size of the project and had started construction without the required approvals from Florida's environmental regulation department and the Army Corps of Engineers. Their blockbuster expose on the project brought these issues to light. When they reported that there was political corruption involved as well, the project was halted. "Carl is a hell of a digger," Brian Duffy confirmed. "He loved to get that telling detail, whether from the fifth re-interview of a source or from a mind-numbing government document."

Hiaasen was glad to be exposing shady construction deals and writing about the environmental damage being done to Florida's natural resources through overdevelopment. This work confirmed the frustration and anger he felt as a child watching his favorite fishing place being bulldozed for housing developments. "Seeing a place you loved cut up and parceled made me cynical at an early age," he asserted. "People say the news business makes you cynical. For me, there were few surprises. Newspaper work only confirmed my worst suspicions —and the reality was worse than I'd feared."

————— " —————

"I would have been in big trouble long ago if I didn't have the columns and the novels as an outlet. I would have ended up either in jail or negotiating to stay out. I've always said that the writing has been a legal and socially acceptable outlet for some of the things I feel. If I didn't have that, God only knows."

————— " —————

Hiaasen views writing as a productive outlet for the anger he feels about what he sees in the world around him. "I would have been in big trouble long ago if I didn't have the columns and the novels as an outlet," he contended. "I would have ended up either in jail or negotiating to stay out. I've always said that the writing has been a legal and socially acceptable outlet for some of the things I feel. If I didn't have that, God only knows."

Hiaasen's ties to South Florida kept him at the *Miami Herald,* even when other newspapers made him offers to leave and work for them. "In the 30 years I've been at the *Herald,* they've lost hundreds of terrific journalists to the *Washington Post, New York Times, Wall Street Journal,*" he asserts. "The difference is that I was born and raised there. It's my home." In 1985 he began writing his own newspaper column in the *Miami Herald.* As a columnist, he was able to turn his anger into sharp satire on a variety of topics that interested him, including the environmental damage that commercial and private development has wreaked on Florida's natural landscape, political corruption, and the impact of government policies and regulation on individuals and the environment.

Hiaasen later collected and published his newspaper columns in two volumes: *Kick Ass* (1999) and *Paradise Screwed* (2004). He has written one longer nonfiction piece: in 1988 he published a scathing critique of the Walt Disney Corporation and its impact on South Florida entitled *Team Rodent: How Disney Devours the World*. In addition to this nonfiction work, Hiaasen has written several novels for adults and two novels for young adults, *Hoot* and *Flush*.

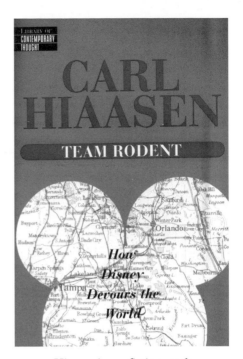

Hiaasen's nonfiction work Team Rodent *was an attack on the Disney Corporation.*

Novels for Adults

Hiaasen began writing fiction in 1976, when William D. Montalbano, an editor at the *Miami Herald*, suggested that they should write a novel together. The result of that collaboration was *Powder Burn* (1981), a crime thriller set in Florida. The two men worked together to write two more thrillers: *Trap Line* (1982) and *A Death in China* (1984).

Hiaasen went on to write several humorous eco-thrillers, which utilize his biting wit and insight into human nature to explore such topics as governmental corruption, corporate greed, and the destruction of Florida's wilderness. His novels feature corrupt politicians, ruthless and greedy developers, and eco-terrorists who seek to preserve Florida's wildlife and wetlands from overdevelopment. They often feature odd characters and wild, improbable plots related to the Everglades.

For example, in one of his early novels, *Tourist Season* (1986), Hiaasen followed the adventures of a group of bumbling environmental activists as they terrorize not only land developers but also the tourists who overrun Florida and spur further development. In *Strip Tease* (1995), Hiaasen explored the world of strip club, corrupt politicians, and custody battles. It was the first of his novels to feature a female protagonist, and the first to

NEW YORK TIMES BESTSELLING AUTHOR

Carl Hiaasen

TOURIST SEASON

"WONDERFUL...LIVELY...FUN."
—Tony Hillerman, *New York Times Book Review*

Tourist Season *was one of Hiaasen's early novels for adults.*

be on the best-seller list. The book was adapted into a movie in 1996 starring Demi Moore and Burt Reynolds. In his next novel, *Stormy Weather* (1995), he took a satirical look at the aftermath of a devastating hurricane and the grifters, opportunists, corrupt politicians, bureaucrats, and developers who try to capitalize on the misfortune of others. His most recent novel, *Skinny Dip* (2004), is a comic novel that once again touches on environmental issues in Florida's Everglades. When a woman discovers her husband is helping a tycoon to illegally dump fertilizer into the Everglades, he unsuccessfully tries to kill her. With the help of a former cop, she seeks her revenge. In fact, this set-up is fairly typical for Hiaasen's novels for adults, which typically feature a contest between unsavory politicians, business leaders, developers, and other characters, and a few do-gooders, who use subterfuge and trickery to overcome.

These satirical books look at the often absurd political, cultural, and social landscape in modern Florida proved to be popular with critics and readers alike. Both critics and readers have enjoyed his use of black humor, slapstick, and moral outrage. "Humor can be an incredible lacerating and effective weapon," Hiaasen emphasized. "And that is the way I use it."

Novels for Young Adults

Hiaasen first started writing for younger readers when a book editor asked him if he would be interested in writing a book for kids. Surprised at first, he dismissed the idea. "An editor had come up with this idea, which I thought was insane — that I should try to write a book for kids, or what you would call the 'Y.A. market,' young adults, young readers. And I just thought it was nuts at first," he recalled. "But you don't want to get on the same bicycle every day, and I thought it might be a nice change of pace. My stepson at the time was about 11, and he was just getting into reading and Harry

Potter and that sort of thing, and then I had nieces and a nephew in that age bracket who had never been able to read any of my other books—for obvious reasons, I wouldn't want them anywhere near them."

Hiaasen knew that kids would enjoy a humorous and interesting story. "I thought it would be nice to have a book I could give them that would have the same sort of [sarcastic] sensibility and the same sort of irreverence in the humor, which is really important to me—to make the books funny as well as tell a good story. At that time, obviously it was just going to be a break between my other novels. I thought the worst that could happen was I would have a book I could give the kids in my family. If it tanked, so what?"

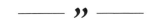

> "*I thought it would be nice to have a book I could give [the kids in my family] that would have the same sort of [sarcastic] sensibility and the same sort of irreverence in the humor, which is really important to me — to make the books funny as well as tell a good story. . . . I thought the worst that could happen was I would have a book I could give the kids in my family. If it tanked, so what?*"

Hoot

In *Hoot* (2002), Hiaasen drew on his childhood experiences sabotaging the work of construction crews that were developing land around his home and destroying the habitat of numerous tiny owls that nested in underground burrows. Set in the fictional town of Coconut Grove, Florida, the novel follows a group of scrappy kids who fight to save a plot of land from being ploughed over to build a pancake house. The land is home to a colony of endangered owls.

The kids turn to eco-terrorism to slow down development, which reflected Hiaasen's own youthful experiences. "We had our own little strategies, some of which surface in this novel," he admitted. "I mean, we pulled up survey stakes or rearranged them just to see if we could slow things down a little bit. It certainly didn't stop anything. But the kids in the book try some stuff like that, because the grown-ups in this book don't behave very well, for the most part, and they act kind of foolishly sometimes, as we do in real life."

The issue of developers vs. burrowing owls in their natural habitat was one from Hiaasen's own childhood. "After the novel was finished, my mom

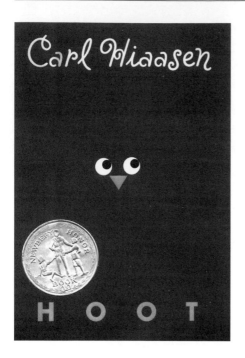

found an old album, a photo album," he explained. "I had taken this little Kodak Instamatic and gone out for a school project to photograph one of the last places where these little burrowing owls nested where I grew up. In the album, you see these tiny, little dots, these little owls standing at their burrows. I could drive you to that site now and it would be under about 25 tons of concrete. These developers came in and put up strip malls, just bulldozed all these little birds and their nests. Even at a very young age, I had a certain amount of anger, frustration, and sadness to see the place that I loved so much disappear."

In writing *Hoot*, Hiaasen showed that he had a lot of respect for kids. "My experience with kids is that they have a marvelously clear and pure instinct about what's right and wrong," he said. "Twenty-nine out of 30 sixth graders would say, 'We love pancakes, but it's wrong to bury these owls. It's just plain wrong.' Take a class that's ready to get their MBAs, and now the issue is clouded with property rights and the free-market economy. My position would be: The kids are right."

Writing for young adults was a challenge, however. "It was definitely hard," Hiaasen admitted. "Changing the language, for one thing. And obviously there are scenes in my other books that would not occur in a book for kids. They are not Disney moments."

Response to the book was very positive—especially considering that *Hoot* was his first book for kids. Readers were quick to fall in love with the novel. "After *Hoot* came out, it achieved a totally unforeseen popularity," Hiaasen said. "It was a real eye-opener. I've gotten hundreds and hundreds of letters from children who read this book. They tune right away into the message and the characters, get right to the heart of what the book is about. They understand where I was coming from. There must be hope for the world because they got it."

Critics also were very positive, praising Hiaasen for his smooth transition into writing for young adults. "Fans of Hiaasen's novels for adults may wonder how well his profane and frequently kinky writing will adapt to a child's audience; the answer is, remarkably well," wrote a reviewer from *Kirkus Reviews*. Critics also praised the novel as engaging and clever and felt the story would appeal to both younger and older readers. As a *Booklist* reviewer asserted, "[Hoot] is full of offbeat humor, buffoonish yet charming supporting characters, and genuinely touching scenes of children enjoying the wildness of nature." *Hoot* was named a 2003 Newbery Honor Book, a runner-up for the Newbery Medal, one of the most prestigious awards in children's literature. Being the author of a Newbery Honor Book is an impressive achievement for a first-time novelist for young readers.

Poster from the movie Hoot.

Hoot was made into a major motion picture released in May 2006. It stars Logan Lerman as Roy Eberhardt; Brie Larson as Beatrice Leep; Cody Linley as Mullet Fingers; Luke Wilson as Officer Delinko, the clueless local cop; and the singer Jimmy Buffett as Mr. Ryan, the science teacher. The book's many fans are eager to see how the story will translate to the big screen.

Flush

In his latest young adult book, *Flush* (2005), Hiaasen told the story of Noah Underwood and his younger sister, Abbey. Their father, an environmentalist, sinks the Coral Queen casino boat, charging that the dastardly owner flushed raw sewage into Florida waters. The brother and sister team up and work together to prove it. In the process, Noah has to face up to the local bully. Hiaasen viewed *Flush* as an opportunity to let characters "do things you wish you could get away with yourself."

Critics found many things to like about *Flush*. A reviewer for *Booklist* wrote that "Hiaasen still succeeds at relating an entertaining story while getting across a serious message about conservation and the results of just plain

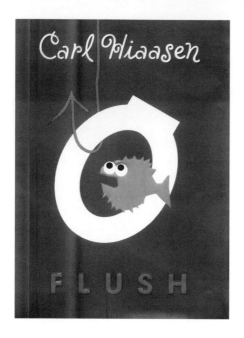

greed." When comparing Hiaasen's two young adult books, however, the reviewer asserted that "the sparkle that catapulted *Hoot* into the limelight isn't quite as brilliant here." But many critics recommended the novel for young readers. According to *School Library Journal,* "This quick-reading, fun, family adventure harkens back to the Hardy Boys in its simplicity and quirky characters." And the reviewer for *Horn Book* magazine suggested that "While the plot offers enough twists and turns to satisfy even the most serious adventure junkies, it is the multidimensional characters who give the novel its vitality. Hiaasen always shows rather than tells, and that showing creates individuals who are simultaneously noble and petty, quirky and realistic, decent and wayward."

Hiaasen was pleased to see readers' favorable response to *Hoot* and *Flush.* He asserted that kids recognize that they are funny books "about something pretty serious and important. Unlike many adults, kids have a fantastic natural instinct for what's right and wrong. With *Hoot,* I think they liked it because the stakes were high, and the children in the story were smarter than most of the adults. That's often true in real life."

Hiaasen also acknowledged the difficulties in writing for younger readers. "The hardest part is reaching kids where they are without talking down to them," he explained in an interview. "As J.K. Rowling and others have proven, kids are sophisticated readers. They're also quite aware when adults are underestimating them."

Advice to Young Writers

Hiaasen has claimed that reading is one of the most important activities for aspiring young authors. "Anybody who wants to be a writer ought to first be a reader," he stated. "Reading not only inspires you to write, it will teach you more about the craft than any teacher or college professor will be able to. Every good writer I know was a hungry reader as a kid."

"Sit down and write stories, write letters, write letters, do journals," he further encouraged young writers. "Journals are great. [Writing a journal] will get you familiar with expressing yourself, putting a thought down exactly as you want it."

MARRIAGE AND FAMILY

On November 12, 1970, Hiaasen married Constance Lyford, a registered nurse and attorney. Their son, Scott Andrew, is also a reporter. Hiaasen and Lyford divorced in 1996. He married his second wife, Fenia Clizer, a restaurant manager, in 1999. They have a son, Quinn.

"Anybody who wants to be a writer ought to first be a reader. Reading not only inspires you to write, it will teach you more about the craft than any teacher or college professor will be able to. Every good writer I know was a hungry reader as a kid."

HOBBIES AND OTHER INTERESTS

Hiaasen enjoys the outdoors, especially riding his boat through the Everglades National Park. He also loves wildlife, and for years raised snakes in his home. "I don't have many free hours, but I try to spend as many as possible with my kids," he said. "Flyfishing is a passion of mine, so I set aside a couple days a month to hang out in the Keys and chase after tarpon or bonefish. I've also taken up golf again after a 30-year break, and I can honestly report that I didn't forget a thing. I'm still a menace on the fairway."

Hiaasen has also been a two-time winner of the Bonefishing World Championship. Bonefishing is a sport in which the fisherman stalks and catches bonefish, a species of fish that is not eaten. He and the other competitors catch and then release the fish. "What drew me to it as a kid was that it's very peaceful," he asserted. "You're out in the shallowest, calmest part of the Florida Bay or even on the ocean side out in the Keys. You may not see any in a whole day or you may see lots, but if you catch just one you've had a good day."

WRITINGS

Fiction for Young Adults

Hoot, 2002
Flush, 2005

Nonfiction for Adults

Team Rodent: How Disney Devours the World, 1998
Kick Ass: Selected Columns of Carl Hiaasen, 1999
Paradise Screwed: Selected Columns of Carl Hiaasen, 2001

Fiction for Adults

Powder Burn, 1981 (with William D. Montalbano)
Trap Line, 1982 (with William D. Montalbano)
A Death in China, 1984 (with William D. Montalbano)
Tourist Season, 1986
Double Whammy, 1987
Skin Tight, 1989
Native Tongue, 1991
Strip Tease, 1993
Stormy Weather, 1995
Naked Came the Manatee, 1996
Lucky You, 1997
Sick Puppy, 2000
Basket Case, 2002
Skinny Dip, 2004

HONORS AND AWARDS

Clarion Award (Women in Communications): 1980
Heywood Broun Award (Newspaper Guild): 1980
National Headliners Award: 1980
Florida Society of Newspaper Editors Award: 1981
Green Eyeshade Award (Sigma Delta Chi): 1981
Investigative Reporters and Editors Award: 1981
Silver Gavel Award (American Bar Association): 1982
Best Books for Young Adults (American Library Association): 2003, for
    Hoot
Notable Book Award (American Library Association): 2003, for *Hoot*; 2005,
    for *Flush*
Damon Runyon Award (Denver Press Club): 2003-2004
Disney Adventures Book Award: 2005, for *Flush*
National Parenting Publications Award: 2005, for *Flush*
Rebecca Caudill Young Readers' Book Award: 2005, for *Hoot*

FURTHER READING

Books

Contemporary Authors New Revision Series, Vol. 45, 1995; Vol. 133, 2004
St. James Guide to Crime & Mystery Writers, 1996

Periodicals

Inspector, Sep. 2005, p.72
Orlando Sentinel, Oct. 2, 2002
Seattle Post-Intelligencer, Sep. 30, 2005, p.44
Smithsonian, June 2003, pp.88
Time for Kids, Dec. 8, 2005
Variety, Sep. 24, 2005, p.E1
Washington Post, Sep.14, 2005, p.C16

Online Articles

http://www.powells.com/authors/hiaasen.html
    (Powells.com, "A Kinder, Gentler Carl Hiaasen," Sep. 29, 2005)
http://books.scholastic.com/teachers
    (Scholastic Authors and Books, "Carl Hiaasen's Biography," undated)

Online Databases

Biography Resource Center Online, 2006, articles from *Contemporary Authors Online*, 2005, and *St. James Guide to Crime & Mystery Writers*, 1996

ADDRESS

Carl Hiaasen
The Miami Herald
1 Herald Plaza
Miami, FL 33101

WORLD WIDE WEB SITES

http://www.carlhiaasen.com
http://www.hootmovie.com

Will Hobbs 1947-

American Young Adult Novelist
Author of *Downriver, Far North,* and *Jason's Gold*

BIRTH

William Carl Hobbs was born on August 22, 1947, in Pittsburgh, Pennsylvania. His father is Gregory J. Hobbs, a civil engineer, and his mother is Mary Ann (Rhodes) Hobbs. Will has three brothers—Greg, Ed, and Joe—and one sister, Barbara.

YOUTH

Because his father was in the U.S. Air Force, Hobbs moved often as a child. When he was only six months old, the family moved to the Panama Canal Zone, where his father was stationed for a time. Later, the family moved to Virginia, Alaska, California, and Texas. Hobbs has said that being close to his siblings made these frequent moves easier to take. All of the Hobbs children were Scouts, giving them an opportunity to frequently experience the outdoors during camping and fishing trips. The family always lived near nature as well. "I consider myself lucky to always have had at least a touch of the wild as an everyday part of my life almost everywhere we lived," Hobbs remarked.

When he was four years old, the family was living in Falls Church, Virginia. Hobbs grew to love the box turtles that he and his older brothers Greg and Ed found in the woods behind the family house. While they routinely captured the box turtles and brought them home, the rule was they could only keep them for three days. On day four, the turtles were returned to the woods and released. "I've since been back to Falls Church to visit," Hobbs remembered. "The woods that were behind our house are all gone. It's all houses. I feel bad that kids living on our street don't have the woods to go to any more."

Hobbs got even closer to nature when he was in third grade and the family moved from Virginia to Alaska. His father was stationed at Elmendorf Air Force Base near Anchorage, Alaska. Here, he learned to fish in the Kenai River with his father and brothers. "Funny," Hobbs recalled, "but the Kenai memory that sticks deepest is my dad undoing the incredible kinks in our lines. Imagine trying to keep three little boys' lines in the water while trying to do any fishing yourself. My father's patience was legendary. . . . I sometimes reflect that the patience it takes me to see one of my novels from that first blank page through all of its revisions comes from my father."

> **"**
>
> *"[The] memory that sticks deepest is my dad undoing the incredible kinks in our [fishing] lines. Imagine trying to keep three little boys' lines in the water while trying to do any fishing yourself. My father's patience was legendary. . . . I sometimes reflect that the patience it takes me to see one of my novels from that first blank page through all of its revisions comes from my father."*
>
> **"**

While attending fourth grade at Mount Spurr Elementary, Hobbs became a voracious reader. He was inspired by the story *Call It Courage* by Armstrong Sperry, read aloud to the class by his teacher. The story of South

Hobbs as a young boy (left), with two of his brothers, Ed and Greg.

Seas adventure enchanted him, even though it was so different from his daily life in Alaska. "On my way to school during those weeks," Hobbs later recalled, "I was in a sort of trance."

The Hobbs family left Alaska in 1957, this time moving just north of San Francisco, California. Again the family lived in an area near woods and farms. He enjoyed working alongside his father in the family vegetable garden. Hobbs grew pumpkins, which he sold for 50 cents apiece at Halloween time. He also read constantly, with *Treasure Island* by Robert Louis Stevenson and *The Adventures of Tom Sawyer* by Mark Twain being his favorite novels.

The family moved to San Bernardino in southern California when Hobbs was in the eighth grade. His father had been transferred to Norton Air Force Base. Six months later, the family moved again, this time to Randolph Air Force Base in San Antonio, Texas. Hobbs attended Central Catholic High School, where he and his brothers joined the ROTC. In Will's senior year, his father was transferred back to California again, this time to the Hamilton Air Force Base in Marin County. Although the family offered him the chance to stay in San Antonio and finish high school there, Hobbs decided to go to California with them and finish his senior year at a new school. He graduated from Marin Catholic High School. During his high school summer breaks, Hobbs worked as a ranger at the Philmont Scout Ranch, taking younger Scouts on treks in the high mountains.

EDUCATION

After graduating from high school, Hobbs decided to attend the University of Notre Dame in Indiana, where his older brother Greg was already a student. One of his instructors praised his class essays and suggested that Hobbs might want to pursue English. In his sophomore year, he transferred to Stanford University in California and declared English his major. He graduated from Stanford in 1969 with a Bachelor of Arts (BA) degree, then entered the school's graduate program. "My intention," Hobbs remembered, "was to specialize in American literature and to teach at the college level." He earned a Master of Arts (MA) degree in 1971, but decided not to continue for a doctorate.

FIRST JOBS

Hobbs spent a number of years teaching school in the West. He started out teaching eighth graders at an elementary school in Upper Lake, California. "I found out that I really liked working with kids," he stated, "getting them excited about reading and writing."

Between 1973 and 1989, Hobbs worked as a teacher of English and reading in the public schools of Pagosa Springs and Durango, both in Colorado. As a writer, he has drawn on his teaching years when creating some of the young characters in his novels. He also learned during his time as a teacher that reluctant readers especially enjoyed reading adventure stories. To reach such readers, Hobbs decided to write adventure stories set in the outdoors that he loves so much.

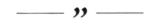

> **"**
>
> *"By high school I was dreaming that one day I would become a writer. In college I studied literature. I became, naturally enough, an English and reading teacher; I liked kids and books, so it was a perfect match. Yet something was missing."*
>
> **"**

BECOMING A WRITER

"By high school I was dreaming that one day I would become a writer," Hobbs explained in the *Seventh Book of Junior Authors and Illustrators*. "In college I studied literature. I became, naturally enough, an English and reading teacher; I liked kids and books, so it was a perfect match. Yet something was missing." While teaching English, Hobbs had accumulated a library of nearly 600 novels for young readers. "Maybe it was the feel of those books in my hands," he recounted. "I couldn't stand it that I wasn't chasing my secret dream. I was a do-it-yourselfer from way back; it was time to write my own book." He wrote the first draft of a novel in the summer of 1980. Six drafts later, that novel was finally published in 1989 as *Bearstone.* His first novel to see publication, *Changes in Latitudes,* took him four years to write and appeared in 1988. In 1990, Hobbs left teaching and began writing full-time.

CAREER HIGHLIGHTS

Hobbs's own experiences in the outdoors have inspired many of his stories. He has written of the canyons of Utah, the Grand Canyon, and the rugged coastline of Alaska. Most of his novels are adventure stories featuring teenaged characters who find themselves by learning how to survive in the wild. Paula Johanson, writing in her biography *Will Hobbs,* noted that "Hobbs's books are a strong example of 'quest' stories, a literary tradition that dates back to Homer's *Odyssey.* A hero goes on a journey, during which he or she is tested, gains self-knowledge, and achieves a prize of value to himself or herself and the community to which he or she returns."

> *"I poured all of my love of the mountains and of bears into the writing, as well as my deep respect for native traditions,"* Hobbs said of writing **Beardance.**

Hobbs's first published novel, *Changes in Latitudes* (1988), is narrated by 16-year-old Travis, whose parents' marriage is falling apart. Travis has traveled to Mexico with his mother and little brother, Teddy. While there, Teddy becomes interested in the ridley sea turtles on the beach. Travis, too, grows more interested in the turtles, but only as a means to forget his parents' troubles. He comes to realize that the turtles are as much "endangered" as is his own family, but he also realizes that he cannot ignore the problems in his life. "Travis's changes in attitudes is what this story is all about," Hobbs wrote on his web site. "Over the course of the novel, he moves from being self-absorbed to caring a whole lot more about his family."

In *Bearstone* (1989), Hobbs told of Cloyd Atcitty, a troubled Ute Indian boy who has been sent to work for Walter Landis, an old rancher in Colorado. Early in the story, Cloyd finds a bearstone at an ancient burial site. The small turquoise fetish symbolizes the special relationship between the Utes and the grizzly bears of the region. Cloyd is happily surprised when he finds what may be the last grizzly bear in Colorado, but his happiness fades when he learns of a hunter who is trailing the bear. Hobbs explained on his web site: "I'd been to the Utes' bear dance and knew how significant the kinship between people and bears was to Ute culture. I thought it would be especially meaningful for a Ute boy to meet the last grizzly." In the sequel, *Beardance* (1993), Cloyd and Walter are searching for a lost Spanish gold mine. Along the way, they are told that a mother grizzly bear and her cubs have been spotted in the area. After an accident claims their mother, Cloyd finds himself taking care of two lost cubs as winter approaches. In a statement posted on his web site, Hobbs said of writing *Beardance*, "I poured all of

WILL HOBBS
BEARSTONE
Face-to-face with the last grizzly in Colorado

my love of the mountains and of bears into the writing, as well as my deep respect for native traditions." In *Beardream* (1997), a picture book for younger readers, Hobbs again presented bears as major characters in the story of a young boy who wakes an oversleeping bear in springtime.

Hobbs drew on his own experiences rafting on the Colorado River to write *Downriver* (1991), the story of seven teenagers who raft down the rapids of the Grand Canyon. Hobbs himself has rafted those rapids 10 times. In the story, 15-year-old Jessie is having trouble with her family back home. She is sent to a wilderness camp, where she and the other kids dare each other into breaking away and rafting the Grand Canyon. A dangerous, unaided journey down the rapids convinces Jessie to rebuild her life at home. Jessie and the other teens from *Downriver* return in *River Thunder* (1997), in which Jessie has the chance to row the Colorado River alone. When the Colorado reaches flood stage, the teens must come together to survive the raging waters. "Most of the same characters are in this story as were in the first book," Hobbs noted on his web site, "and they all grow and change when faced with the incredible danger of the high water."

The Big Wander (1992) is set in Utah in 1962. In this story, Hobbs told the story of Clay Lancaster, who is looking for a missing uncle, a former rodeo star trying to save a herd of wild horses in the Escalante Mountains. Along the way, Clay and his burro travel through desolate canyons, visit a Navajo family, and escape a flash flood before locating the lost uncle. Clay also meets Sarah, a ranch girl who loves the canyons as much as he does. Hobbs explained on his web site that *The Big Wander* "began with the image of a boy, a burro, and a dog wandering in the canyon country. I was inspired by the real-life wanderings of a remarkable young man named Everett Ruess, who disappeared in the canyons of the Escalante River in Utah in the early 1930s. I didn't want to write Everett's story; I wanted to make up a story that would be a tip of the hat to him."

─────── " ───────

"I lived in Alaska when I was a kid. As I wrote **Far North** *it was all coming back; the raw vastness of the land, the winter darkness, the northern lights. . . . Of course I drew heavily on our summertime experiences on the Nahanni. . . . I couldn't have done nearly as well writing convincing descriptions unless I'd seen that country myself and fallen in love with it."*

─────── " ───────

Hobbs set his next novel in northern New Mexico. In *Kokopelli's Flute* (1995), 13-year-old Tepary Jones decides that the ancient cliff dwellings near his family's seed farm would be the perfect place to watch his first full eclipse of the moon. But that night, he finds grave robbers digging at the site. They run off, leaving behind a small flute. When Tepary tries to play it, he discovers the ancient piece holds a secret that takes him on a strange and incredible journey. "Hobbs vividly evokes the Four Corners region and blends fantasy with fact so smoothly that the resulting mix can be consumed without question," Darcy Schild wrote in *School Library Journal*. "Subplots flow together naturally, and ancient stories and sensibilities become one with modern lives. Outstanding characters, plot, mood, and setting combine in this satisfying and memorable book."

Hobbs turned to Canada's Northwest Territories for the setting of his novel *Far North* (1996). In this tale, 15-year-old Gabe Rogers has flown with his boarding school roommate, a Canadian Indian boy named Raymond Providence, to the Nahanni River. When the small bush plane sets down in the upper river, the engine quits. The plane is soon caught in the river's mighty current, headed straight for Virginia Falls. Gabe and Raymond escape from the plane, only to find themselves facing winter in the wilderness. They have to survive in the rugged terrain while coming to terms with their different cultural backgrounds. "I lived in Alaska when I was a kid," Hobbs remembered on his web site. "As I wrote *Far North* it was all coming back; the raw vastness of the land, the winter darkness, the northern lights. My winter experiences in Colorado, where we now live, helped as well. . . . Of course I drew heavily on our summertime experiences on the Nahanni. . . . I couldn't have done nearly as well writing convincing descriptions unless I'd seen that country myself and fallen in love with it." The Nahanni River was also the setting for the picture book *Howling Hill* (1998), which tells the story of a young wolf pup who becomes separated from her family along the river.

Ghost Canoe (1997), winner of an Edgar Allan Poe Award for best young adult mystery, is the story

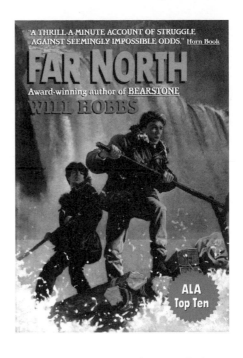

"A THRILL-A-MINUTE ACCOUNT OF STRUGGLE AGAINST SEEMINGLY IMPOSSIBLE ODDS." Horn Book

FAR NORTH

Award-winning author of BEARSTONE

WILL HOBBS

ALA Top Ten

of a lighthouse keeper's son, Nathan MacAllister, who refuses to believe there are no survivors of a nearby shipwreck, despite what the authorities say. He has seen strange footprints on the beach, and there are reports of a hairy man hiding in the woods. When the ship captain's body is washed ashore with a stab wound to the heart, Nathan knows there is more to the wreck than he has been told. Set in 1874 along the rugged Washington coastline, the story follows not only Nathan's investigation into the mystery, but his growing friendship with a local Makah Indian who delivers mail to the lighthouse by canoe. Chris Sherman in *Booklist* found that, "as always, Hobbs delivers well-developed characters and a plot that never falters."

In *The Maze* (1998), Rick Walker has lived in a series of foster homes and is now on the run, desperate to leave the past behind him. But he stumbles into The Maze, a desolate region of the Canyonlands National Park in Utah that is filled with deep, treacherous canyons. Rick wanders into the camp of Lon Peregrino, who is working to release California condors into the wild. From Lon, Rick is learning about the birds, about life, and about hang-gliding. When strangers with an axe to grind try to stop Peregrino from doing his work, Rick must pilot the hang-glider himself to save Lon. Although Hobbs has never flown a hang-glider, he does have a friend who has been a hang-glider pilot for many years. "I asked him if I could hang out with him and his buddies when they went flying," Hobbs explained on

Hobbs's love of the outdoors, adventure, and the West is evident in his novels and in his hobbies. He's shown here backpacking in the mountains in Colorado.

his web site. "I got to watch them assemble their hang gliders and run off the cliffs. . . . My friend talked me through what he was doing as he was flying the hang glider, how he finds and uses thermals and so on. After I'd written the story, I showed him all the parts that have hang gliding in them so he could check that they were correct." Mary M. Burns in the *Horn Book* magazine concluded: "Hobbs spins an engrossing yarn, blending adventure with a strong theme, advocating the need for developing personal values."

Hobbs set his story *Jason's Gold* (1999) during the Klondike Gold Rush of Canada's Yukon Territory in 1897. Thousands of gold-seekers made the trek into the rough country of the Yukon, hoping to strike gold and become rich. Hobbs tells of adventurous 15-year-old Jason Hawthorn, who sets out for the goldfields on his own. Along the way, he makes friends with Jamie, a Canadian girl, and with Jack London, author of *White Fang* and other adventure novels. London actually did participate in the Klondike Gold Rush, although he came back penniless. A reviewer for *Horn Book* magazine found that "Hobbs is right on target, blending fact and fiction to create a believable story that is fast reading but never simplistic." Jason returns in *Down the Yukon* (2001), working at his family's Yukon lumber mill along with his two older brothers. When Jason's brother gambles the mill away, Jason must get it back. He enters a river race down the Yukon that offers a $20,000 grand prize. Jason and Jamie race hundreds of others from Dawson to

Nome. But Cornelius Donner, the unscrupulous man who won the mill, will stop at nothing to prevent them from winning. Michele Winship, writing in *Kliatt,* noted that "Hobbs gives his readers a taste of life at the turn of the century as well as a vivid description of the Yukon wilderness."

Present-day Alaska is the setting for *Wild Man Island* (2002). Andy Galloway is with a kayak tour group when he sneaks away from the others in a remote corner of southeastern Alaska. He plans to visit Hidden Falls, where his archeologist father died in an accident nine years before. He only plans to be gone for a few hours before rejoining the group. But a sudden storm drives him 20 miles across the strait to Admiralty Island, where he encounters brown bears, wolves, and a hermit living by prehistoric means. He also finds a cave containing evidence to prove his father's archeological theories about early humans in the region. The story provides, Chris Sherman noted in *Booklist,* "a wealth of information about early human migration in North America." According to James Blassingame, writing in the *Journal of Adolescent & Adult Literacy,* "Hobbs seamlessly combines outdoor action/adventure and archeological mystery."

"I love living in [south-western Colorado] because everything is so close: mountains, canyons, rivers. We're in the Four Corners area, where Colorado, New Mexico, Arizona, and Utah all touch. Our house . . . is at the very edge of Durango, bordering a large wildlife preserve. From our windows we see elk, deer, eagles, bears, even an occasional mountain lion."

Jackie's Wild Seattle (2003) tells of a Seattle animal shelter of the same name that takes in injured or orphaned wild animals. Shannon, who is 14, and her younger brother, Cody, are spending the summer with their Uncle Neal, an animal rescuer with the shelter. But when Uncle Neal is injured by a hawk, Shannon and Cody find that they need to pitch in and help save the animals themselves. Shannon especially becomes involved, even rappelling down a cliff to save an injured seal. Another shelter volunteer, 15-year-old Tyler, is afraid of his violent father, while Shannon is unsure of Tyler, who once abused animals. Once again, Hobbs drew on personal experience for his story. In an interview for the *Journal of Adolescent & Adult Literacy,* Hobbs explained: "The last few summers I've been spending time with volunteers who work with urban and suburban wildlife. I ran into some amazing stuff, for example, the rescue of a coyote from an elevator in a downtown Seattle office building."

Leaving Protection (2004) tells of Robbie Daniels, a 16-year-old who signs on to an Alaskan fishing trawler owned by tough Norwegian Tor Torsen. The days are busy as the king salmon season is in full swing, but Robbie accidentally discovers something that puts his life in danger. Tor is also looking for "possession plaques," metal plaques left behind by the first Russian explorers in the area in order to lay claim to the Alaskan territory. These plaques are worth a great deal of money, and Tor intends to sell them illegally on the black market. He does not want anyone to get in his way. Robbie's knowledge may mean trouble. But a terrible storm soon threatens to sink the troller, and Tor and Robbie must work together to save themselves. Todd Morning, writing in *Booklist,* called the story "a taut, exciting novel."

Hobbs's most recent novel is *Crossing the Wire,* published in early 2006. It tells the story of 15-year-old Victor Flores, who lives in central Mexico. Ever since the death of his father, the boy has been supporting his family by farming, but the collapsing price of corn makes that impossible. After his best friend, Rico, leaves home to seek a better life in the United States, Victor decides to try to cross the border ("cross the wire"). He hopes to find work in the U.S. and send money back home to his family. Through the story of Victor's desperate and dangerous attempt to sneak across the border and

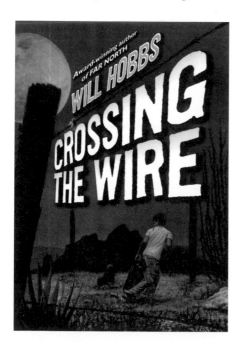

become an illegal worker, Hobbs explored controversial issues related to immigration and security that are currently facing the United States. "Victor's story is riveting, and the reader is immersed in striking natural landscapes while experiencing at first hand the controversial drug, labor, and immigration politics of the Arizona-Mexico border region," Walter Hohan wrote in *VOYA.* "While obviously sympathetic to migrant workers and illegal aliens, Hobbs is unsentimental in his portrayal of the hard lives and unpleasant choices facing impoverished Mexican villagers. . . . It is an exciting story in a vital contemporary setting."

Advice for Young Writers

Hobbs offered the following advice to aspiring writers. "Learning to write well takes practice and dedication, just like learning to play a musical instrument or a sport. It takes patience too, because revision is a big part of it. My biggest breakthrough was learning to write with the five senses. In the world of the story, both writer and reader are imagining what it's like to be someone else, so you want to let the reader hear, see, taste, touch, and smell what your characters are experiencing."

> "My biggest breakthrough was learning to write with the five senses. In the world of the story, both writer and reader are imagining what it's like to be someone else, so you want to let the reader hear, see, taste, touch, and smell what your characters are experiencing."

MARRIAGE AND FAMILY

Hobbs married Jean Loftus, a teacher, in December 1972. The following year the couple moved to southwestern Colorado. On his web site, he said that "I love living in this area because everything is so close: mountains, canyons, rivers. We're in the Four Corners area, where Colorado, New Mexico, Arizona, and Utah all touch. Our house . . . is at the very edge of Durango, bordering a large wildlife preserve. From our windows we see elk, deer, eagles, bears, even an occasional mountain lion."

HOBBIES AND OTHER INTERESTS

Hobbs has said he enjoys mountain hiking, whitewater rafting, archeology, and natural history.

WRITINGS

Changes in Latitudes, 1988
Bearstone, 1989
Downriver, 1991
The Big Wander, 1992
Beardance, 1993
Kokopelli's Flute, 1995
Far North, 1996
Beardream, 1997
Ghost Canoe, 1997
The Maze, 1998

Howling Hill, 1998
Jason's Gold, 1999
Down the Yukon, 2001
Wild Man Island, 2002
Jackie's Wild Seattle, 2003
Leaving Protection, 2004
Crossing the Wire, 2006

SELECTED HONORS AND AWARDS

Best Book for Young Adults (American Library Association): 1989, for *Bearstone*; 1991, for *Downriver*; 1992, for *The Big Wander*; 1993, for *Beardance*; 1996, for *Far North*; 1998, for *The Maze*; and 1999, for *Jason's Gold*

Books for the Teen Age (New York Public Library): 1992, for *Downriver*; 1993, for *The Big Wander*; 1994, for *Beardance*; 1997, for *Far North*; 1998, for *Ghost Canoe*; 1998, for *River Thunder*; 2000, for *Jason's Gold*; 2002, *Down the Yukon*; 2004, for *Jackie's Wild Seattle*; 2005, for *Leaving Protection*

100 Best of the Best Young Adult Books of the 20th Century (American Library Association): 1992, for *Downriver*; 1997, for *Far North*

Quick Picks for Reluctant Young Adult Readers (American Library Association): 1992, for *Downriver*; 1997, for *Far North*; 1999, for *The Maze*; 2000, for *Jason's Gold*

Spur Award (Western Writers of America): 1993, for *Beardance*; 1996, for *Far North*

Notable Children's Trade Book in the Field of Social Studies (National Council for Social Studies-Children's Book Council): 1989, for *Changes in Latitudes*; 1990, for *Bearstone*; 1996, for *Kokopelli's Flute*; 1997, for *Far North*; 2000, for *Jason's Gold*

"Books in the Middle" Outstanding Titles (*VOYA*): 1997, for *Far North*; 1998, for *Ghost Canoe*; 2000, for *Jason's Gold*

Edgar Allan Poe Award (Mystery Writers of America): 1998, for *Ghost Canoe*

Outstanding Science Trade Book for Students (National Science Teachers Association): 2003, for *Wild Man Island*; 2004, for *Jackie's Wild Seattle*

FURTHER READING

Books

Authors and Artists for Young Adults, Vol. 39, 2001
Contemporary Authors New Revision Series, Vol. 124, 2004
Hipple, Ted, ed. *Writers for Young Adults*, Vol. 2, 1997
Holtze, Sally Holmes. *Seventh Book of Junior Authors & Illustrators*, 1996
Johanson, Paula. *Will Hobbs*, 2006
Major Authors and Illustrators for Children and Young Adults, 2002

Marcovitz, Hal. *Who Wrote That? Will Hobbs*, 2006
McElmeel, Sharron R. *Children's Authors and Illustrators Too Good to Miss: Biographical Sketches and Bibliographies*, 2004
Something about the Author, Vol. 72, 1993; Vol. 109, 2000; Vol. 127, 2002
St. James Guide to Young Adults Writers, 1999

Periodicals

Booklist, May 1, 1997, p.1489; Apr. 15, 2002, p.1395; Mar. 1, 2004, p.1183
Horn Book, Sep.-Oct. 1998, p.609; Sep. 1999, p.612
Journal of Adolescent & Adult Literacy, Feb. 2003, pp.442, 444
Kliatt, July 2002, p.20
Writing!, Oct. 2003, p.4

Online Databases

Biography Resource Center Online, 2005, articles from *Authors and Artists for Young Adults,* 2001; *Contemporary Authors Online,* 2004; *Major Authors and Illustrators for Children and Young Adults,* 2002; and *St. James Guide to Young Adult Writers,* 1999

ADDRESS

Will Hobbs
Author Mail
HarperCollins Books for Young Readers
1350 Avenue of the Americas
New York, NY 10019

WORLD WIDE WEB SITE

http://www.willhobbsauthor.com

Kathryn Lasky 1944-
American Writer for Children and Young Adults
Prolific Author of Nonfiction Works, Historical Novels,
and Fantasy Novels

BIRTH

Kathryn Lasky was born on June 24, 1944, in Indianapolis, Indiana. She was the second child of Marven Lasky, a wine bottler who started his own business, and Hortense Lasky, a social worker. Her sister Martha is five years older, a big age difference when they were young. "I worshiped her," Lasky noted on her web site. "She was very smart and musically gifted."

YOUTH

Although Lasky loved reading and making up stories as a child, she wasn't the best student. "I feel like I was always daydreaming and I was always distracted," she observed. Her mother was a great encouragement to her at this time, according to Lasky: "She thought I was smart even when the teachers didn't." She would tell them that her daughter daydreamed to exercise her creativity. As a young student, Lasky had no thought of becoming a writer. "I loved to read, and if I could have been a professional reader, that's probably what I would've wanted to be! Somehow, it just evolved—if you like reading, I think you like writing. But I never really thought anybody could get paid for writing!" It took the encouragement of her mother to put the idea of writing as a career into her head. "She said, 'Kathy, you love words. And you have such a great imagination. You should be a writer.'"

> "I loved to read, and if I could have been a professional reader, that's probably what I would've wanted to be! Somehow, it just evolved—if you like reading, I think you like writing. But I never really thought anybody could get paid for writing!"

Lasky entered Tudor Hall, a private all-girls' school, at the age of eight. It wasn't the best fit for her; the teachers were very strict and there was little chance for her to exercise her imagination. Subjects she would later love to write about, like the natural sciences, were presented in a very boring manner. In addition, she was a Jewish student in a Christian school, and she often felt out of place while attending chapel with her schoolmates. Luckily, Lasky had a very supportive and loving family, and lakeside summer vacations and Florida winter vacations provided a break from the pressures of school.

EARLY MEMORIES

Lasky has often described the summer night her mother inspired her choice of career. She was 10 years old and her family was driving in their convertible. "There were no stars that night, but there were clouds, thick and woolly. Suddenly an image struck me. 'It's a sheepback sky,' I said to no one in particular. Hearing me my mother turned around and said, 'Kathy, you should be a writer.'"

EDUCATION

After graduating from Tudor Hall, Lasky enrolled at the University of Michigan. A self-described "late bloomer," she blossomed as a scholar there. At Michigan she studied English literature, reading all types and periods of literature. She earned her Bachelor of Arts (BA) degree in 1966 in English. In 1974 she entered Wheelock College in Boston, Massachusetts, earning a Master of Arts (MA) degree in teaching reading two years later.

MARRIAGE AND FAMILY

After moving to Massachusetts, Lasky met Christopher G. Knight, a professional photographer and documentary filmmaker, in 1968. They married on May 30, 1971, and raised two children: Max, born in 1977, and Meribah, born in 1982. Since their marriage, Lasky and her husband have frequently collaborated on nonfiction picture books, with Knight providing the photographs for his wife's text. They live in Cambridge, Massachusetts.

CAREER HIGHLIGHTS

Becoming a Writer

Lasky's first jobs after college were forgettable: substitute teaching, then writing on fashion and social events for *Town and Country* magazine in New York City. Her adventures began after meeting and marrying her husband. Her parents had given them a 30-foot sailboat for a wedding gift, and Lasky and her husband decided to sail across the Atlantic Ocean. They sailed to Europe in 1974, spent the next summer exploring the waters around the continent, then sailed back to America in 1976. The return journey was challenging, as they faced high winds and cold rains. Her shipboard experiences proved important to her career, however. She gained writing credits by contributing to *Sail* magazine during those years, and later wrote a book for adults, *Atlantic Circle* (1985), about their ocean journeys.

At the same time Lasky was discovering the seas, she was also studying to become a reading teacher. She discovered that the materials she was supposed to use with her students were just as boring as the ones she hated as a child. She believed she could write stories that would encourage children to read. While working on her master's degree, she began her first books for children. In 1976 she published her first picture book, *I Have Four Names for My Grandfather.* It depicts young Tom as he spends quality time with "Poppy," "Pop," "Grandpa," and "Gramps." Although the name Tom calls his grandfather changes, the love they share as they go fishing, plant flowers, and watch trains never does. The book is illustrated with photos by Lasky's husband, Christopher Knight, the first of their many collaborations.

In 1977, Lasky published her first nonfiction book for children, *Tugboats Never Sleep*, inspired by the boats she saw outside her house on Boston harbor. It, too, was illustrated with photographs by Knight, as was her next nonfiction book, *Tall Ships* (1978). The couple had discovered that by working together, they could produce nonfiction books where the words and pictures worked together to tell the story. In addition, Lasky learned to focus on the people related to her nonfiction subjects. "I didn't like nonfiction as a kid—the nonfiction books were really dry back then," the author recalled. "But then I realized that you can make the characters in nonfiction as fascinating as those in fiction."

I Have Four Names for My Grandfather

by
KATHRYN LASKY
Photographs by
CHRISTOPHER G. KNIGHT

Since that time, Lasky has created a wide range of books. She has written mystery novels for adults under her married name (Kathryn Lasky Knight), stories for elementary school age readers, and many nonfiction and fiction books for young adults. She has written nonfiction works on a wide range of subjects, including science, history, and biography. These include several photoessays, which are narrative works illustrated with her husband's photographs. In addition, she has written a wide variety of fictional works, including historical fiction, both in novel and diary form; contemporary fiction; and science fiction and fantasy. A prolific author, Lasky has won the hearts of both readers and critics, who have rewarded her works with many honors and awards.

Nonfiction

Lasky has written many nonfiction works, revealing a gift for finding the characters and drama in her real-life subjects. In *The Weaver's Gift* (1981), she detailed the creation of a blanket. Focusing on a Vermont farmer and weaver who raises sheep for their wool, she showed the process from sheep's wool to woven finish. *The Weaver's Gift* won the 1981 *Boston*

Globe/Horn Book Award for Nonfiction. Another book about a traditional craft, *Sugaring Time* (1983), follows the activities of the Lacey family as they spend the month of March producing maple syrup on their Vermont farm. *Sugaring Time* was named a 1984 Newbery Honor Book by the American Library Association. The Newbery Honor is a runner-up for the Newbery Medal, one of the most prestigious awards in children's literature. Winning the Newbery Honor was a rare accolade for a nonfiction book. In these and other nonfiction works, critics praised Lasky's vivid writing, exciting stories, and ability to communicate a sense of wonder about her subject. In 1986 she received the *Washington Post*/Children's Book Guild Nonfiction Award for her body of work.

Lasky has found subjects for her nonfiction writing in many areas, including the natural world, which has been the subject of several of the photoessays created with her husband. For *Dinosaur Dig* (1990), Lasky took her entire family to Montana to dig for fossils. This account not only conveys fascinating facts about paleontology (the study of fossils), but also shows the excitement the participants feel as they uncover a possible Triceratops skeleton. In *The Most Beautiful Roof in the World: Exploring the Rainforest Canopy* (1997), Lasky again communicated the fun of scientific study by following the efforts of scientists to explore their subject, in this case the biology of the Central American rainforest in Belize.

In *Shadows in the Dawn: The Lemurs of Madagascar* (1998), Lasky followed another kind of biologist: a primatologist, someone who studies apes and monkeys. In this case the scientist is tracking lemurs on the African island nation of Madagascar. Showing the animals in action, Lasky also gave a fascinating glimpse into the methods scientists use to study them. The photoessay *Interrupted Journey: Saving Endangered Sea Turtles* (2001) begins with a very urgent story: a boy discovers an injured turtle on Cape Cod. The book traces the efforts of local vets and marine biologists to save it. Critics have praised these photoessays for reading like fiction despite being true stories.

Lasky has not limited her nonfiction work to the nature-based photoessay. Her book *Traces of Life: The Origins of Humankind* (1989), for instance, is a thorough survey of the history of human evolution, a particular interest of the author. In this book, she examines the history of research into pre-human species (known as hominids) and speculates as to what the lives of these pre-humans might have been like. Another nonfiction book, *Searching for Laura Ingalls: A Reader's Journey* (1993), is a photoessay, but a bit different from her previous works of this kind. Its subject is more personal: the travels of Lasky and her family to find and explore the locations behind Laura Ingalls Wilder's beloved "Little House" books. Lasky included her daughter Meribah's journal entries in this travel story. *Searching for Laura Ingalls: A Reader's Journey* was awarded the Best Western Juvenile Nonfiction Award from the Western Writers of America in 1993.

"I love writing for adolescents. I feel the same vulnerability that they feel. When I was young, my mother used to say, 'Don't believe people who tell you that this is the best time of your life. It isn't. It's the worst.' Kids are trying to define themselves, find out who they are. I can connect pretty well with that feeling."

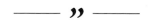

Lasky has also written several biographies in the picture book format, giving readers simple yet entertaining introductions to the lives of real people. Her subjects have ranged from very famous historical figures, to lesser-known groundbreakers, to her own family. In *The Librarian Who Measured*

99

the Earth (1994), for instance, Lasky wrote about the ancient Greek scholar Eratosthenes, who was head of the wondrous library of the city of Alexandria. Eratosthenes was the first person to calculate the circumference of our planet. He looked at the angles of shadows in two different places, measured the distance between them, and then calculated the curvature and circumference of the earth by using geometry. In her 1997 biography *Marven of the Great North Woods,* Lasky writes about her own father. The son of Russian Jewish immigrants, he was sent to a north Minnesota logging camp during the flu epidemic of 1918. He was only 10 years old at the time and found the logging lifestyle strange, without kosher food. He overcomes this strangeness to befriend the lumberjacks at the camp and ends up waking them for work each day. This biography of her father earned Lasky a National Jewish Book Award in 1997.

——— *“* ———

“I can't stand doing the same thing twice. I don't want to change just for the sake of change. But the whole point of being an artist is to be able to get up every morning and reinvent the world.”

——— *”* ———

One of her favorite authors became the subject of *A Brilliant Streak: The Making of Mark Twain* (1996). This biography traces the famous author's childhood in Missouri and his experiences on the Mississippi River as a young man. Lasky used Twain's own writings as a source for many of the amusing stories about his youth. Self-made businesswoman Sarah Breedlove Walker is the subject of *Vision of Beauty* (2000). By creating hair-care products, Walker became the first African-American woman to earn a million dollars. She worked as a feminist and civil rights pioneer and encouraged women to gain self-confidence through beauty. In *The Man Who Made Time Travel* (2003), Lasky focuses on a British scientific pioneer. John Harrison was a self-taught watchmaker who was the first to create an accurate method of measuring longitude (a precise point east or west of the Prime Meridian). Lasky relates the history of Harrison's era, noting the importance of sea travel in the 18th century as well as his lifelong efforts to perfect his seaworthy timepiece and win recognition for its success.

Historical Fiction

Lasky has also written historical fiction, combining her gift for storytelling with her fascination with the past. Indeed, she has even admitted that she has “a favorite kind of book, and that is historical fiction.” Lasky hadn't originally planned to write historical fiction for her first novel, *The Night Journey* (1981); instead, it grew out of her own family history. Her father's parents emigrated from Russia in the 1800s, escaping religious persecution during the rule of the czars. *The Night Journey* is Nana Sashie's account of her childhood in Russia and escape to America, told to her 13-year-old granddaughter Rachel. Although Sashie's story includes the murders of her grandparents, it is her stories of their everyday lives in the village that stick with Rachel and give her a sense of family. *The Night Journey* earned Lasky a National Jewish Book Award and the Sydney Taylor Book Award.

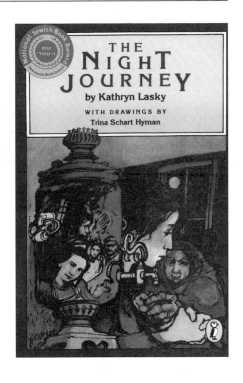

In her novel *Beyond the Divide* (1983), Lasky told the story of pioneer girl Meribah Simon as she travels with her father from Pennsylvania Amish country to the California of the Gold Rush. She encounters hardships on the cross-country journey: her close friend is raped and commits suicide, and her father is wounded and dies of an infection. Left to fend for herself, the 14-year-old Meribah barely survives the wild until she meets a tribe of Yana. These Native Americans help the girl stay alive until she finds a place to settle. "The novel is so realistic it would be easy to believe that *Beyond the Divide* is directly from the diary of a young girl going west," noted a writer for the *St. James Guide to Young Adult Writers*.

Lasky's novel *The Bone Wars* (1988), about competition for dinosaur fossils during the late 19th century, also makes use of the author's research into the American West. It is set against the backdrop of the Sioux Indian Wars, when General George Custer and Chief Crazy Horse led battles over the northern plains of South Dakota and Montana. At the same time, rival scientists vied to find and excavate the best dinosaur fossils in that area. Two 14-year-old boys witness these struggles: Thaddeus, an orphaned American, and Julian, the son of a famous British paleontologist. They dislike the tactics the scientists use to promote their careers, so when they find a dinosaur skeleton they decide to uncover it in secret and donate it to a mu-

Lasky hiking out west, doing research for her western fiction.

seum. As critic Joanne Brown noted in *Presenting Kathryn Lasky,* by exploring issues of bigotry, history, and growing up, *The Bone Wars* "weaves several major themes into its adventure story, most of them common to Lasky's fiction."

In choosing topics for her historical novels, Lasky has selected subjects that "I don't feel have been given a fair shake in history. Where people fell into kind of easy answers or stereotypical thinking—I always feel [that] there's an understory that people should explore." Living in Massachusetts, for instance, she was uncomfortable with the way the village of Salem was presented as a tourist attraction. This home of the notorious witch trials of the 17th century was the scene of what she called "a terrible tragedy, and a shameful moment in our history." The resulting novel was *Beyond the Burning Time* (1994), told from the viewpoint of 12-year-old Mary Chase, whose mother has been accused of witchcraft and sentenced to hang. The author used actual court records and journals of the era in her research, bringing realistic details to Mary's attempts to free her mother from a community's obsession with destroying "evil."

Lasky explored another emotional historical subject in the novel *True North* (1996), set in Boston in 1858. When 14-year-old Lucy discovers young Afrika, a runaway slave, hiding in her late grandfather's house, Lucy must decode his notes in order to help Afrika continue her journey along the Underground Railroad. As the two girls make the dangerous trip to Canada and freedom, Lucy learns more about the horrible conditions

Afrika faced as a slave in the South. Lasky created another novel set in mid-19th-century America in *Alice Rose and Sam* (1998). In this novel, 12-year-old Alice Rose is a newspaperman's daughter living in a Nevada mining town in 1863. When she witnesses a murder, she enlists the assistance of a young reporter to investigate — not a safe or easy task for those living in the Wild West, where lawmen can be corrupt and people take the law into their own hands. With the help of Sam Clemens — readers might recognize him as the future Mark Twain — Alice Rose finds the killer and also helps uncover a Confederate plot. The novel won the Western Heritage Award from the National Cowboy Hall of Fame.

In her novel *Broken Song* (2005), Lasky again used her family history as the inspiration for a moving tale of struggle. Reuven Bloom is a 15-year-old living in a Russian *shtetl* (a Jewish village) at the end of the 19th century. He aspires to become a violinist, but life changes when anti-Semitic soldiers of the Russian army overrun the area. First Reuven's best friend is pressed into the army; then an attack leaves his parents and older sister dead and Reuven alone with his baby sister. He escapes on foot, ending up in Poland working for a revolutionary group. Eventually he leaves the violent struggle for the promise of a new life in America. Critics noted the powerful story reads like an adventure while still featuring Lasky's usual thorough historical research.

> **"**
>
> *Research takes up most of Lasky's time — around four times as long as the actual writing. "I love doing research," she maintained. "It's really fun. It's like a treasure hunt."*
>
> **"**

Historical Fiction in Diary Form

As the author of historical novels, it was a natural step for Lasky to make use of the diary format in her historical fiction. She first contributed to Scholastic's "Dear America" series with *A Journey to the New World: The Diary of Remember Patience Whipple* (1996). Since then, she has written over a dozen novels using the very personal point of view of the diary form. Her entries in the "Dear America" series include Remember Patience Whipple's voyage on the *Mayflower*, Zipporah Feldman's immigrant experience in New York in 1903 (*Dreams in the Golden Country*, 1998), and Kathryn Bowen's work as a suffragette in 1917 (*A Time for Courage*, 2002). Although these characters are fictional, they are also believable, and their detail-packed stories entertain readers as well as inform them about history. Other

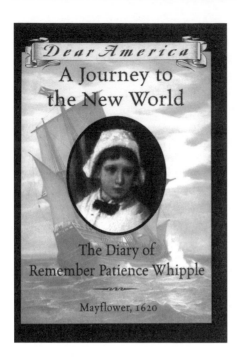

fictional "diaries" Lasky has written about American history include *The Journal of Augustus Pelletier* (2000), about the Lewis and Clark expedition of 1804, and a trilogy (*Hope in My Heart, Home at Last,* and *An American Spring,* 2003-2004) about a young Italian girl's experience of immigrating to the United States.

Lasky has also used the diary format to bring personal immediacy to the lives of famous historical figures. Her "Royal Diaries" series brings to life the early years of princesses of various eras and cultures. In *Elizabeth I: Red Rose of the House of Tudor* (1999), Lasky explored the years the future queen of England lived with her famous father, King Henry VIII, and his wife Catherine Parr. In *Marie Antoinette: Princess of Versailles* (2000), the author related the early teen years of the archduchess of Vienna, before she became queen of France and was beheaded during the French Revolution. In *Mary, Queen of Scots: Queen without a Country* (2002), Lasky recalled the years the Scottish queen spent growing up in France, before her cousin Elizabeth I had her executed as a threat to the English throne. Lasky also portrayed lesser-known historical figures in this series, including the daughter of the Moghul Emperor and builder of the Taj Mahal, Shah Jahan (*Jahanara: Princess of Princesses,* 2003), and a Japanese princess who must marry to support her brother, the Emperor Komei (*Kazunomiya: Prisoner of Heaven,* 2005). In each of these fictional diaries, Lasky offered readers glimpses into the lives of these famous young women, as well as historical notes that provided perspective on broader issues of the era.

Contemporary Fiction

In addition to historical novels, Lasky has also written contemporary novels for young adults. Some of these have drawn on her personal background, including the novel *Pageant* (1986), considered her most autobiographical book. Its protagonist, Sarah Benjamin, is a Jewish teenager attending a Christian high school in the early 1960s—just as Lasky did. Every year

Sarah is cast as a shepherd in the school's nativity play because she is too dark to play an angel. She has a growing difficulty coping with other people's expectations of her, as well as their narrow-minded ideas about gender and race. Despite having loving parents, she runs away to New York to visit her older sister. Along the way she hears that her idol, President John F. Kennedy, has been shot and killed. She also discovers her sister is living with a man. Despite these painful surprises, Sarah learns she can control her own destiny. She earns her high school diploma and enters the Peace Corps.

Not all the families in Lasky's contemporary novels are supportive. In the novel *Prank* (1984), Birdie Flynn's brother has desecrated a synagogue. As Birdie researches the Nazi holocaust, she becomes more aware of her parents' bigotry and anti-Semitism, as well as other problems at home. She also develops the determination she needs to escape her poor neighborhood and leave her abusive family. In the novel *Memoirs of a Bookbat* (1994), Harper Jessup's father used to be an alcoholic who beat his wife and couldn't keep a job. Then he became involved in a fundamentalist religious group that works to ban "bad" books. Unfortunately, Harper loves to read all kinds of books. To help keep her family together, Harper pretends to follow her parents' teachings; in secret, she is reading the same books they despise. Eventually, moved by letters from a favorite author, Harper leaves her family to strike out on her own as an independent thinker.

It is not surprising that Lasky can create such vibrant, believable characters in her young adult novels. "I love writing for adolescents. I feel the same vulnerability that they feel," she noted. "When I was young, my mother used to say, 'Don't believe people who tell you that this is the best time of your life. It isn't. It's the worst.' Kids are trying to define themselves, find out who they are. I can connect pretty well with that feeling." This gives her young adult fiction an immediacy and authenticity that appeal to readers.

Science Fiction and Fantasy

Lasky has also written science fiction and fantasy for young adults, including individual works as well as multi-volume series. In her "Starbuck Family" series, she featured two sets of twins who can communicate using only their minds. Liberty and her twin brother July are 12-year-old telepaths; they can also "teleflash" their younger identical twin sisters, five-year-old Charley and Molly. In their first book, *Double Trouble Squared* (1991), the four siblings visit London, where they encounter a mystery involving the home of Sir Arthur Conan Doyle, author of the "Sherlock Holmes" mysteries. In the sequel, *Shadows in the Water* (1992), the four Starbuck siblings are in Florida, where their father is hunting the source of a toxic waste spill. Using detective skills and their ability to communicate with dolphins, the kids catch the polluters—and the attention of Hollywood. The American Southwest provides the setting for a third novel, *A Voice in the Wind* (1993). The ownership of Native American artifacts serves as a backdrop for this mystery, another fun adventure.

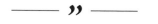

> *"I feel honored by any young person who breaks away from all those demands on their time and picks up my books. I just hope they read them to enjoy them and not just because they have to write a report!"*

In her science fiction novel *Star Split* (1999), Lasky set her story over 1000 years in the future to look at the issues involved in genetic engineering. Darci is 13 years old; like most people around her, she is a genetically enhanced "Genhant," her DNA selected by her parents. She sometimes wonders what it would be like to be an "Original," a human created through old-fashioned reproduction, and whether they have more choice in their future than she seems to have. When Darci discovers an illegal clone of herself, she must consider these issues even more carefully. In *Star Split* Lasky included an afterword to explain the science of cloning—giving her speculative fiction, like her historical fiction, a through grounding in reality.

Lasky mixed fantastic and historical fiction in her novel *Blood Secret* (2004). After bouncing between orphanages, Jerry has come to live in New Mexico with her great-great-aunt Constanza. Jerry's mother mysteriously disappeared several years ago, and the trauma has left the 14-year-old girl unable to speak. When she discovers an old trunk in her aunt's basement, the objects within transport her through time to experience her family's past. These episodes begin with a Jewish girl baptized by force in 14th-century Spain and continue through immigrant experiences in America, and Catholic Jerry comes to learn that some of her ancestors were Jewish. Her understanding of her family history, along with the love of her aunt and the compassion of a new school friend, help bring Jerry out of her shell.

Lasky conducted thorough research to create the fantasy world of owls in her popular "Guardians of Ga'Hoole" series. Using her knowledge of actual owl behavior, the author created a soci-

ety in which the owls celebrate such milestones as "First Fur" and "First Meat" and tell stories of the chivalrous and noble Guardians of Ga'Hoole. In the opening novel, *The Capture* (2003), baby barn owl Soren is knocked from his family's nest by an older brother. He is taken away to the St. Aegolius Academy for Orphaned Owls, where he and the other fledglings are brainwashed by the light of the moon. With the secret help of an older owl, Soren and his friend Gylfie learn to fly and escape St. Aegolius. In the series' second volume, *The Journey* (2003), Soren and his friends search for the legendary Great Ga'Hoole tree. There they find a school for young owls that teaches teamwork and important skills like navigation and rescue operations. Further novels pit Soren and his friends against the evil forces led by Soren's brother, detailing their various struggles to find allies, avoid unexpected betrayals, and put the rightful heir on the throne of Ga'Hoole. Lasky also plans several future novels exploring the history of Ga'Hoole. The series has proven so successful that in 2005, the author signed a deal with Warner Brothers to bring "The Guardians of Ga'Hoole" to the big screen as an animated film. She will write the screenplay and help produce the film, as well.

In publishing some 100 books on various subjects for audiences from the very young to adults, Lasky always looks for new challenges. "I can't stand doing the same thing twice," she said. "I don't want to change just for the sake of change. But the whole point of being an artist is to be able to get up every morning and reinvent the world." She never has writer's block or a shortage of ideas, explaining that "I think I am just a good observer, and perhaps I see things and wonder about them in odd ways; and this means sometimes making up stories about them." She has gotten many of her ideas from reading, especially the newspaper. Research takes up most of her time—around four times as long as the actual writing. "I love doing research," she maintained. "It's really fun. It's like a treasure hunt." She considers research to be an important part of her work, whether writing fiction or nonfiction. "My responsibility as a writer for authenticity and accuracy does not vary whether the character is real or fictional."

————— *"* —————

"Facts are quite cheap, but real stories are rare and expensive. . . . I really do not care if readers remember a single fact. What I do hope is that they come away with a sense of joy—indeed celebration—about something they have sensed of the world in which they live."

————— *"* —————

Lasky feels strongly that writing for children—all ages of children—is a valuable occupation. "I feel honored by any young person who breaks away from all those demands on their time and picks up my books. I just hope they read them to enjoy them and not just because they have to write a report!" What is more important to her than communicating facts is telling a good story: "Facts are quite cheap, but real stories are rare and expensive. . . . I really do not care if readers remember a single fact. What I do hope is that they come away with a sense of joy—indeed celebration—about something they have sensed of the world in which they live."

HOBBIES AND OTHER INTERESTS

Lasky enjoys reading, which she offers as the ideal activity for aspiring writers. She also enjoys art, music, and movies, finding inspiration in all forms of creative expression. When not writing, she enjoys working in her garden. She still goes sailing with her husband, but limits her journeys to the coastal waters near their summer home in Maine.

SELECTED WRITINGS

Fiction

I Have Four Names for My Grandfather, 1976
Jem's Island, 1982
Prank, 1984

Pageant, 1986
Double Trouble Squared, 1991 ("Starbuck Family")
Shadows in the Water, 1992 ("Starbuck Family")
A Voice in the Wind, 1993 ("Starbuck Family")
Memoirs of a Bookbat, 1994
Star Split, 1999
Blood Secret, 2004

Nonfiction

Tugboats Never Sleep, 1977
Tall Ships, 1978
The Weaver's Gift, 1981
Sugaring Time, 1983
A Baby for Max, 1984
Traces of Life: The Origins of Humankind, 1989
Dinosaur Dig, 1990
Searching for Laura Ingalls: A Reader's Journey, 1993
Monarchs, 1993
The Librarian Who Measured the Earth, 1994
A Brilliant Streak: The Making of Mark Twain, 1996
The Most Beautiful Roof in the World: Exploring the Rainforest Canopy, 1997
Marven of the Great North Woods, 1997
Shadows in the Dawn: The Lemurs of Madagascar, 1998
Vision of Beauty: The Story of Sarah Breedlove Walker, 2000
Interrupted Journey: Saving Endangered Sea Turtles, 2001
The Man Who Made Time Travel, 2003
A Voice of Her Own: The Story of Phillis Wheatley, Slave Poet, 2003

Historical Fiction

The Night Journey, 1981
Beyond the Divide, 1983
The Bone Wars, 1988
Beyond the Burning Time, 1994
True North: A Novel of the Underground Railroad, 1996
Alice Rose and Sam, 1998
The Journal of Augustus Pelletier, 2000
Hope in My Heart: Sofia's Ellis Island Diary, 2003
Home at Last: Sofia's Immigrant Diary, 2003
An American Spring: Sofia's Immigrant Diary, 2004

Dancing through Fire, 2005
Broken Song, 2005

"Dear America" Series

*A Journey to the New World: The Diary of Remember Patience Whipple,
Mayflower, 1620,* 1996
Dreams in the Golden Country: The Diary of Zipporah Feldman, 1998
Christmas After All: The Great Depression Diary of Minnie Swift, 2001
A Time for Courage: The Suffragette Diary of Kathleen Bowen, 2002

"Royal Diaries" Series

Elizabeth I: Red Rose of the House of Tudor, England 1544, 1999
Marie Antoinette: Princess of Versailles, Austria-France 1769, 2000
Mary, Queen of Scots: Queen without a Country, France 1553, 2002
Jahanara: Princess of Princesses, India 1627, 2002
Kazunomiya: Prisoner of Heaven, Japan 1858, 2005

"Guardians of Ga'Hoole" Series

The Capture, 2003
The Journey, 2003
The Rescue, 2004
The Siege, 2004
The Shattering, 2004
The Burning, 2004
The Hatchling, 2005
The Outcast, 2005
The First Collier, 2006

SELECTED HONORS AND AWARDS

Boston Globe-Horn Book Award for Nonfiction: 1981, for *The Weaver's Gift*
National Jewish Book Award (Jewish Welfare Board Book Council): 1982,
for *The Night Journey;* 1997, for *Marven of the Great North Woods*
Sydney Taylor Book Award (Association of Jewish Libraries): 1982, for *The
Night Journey*
Best Book for Young Adults (American Library Association): 1983, for
Beyond the Divide; 1984, for *Prank;* 1986, for *Pageant*
Washington Post/Children's Book Guild Nonfiction Award: 1986, for body
of work

Golden Trilobite Award (Paleontological Society): 1990, for *Traces of Life: The Origins of Humankind*

Best Western Juvenile Nonfiction Award (Western Writers of America): 1993, for *Searching for Laura Ingalls*

Sequoyah Young Adult Book Award: 1994, for *Beyond the Burning Time*

Western Heritage Award (National Cowboy Hall of Fame): 1999, for *Alice Rose and Sam*

FURTHER READING

Books

Authors and Artists for Young Adults, Vol. 19, 1996

Brown, Joanne. *Presenting Kathryn Lasky,* 1998

Contemporary Authors New Revision Series, Vol. 141, 2005

Gallo, Donald R., ed. *Speaking for Ourselves, Too: More Autobiographical Sketches by Notable Authors of Books for Young Adults,* 1993

Hipple, Ted, ed. *Writers for Young Adults,* Vol. 2, 1997

Major Authors and Illustrators for Children and Young Adults, 2002

Silvey, Anita, ed. *The Essential Guide to Children's Books and Their Creators,* 2002

Something about the Author, Vol. 69, 1992; Vol. 112, 2000

St. James Guide to Young Adult Writers, 1999

Periodicals

Horn Book, Sep.-Oct. 1985, p.527; Nov.-Dec. 1991, p.705

Teaching PreK-8, May 1999, p.42

Online Articles

http://www.eduplace.com/kids/hmr/mtai/lasky.html
(Houghton Mifflin, "Meet the Author: Kathryn Lasky," undated)
http://books.scholastic.com/teachers
(Scholastic Authors and Books, "Kathryn Lasky's Biography" and "Kathryn Lasky's Interview Transcript," 2005)

Online Databases

Biography Resource Center Online, 2006, articles from *Authors and Artists for Young Adults,* 1996; *Contemporary Authors Online,* 2005; *Major Authors and Illustrators for Children and Young Adults,* 2002; and *St. James Guide to Young Adult Writers,* 1999

ADDRESS

Katherine Lasky
Scholastic Inc.
557 Broadway
New York, NY 10012

Katherine Lasky
HarperCollins Children's Books
1350 Avenue of the Americas
New York, NY 10019

WORLD WIDE WEB SITE

http://www.kathrynlasky.com

Arnold Lobel 1933-1987

American Author and Illustrator
Creator of the "Frog and Toad" Series, *Fables*, and
Other Beloved Books for Children

BIRTH

Arnold Stark Lobel was born on May 22, 1933, in Los Angeles,
California. His parents, Joseph Lobel and Lucille (Stark)
Lobel, divorced when he was a baby, and he and his mother
moved back to her hometown of Schenectady, New York. He
was an only child.

YOUTH

Lobel described his early childhood as "quite happy," even though his family situation made him feel like an outsider. His parents had divorced, which was very unusual at the time. He lived with his mother and her parents. His grandmother took care of him while his mother worked full time. His father lived far away in California. Other problems made him feel like an outsider also. Not long after he started school, a series of illnesses forced him into the hospital for long periods of time. "I can remember sitting on the sundeck of the hospital looking out at the school playground across the street and feeling isolated and separate from the children I saw playing there."

When Lobel finally returned to school in the third grade, he recalled, he was "the skinny kid with glasses all the other kids loved to beat up." Telling stories and drawing pictures became a way for him to fit in with his classmates. One afternoon, a teacher invited a student to share a story or experience. "Well, I told a story. I make it up out of my head as I went along," Lobel recalled. "To my enormous surprise, the story had plot, characterization, dialogue; I picked up a piece of chalk and drew on the blackboard—the story had illustration. . . .The class was enthralled, and I was elevated to a position of high social esteem which lasted for a couple of years, until I myself put a stop to it."

> *One afternoon, a teacher invited a student to share a story. "Well, I told a story. I make it up out of my head as I went along," Lobel recalled. "To my enormous surprise, the story had plot, characterization, dialogue; I picked up a piece of chalk and drew on the blackboard—the story had illustration. . . . The class was enthralled, and I was elevated to a position of high social esteem which lasted for a couple of years, until I myself put a stop to it."*

Stories were always important to Lobel. One of his favorite things was to take a stack of newly checked-out library books and read them beneath the tree in front of his grandparents' "large and ramshackle" house. He especially loved *The 500 Hats of Bartholomew Cubbins* by Dr. Seuss and the nonsense verse of Edward Lear, a writer and artist who lived in the 1800s in England. Lear is most famous for his nonsense poem "The Owl and the Pussycat."

Lobel also loved stories told on television and in movies and plays. Every day he hurried to the TV to watch "Kuklapolitan Players." This popular show featured the humorous adventures of two male puppet friends, Kukla and Ollie, and their human pal, Fran. "I prolonged my childhood as long as possible, and the time with Kukla and Ollie was really the most important part of my day, all through high school," Lobel recalled.

Lobel enjoyed acting out stories in a theater that he created with back-drops painted on bed sheets in his grandparents' basement. Later, in high school and college, he took part in school productions as an actor and director. Although he had many different interests and talents, Lobel felt sure he wanted to be an artist. In his later career as a creator of picture books, the worlds of drama and art came together. As an adult, he wrote, "There is a little world at the end of my pencil. I am the stage director, the costume designer, and the man who pulls the curtains."

EDUCATION

After he graduated from the local high school in Schenectady, Lobel was accepted at the Pratt Institute, a prestigious art school in Brooklyn in New York City. "The sense of independence and the excitement of the Big City was a heady combination for a young man fresh from a quiet town in upstate New York," he said. "In settling down to my studies at Pratt, I discovered that book illustration was a special branch of the art that intrigued me the most." In 1955, he received his Bachelor of Fine Arts (BFA) degree from Pratt.

CAREER HIGHLIGHTS

The creator of many beloved books for young children, Lobel is admired for the gentle and often absurd humor in his books. In his words and drawings he often celebrated such simple pleasures as friendship, nature, and the comforts of home. These traits shine most brilliantly through his beloved "Frog and Toad" stories, four books about a pair of amphibian friends, and his *Fables*, a collection of animal stories each with a light-hearted lesson attached. The "Frog and Toad" stories and *Fables* are perhaps his best-known and best-loved works. In all, Lobel wrote and illustrated more than 25 books, as well as creating the pictures for at least 70 books by other authors. He also wrote the texts for four books illustrated by his wife, Anita Lobel.

First Publications

Lobel began his career as an artist doing artwork for advertisements, "and I hated it," he said. When he started his career in the mid-1950s,

publishers did not produce very many books for children. Although it was a difficult way to earn money, he was eager to become a children's book illustrator. He started to "do the rounds," visiting New York publishers looking for work.

One day, his drawing of a grasshopper caught the eye of Susan Hirschman, an editor at Harper and Row publishers. When she asked if he could "do" salmon Lobel gave a resounding "yes," even though he had never drawn one. *Red Tag Comes Back* by Fred Phleger, about a salmon swimming upstream, became the first book Lobel illustrated, in 1961. Around that time, the U.S. government began to pour resources into helping children learn to read better. As a result, many more publishers started to hire artists and writers for children's books.

In 1962, Lobel produced his first book as author and illustrator, *A Zoo for Mister Muster*. "I turned to writing only as a kind of economic expedience, because you quickly learn that when you're illustrating for another author you get five percent of royalties, and when you're writing your own story you get ten percent," he said. "That makes a big difference." The Mister Muster story was inspired by the Prospect Park Zoo in Brooklyn, where Lobel often took his two children. In the story, the zoo animals become so devoted to the loving Mister Muster that they escape their cages and come to live in his apartment.

"I find that the majority of my books have as their central characters 'child substitutes' rather than real children," Lobel said. "[Mr. Muster] would most certainly fit into that description. A portly and friendly little man, he has all the attributes of a child, but moves through the world with the independence of an adult." Mr. Muster reappeared in 1963 in *A Holiday for Mister Muster*, which describes the hero taking his beloved animals on vacation to the seaside.

"I Can Read" Books

Lobel's next two books as author and illustrator, *Prince Bertram the Bad* (1963) and *Giant John* (1964), also featured "child substitutes" in the lead roles. He said he drew these in a "cartoony" style, influenced by the television programs his young children watched in their apartment while he was drawing. With a young family to support, Lobel usually agreed to publish any manuscript that publishers offered him. Some critics note that the early, cartoon-like drawing style he used in these early books was rigid and not as pleasing or expressive as later work.

But reviewers note that a more lively, distinctive style started to emerge in such books as *Red Fox and His Canoe* (1964) by Nathaniel Benchley. As his style continued to evolve, Lobel illustrated many books in a new series launched by Harper and Row. The "I Can Read" series was aimed at beginning readers who did not yet know a lot of words, but still craved engaging stories and colorful characters. *Lucille* (1964) was the first book that Lobel wrote and illustrated for "I Can Read." He eventually created some of his most popular titles — including the "Frog and Toad" stories — for the series.

"Drawing the pictures is nothing for me. I know how to draw pictures," Lobel said. *"With writing, I'm in quicksand a bit. I don't really know what I'm doing."*

"Frog and Toad" Stories

By 1970, Lobel was developing a personal and individual style as an artist, but he was slow to gain confidence as a writer. "Drawing the pictures is nothing for me. I know how to draw pictures," he said. "With writing, I'm in quicksand a bit. I don't really know what I'm doing." At around this time, his family spent time on a lake in southern Vermont, where his daughter liked to catch toads and frogs. She was appalled when he didn't know the difference between the two.

"I thought about the frogs and toads and how much I liked them," Lobel recalled, "and I picked up my ballpoint writing pen and I wrote on the notebook, 'Frog ran up the path to Toad's house.'" Thus began *Frog and Toad Are Friends*, the first of four books about the pair of friends. Lobel soon found that the story flowed easily from his pen. "Somehow in the writing of the manuscript for Frog and Toad, I was, for the first time, able to write about myself," he said. "Frog and Toad are really two aspects of myself."

Readers and critics appreciate how the friends' personalities make a funny contrast, and also balance each other out. Frog is the more vigorous, practical, and active of the two. He tends to remain calm and helpful, whatever the situation. Toad, on the other hand, is a great worrier, pessimistic, and more childlike in his extreme behavior. For example, he often screams, jumps up and down in anger, or grumbles. His negative nature is captured by his favorite expression, "Blah!"

In one story, Toad makes a to-do list that includes items like get up, go for a walk with Frog, etc. All goes well until the list blows away. Toad can't chase it, because that isn't on the list of things to do. In fact, without the list to guide him, he refuses to do anything. Other adventures include searching for a lost button or trying to avoid the temptation of a plateful of cookies.

Children can relate to Toad's fears about loss and responsibilities. The stories are shadowed with his anxiety. But they are shot through with gentle humor. They take place in a timeless and idyllic setting. And Frog's constant reassurance and encouragement strikes an ever-positive tone. At the heart of each episode is Frog and Toad's warm friendship, captured by the ending of one story. "Frog and Toad stayed on the island all afternoon . . . they were two close friends sitting alone together."

Lobel Laughing at Himself

Lobel's wife Anita believed that the *Frog and Toad Are Friends* was the first book that he "felt very deeply," she said. "He was not just manufacturing stories. He was talking about important subjects like friendship, fear, loneliness." His friends and family say that he saw the world as a place that didn't really make sense. But that was all right, because he could laugh at it and himself. He thought people's behavior was basically comical—especially his own. He made fun of himself as a "morbidly tidy person," and the character of Toad who frets over details is usually seen as Lobel's most vivid caricature of himself.

Lobel acknowledged that the stories are probably more about grown-ups than kids. "All the Frog and Toad stories are based on adult preoccupations, really," he said. "I was able to tilt them somehow so that a child could appreciate them, too, but I think that adults also enjoy them—and I think that's probably why. It's because they're really adult stories, slightly disguised as children's stories.

Frog and Toad were warmly received from the start. The other three books—*Frog and Toad Together* (1972), *Frog and Toad All Year* (1976), and *Days with Frog and Toad* (1979)—were equally well received. Critics especially marveled that he could create warmly drawn characters and memorable situations using only the simple words of beginner readers. In fact, the first book in the series, *Frog and Toad Are Friends*, was named a Caldecott Honor Book. The Honor Book is a runner up for the Caldecott Award, a prestigious award given to children's book illustrators. One critic claimed that "Lobel made beginning reading more fun when he created Frog and Toad, and in doing so, loosened the restrictions of the easy-to-read form." Other critics have compared Lobel with such classic children's authors as Beatrix Potter, the writer and artist who created Peter Rabbit, and A.A. Milne, who wrote the Winnie the Pooh books. According to George Shannon, the Frog and Toad books create a "world of friendship and comedy, obsession and gentleness, foolishness and thoughtfulness, in which story, song, and laughter were the greatest gifts."

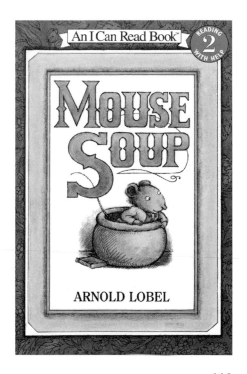

Other Animal Tales

Frog and Toad may be the characters for which Lobel is best remembered. But his many books are crowded with a number of other appealing creatures. *Mouse Tales* (1972) includes a series of stories that a father mouse tells to his seven children, while *Mouse Soup* (1977) involves a mouse who must distract a weasel with stories to avoid becoming the main ingredient in his supper.

Grasshopper on the Road (1978) relates the adventures of a traveling insect. *Uncle Elephant* (1981) tells the story of an elderly elephant that has a warm relationship with his nephew. The story, inspired by the illness of Lobel's beloved grandmother, reflected his tender closeness to her. *Owl at Home* (1987) features a warm-hearted but extremely neurotic owl. His nature is so depressive that he makes tea from his own tears.

Lobel liked using animal characters. He said that by drawing animals, he could represent people of every nationality, shape, and color. "Everyone can relate to Frog and Toad because they don't exist in this world," Lobel said. "Frog and Toad belong to no one, but they belong to everyone, every sector: rich children, poor children, white children, black children."

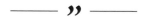

"Everyone can relate to Frog and Toad because they don't exist in this world," Lobel said. "Frog and Toad belong to no one, but they belong to everyone, every sector: rich children, poor children, white children, black children."

Timeless Settings and Themes

Like many of his other characters, Frog and Toad are depicted in a timeless setting, wearing old-fashioned clothes seemingly from the 19th century. Dressing his characters in period outfits and placing them in bygone days was another means Lobel used to be inclusive. "I don't like drawing people in contemporary clothes," he said. "There was a time when I was getting all these manuscripts about Mommy and Daddy in the kitchen. . . . I didn't have a Mommy and Daddy in the kitchen and I don't know what Mommy and Daddy are like in the kitchen anymore anyway." Lobel didn't want to place his readers in the real world. "I make a conscious attempt to pull the child away from his or her environment," he said. "I think a child wants to read for escape."

Like his settings, Lobel's themes are also timeless. The importance of friendship underscores nearly all of his work. Books like *Prince Bertram the Bad* (1963), *Giant John* (1864), *Martha the Movie Mouse* (1966), and *Small Pig* (1969) all describe to some degree developing friendships. The warmth of home, family, and loved ones was very important to Lobel. In a questionnaire in 1969, he wrote, "[I] get much comfort from the companionship of my wife and a few close friends."

HOW THE ROOSTER SAVED THE DAY

BY ARNOLD LOBEL · PICTURES BY ANITA LOBEL

Critics agree that humor is the key to much of Lobel's work. "[It] seems to me that one thing that doesn't change much as we grow older is our sense of humor. I think a child's sense of humor and an adult's sense of humor are rather the same. . . . We laugh at incongruity and we laugh at a lack of dignity. If a man's pants fall down, everybody laughs, children, adults."

Collaborations with Anita Lobel

Lobel's wife is Anita Lobel, also a celebrated illustrator and author for children. Although for decades the two worked side by side at their drawing tables, they never collaborated on a book. But one day, Lobel began to write a European-style folk tale about a rooster and a farmer. "I thought, 'This is a story Anita could illustrate more successfully than I,'" he said. According to Anita, when she started her illustrations, he protested, "What are you doing to my story?"

Nevertheless, their first collaboration, *How the Rooster Saved the Day* (1977), was a success. Two years later Lobel wrote another folk tale, *A Treeful of*

Pigs (1979), and again allowed his wife to create the pictures. Later, they collaborated on the alphabet book, *On Market Street* (1981), a colorful account of what shoppers can get at a busy market — from apples to zippers. Their final collaboration, *The Rose in My Garden* (1984), surveys the blooms and the animals in a lush landscape. Critics often cite it as one of Anita Lobel's best efforts as an illustrator.

Fables

With *Fables* (1980), Lobel presented his take on simple tales that end with a moral, or lesson. Originally, he accepted an assignment to illustrate the fables of Aesop, an ancient Greek writer. Aesop's tales of the tortoise and the hare, and the fox who hungered for grapes, are well known. But after Lobel carefully read the fables, he said, "I found a dog tearing sheep into pieces. I found deer being chewed to bits by lions. I came upon harsh cruelties and bitter ironies of every sort." The gentle-natured Lobel decided that Aesop's stories were "not intended for children," and told his publisher he had changed his mind.

> **Like the Frog and Toad stories, Fables *tapped right into Lobel's own personality. He said,* "Many of the things in the book are very personal; the animals are mouthpieces for different aspects of myself."**

But a couple of months later, when he was housebound with a broken ankle, Lobel found himself inventing his own fables. He started by making a list of all the animals he loved, but never had had a chance to draw. These included a hippo, an ostrich, and a crocodile. Writing never came easily to him. As he admitted, "I feel that I'm a trained illustrator and a lucky amateur in terms of writing." But, in this instance, he was amazed to find that the stories poured out of him.

Each fable is acted out by one of Lobel's fanciful animal characters. The hippopotamus overeats hugely at dinner — and the story concludes wryly, "Too much of anything leaves one with a feeling of regret." In another, a wolf disguises himself as an apple tree while trying to catch a hen. But the wise fowl is on to him when she spies his ten furry toes. And what's the moral? "It is always difficult to pose as something that one is not." Like the Frog and Toad stories, *Fables* tapped right into Lobel's own personality, as he later admitted: "Many of the things in the book are very personal; the

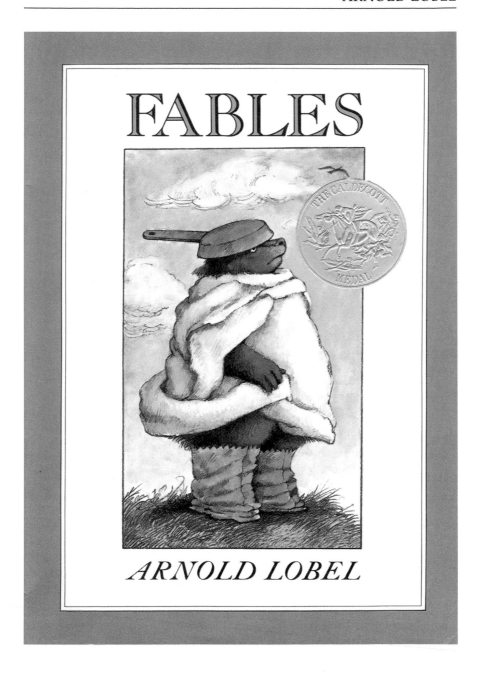

animals are mouthpieces for different aspects of myself." *Fables* was a delight for readers and critics, winning the Caldecott Medal in 1981. The Caldecott, a prestigious award given by the American Library Association, is awarded to the best illustrated children's book of the year.

Later Works

In the 1980s, Lobel collaborated with the popular children's poet Jack Prelutsky to create a large, illustrated volume of children's verse, *The Random House Book of Poetry for Children* (1983). Lobel also selected and illustrated a companion book of Mother Goose nursery rhymes, called *The Random House Book of Mother Goose* (1986).

These illustrations exemplify the whimsy, humor, and skill of Lobel's artistic style. "I never like to use the same illustrative technique over and over, but rather to use a repertory of styles as they suit the mood of the manuscript," he said. "I cannot think of any work that could be more agreeable and fun than making books for children."

―――― **"** ――――

"I cannot think of any work that could be more agreeable and fun than making books for children."

―――― **"** ――――

MARRIAGE AND FAMILY

Lobel met Anita Kempler, a fellow student at the Pratt Institute of Art, when he directed her in a play called "The Marriage Proposal" in the early 1950s. Anita was a native of Krakow, Poland. Her Jewish family had survived the Holocaust, the organized killing of millions of Jews and other people by the German government during World War II (1939-1945). Anita had lived in the United States for less than 10 years when they met. She and Lobel married in 1955, the year he graduated from college. Their daughter, Adrianne, was born the same year, and their son, Adam, a few years later.

Anita Lobel was a book illustrator and author like her husband. From the early days, the two worked from home in Brooklyn and shared child care. Anita remembered: "When the children were little, Arnold would often take them to the park―a perfectly normal occurrence today, but in the late '50s fathers did not necessarily spend hours at the sandbox with their babies." After their children went to bed at night, Arnold and Anita often worked side by side, sharing an artists' table they had made out of an old door. Though one would often jiggle the other's work (and the two bickered about it), they worked companionably into the night. The two were "by turns mutually irritating and helpful to each other," Lobel said. Even after they got separate tables, and a larger studio space, the couple made sure their drawing tables faced each other or stood side by side. "We're two flying buttresses, supporting the work we are both doing in the room," Anita Lobel wrote in 1981.

The couple remained supportive friends, even after they separated in the early 1980s. During this period, Arnold Lobel acknowledged that he was homosexual, and both he and Anita got involved with other romantic partners. Lobel was 54 when he died from Acquired Immune Deficiency Syndrome (AIDS) in 1987.

The Lobels' children carry on their parents' artistic natures. Adam became a photographer and a musician, and Adrianne is a successful set designer. In 2002 she produced a musical play based on *A Year with Frog and Toad* that ran originally in New York City and has become a favorite in children's theaters.

HOBBIES AND INTERESTS

Adrianne Lobel said about her father: "He was a lot like Frog and Toad mixed together. He was a stay-at-home person. He didn't like traveling. He loved work, which had its good points and its bad points. And I think he taught me that work was the most fun you could possibly have."

Lobel also loved cats. One of his favorites was named Orson, who was "devoted to Arnold," according to Anita Lobel. "When my husband goes away even for a short time the cat seems visibly bereft." Lobel enjoyed needlepoint and would create stitched portraits of fantastic animals.

Lobel began to take voice lessons later in his life. At the urging of Anita he even gave a concert in New York City in the 1980s. He explained the unexpected career swerve to a journalist in 1983: "I've written and illustrated about 80 books in 23 years. It's been a totally satisfying career. But working at home alone so much, I was turning into Grace Poole, the crazy lady they locked up in *Jane Eyre* [a 19th-century English novel by Charlotte Bronte]. I tried jogging but that didn't work." Lobel used to practice singing on the subway train in New York City. "I tap my feet so people don't think I'm talking to myself," he said. "Some do move away. But subways are like showers. The sound accompanies you."

SELECTED WRITINGS

As Author and Illustrator

A Zoo for Mister Muster, 1962
A Holiday for Mister Muster, 1963
Prince Bertram the Bad, 1963
Giant John, 1964
Lucille, 1964

Martha the Movie Mouse, 1966
The Great Blueness and Other Predicaments, 1968
Small Pig, 1969
Frog and Toad Are Friends, 1970
The Ice-Cream Cone Coot and Other Rare Birds, 1971
On the Day Peter Stuyvesant Sailed into Town, 1971
Frog and Toad Together, 1972
Mouse Tales, 1972
The Man Who Took the Indoors Out, 1974
Frog and Toad All Year, 1976
Mouse Soup, 1977
Grasshopper on the Road, 1978
Days with Frog and Toad, 1979
Fables, 1980
Uncle Elephant, 1981
Ming-Lo Moves the Mountain, 1982
The Book of Pigericks: Pig Limericks, 1983
Whiskers and Rhymes, 1985
The Random House Book of Mother Goose, 1986 (selected by Arnold Lobel)
Owl at Home, 1987
The Turnaround Wind, 1988
Arnold Lobel's Mother Goose for Babies, 2004

As Author (all works illustrated by Anita Lobel)

How the Rooster Saved the Day, 1977
A Treeful of Pigs, 1979
On Market Street, 1981
The Rose in My Garden, 1984

As Illustrator

Red Tag Comes, 1961 (by Fred Phleger)
Red Fox and His Canoe, 1964 (by Nathaniel Benchley)
Let's Get Turtles, 1965 (by Millicent Selsam)
Someday, 1964 (by Charlotte Zolotow)
Benny's Animals and How He Put Them in Order, 1966 (by Millient Selsam)
The Four Little Children Who Went around the World, 1968 (by Edward Lear)
I'll Fix Anthony, 1969 (by Judith Viorst)
Hildilid's Night, 1971 (by Cheli Duran Ryan)
Seahorse, 1972 (by Robert A. Morris)
The Clay Pot Boy, 1973 (adapted from the Russian by Cynthia Jameson)

Dinosaur Time, 1974 (by Peggy Parish)
Miss Suzy's Birthday, 1974 (by Miriam Young)
As I Was Crossing Boston Common, 1975 (by Norma Farber)
As Right as Right Can Be, 1976 (by Anne K. Rose)
Nightmares: Poems to Trouble Your Sleep, 1976 (by Jack Prelutsky)
Merry Merry FIBruary, 1977 (by Doris Orgel)
Tales of Oliver Pig, 1979 (by Jean Van Leeuwen)
The Headless Horseman Rides Tonight: More Poems to Trouble Your Sleep, 1980
    (by Jack Prelutsky)
More Tales of Oliver Pig, 1981 (by Jean Van Leeuwen)
The Random House Book of Poetry for Children, 1983 (compiled by Jack
    Prelutsky)
The Devil and Mother Crump, 1987 (by Valerie S. Carey)

SELECTED HONORS AND AWARDS

Outstanding Children's Book (National Education Association): 1965, for
    Someday
Outstanding Children's Book (American Library Association): 1965, for
    Someday
Notable Book Citation (American Library Association): 1970, for *Frog and
    Toad Are Friends;* 1971, for *On the Day Peter Stuyvesant Sailed into Town;*
    1972, for *Frog and Toad Together*
Best Illustrated Children's Books of the Year (*New York Times*): 1974, for *The
    Man Who Took the Indoors Out* and *Miss Suzy's Birthday;* 1976, for *As
    Right as Right Can Be;* 1977, for *Merry Merry FIBruary;* 1980, for *The
    Headless Horseman Rides Tonight: More Poems to Trouble Your Sleep*
George G. Stone Award (Claremont College): for the *Frog and Toad* series
Caldecott Medal (American Library Association): 1981, for *Fables*
Parents' Choice Award for Illustration (Parents' Choice Foundation): 1982,
    for *Ming-Lo Moves the Mountain*
Silver Medallion (University of Southern Mississippi School of Library
    Service): 1985, for distinguished service to children's literature
Golden Kite Award (Society of Children's Book Writers): 1987, for *The
    Devil and Mother Crump*

FURTHER READING

Books

Contemporary Authors New Revision Series, Vol. 79, 1999
De Montreville, Doris, and Donna Hill. *Third Book of Junior Authors,* 1972

Hopkins, Lee Bennett. *Books Are by People: Interviews with 104 Authors and Illustrators of Books for Young Children,* 1969
McElmeel, Sharon L. *100 Most Popular Picture-Book Authors and Illustrators,* 2000
Rockman, Connie. *Ninth Book of Junior Authors & Illustrators,* 2005
Shannon, George. *Arnold Lobel,* 1989
Silvey, Anita, ed. *100 Best Books for Children,* 2004
Silvey, Anita, ed. *Children's Books and Their Creators,* 2004
Something about the Author, Vol. 55, 1989
St. James Guide to Children's Writers, 1999

Periodicals

Horn Book, Aug. 1981, p.400
Pittsburgh Post-Gazette, Oct. 10, 2004, p.B5
Seattle Times, Mar. 26, 2005, p.C1
Washington Post, Jan. 10, 1988, p.X7
Washington Post Book World, June 13, 1982, p.6

Online Databases

Biography Resource Center Online, 2006, articles from *Contemporary Authors Online,* 2004; *St. James Guide to Children's Writers,* 1999

Online Articles

http://bccb.lis.uiuc.edu/0502gone.html
(Bulletin of the Center for Children's Books, "Gone But Not Forgotten: Arnold Lobel," May 1, 2002)
http://www.edupaperback.org/showauth.cfm?authid=242
(Educational Paperback Association, "EPA's Top 100 Authors: Lobel, Arthur," 1999)
http://www.harpercollins.com/authors.asp
(HarperCollins, "Arnold Lobel: Biography," undated)
http://www.eduplace.com/kids/hmr/mtai/lobel.html
(Houghton Mifflin, "Meet the Author/Illustrator: Arnold Lobel," undated)
http://www.parents-choice.org/full_abstract.cfm?art_id=35%15&the_page=editorials
(Parents' Choice Foundation, "Arnold Lobel," undated)

Janet McDonald 1953-
American Novelist for Young Adults
Winner of the 2003 Coretta Scott King/John Steptoe
Award for New Talent for *Chill Wind*

BIRTH

Janet McDonald was born in 1953 in Brooklyn, New York. Her
father, William, was a postal clerk, and her mother, Florence,
was a homemaker. William and Florence were childhood
sweethearts growing up in Decatur, Alabama. They left their
hometown to find work in New York City after William was released from the army on V-J Day in 1945. They were married a
few years later and settled in Brooklyn. Janet has four brothers
and two sisters: Luke, Ernest, Ann, Jean, Victor, and Kevin.

A 1952 photo of the Farragut Houses in Brooklyn, the projects where McDonald grew up.

YOUTH

McDonald grew up in a small 12th-floor apartment in a large public housing project in Brooklyn called the Farragut Houses. Public housing, or the projects, as it's also known, has usually been a block of housing units, typically apartments, subsidized by the government, built in large cities, and often inhabited by lower-income families. At first these public housing projects were fairly stable and included residents with a mix of incomes. But in the past 40 years, many public housing projects around the U.S. have significantly deteriorated, in many cases becoming concentrations of poverty, crime, and drugs.

In interviews, McDonald has described her childhood as happy. "As I show in my memoir *Project Girl*, growing up in the projects before they were the troubled places they are nowadays was cool. Lots of other kids to play with, ice cream trucks to chase, neighborhood basketball games to watch. I had two parents, both of them great cooks, nice teachers, and friendly neighbors. So yes, I would say I had a happy childhood."

McDonald has described herself as a good child: quiet, polite, and respectful to adults. She reflected that her eagerness to please others may have hurt her in the long run. She wrote, "I now regret this early training in stuffing emotions; perhaps having a wider range of expression then would have spared me the destructive outbursts I experienced later."

McDonald's father pushed her and the rest of his children to do well in school. "Schooling meant everything to him, and I learned early that it should mean everything to me as well," she stated in *Project Girl*. "Fortunately, I had a knack for it. Shining in school was guaranteed to keep me in his good favor, so I shone." She discovered at an early age that reading provided an escape from her family's small, cramped apartment and increasingly dangerous neighborhood. Reading allowed her to experience new places and fun adventures. In particular, she enjoyed reading Nancy Drew mysteries and other stories that featured young women in faraway places.

However, her academic success separated her from other kids growing up in the projects. McDonald soon began to evaluate her identity and sense of self in relation to what she believed a girl from the projects should be like. "I have always felt like an outsider," she realized later. "In the projects, I was a bookish nerd, definitely outside the hip, sassy, project girl norm."

McDonald started school in 1958, attending a local elementary school with a predominantly African American and Puerto Rican student body taught by almost exclusively white teachers. In fact, she recalls that she only had two black teachers through the ninth grade. It was her first experience with integration; her neighborhood in Brooklyn was primarily African American. She describes her teachers as passionate and committed to providing the students in her less privileged school with a quality education.

> *"[Growing] up in the projects before they were the troubled places they are nowadays was cool. Lots of other kids to play with, ice cream trucks to chase, neighborhood basketball games to watch. I had two parents, both of them great cooks, nice teachers, and friendly neighbors. So yes, I would say I had a happy childhood."*

Experiencing Racism

After getting a high score on a city-wide reading test, McDonald skipped from fourth to six grade. That summer she traveled with her family to her parents' hometown in Alabama, where she experienced segregation and racism on a personal level. She felt that many people seemed to accept discrimination, at a time when the civil rights movement was helping African Americans to fight for their rights.

"I have often wondered why no one expressed anger or resentment, why no outraged explanation was given me, no sense of wrongness conveyed," she reflected later. "Perhaps they thought me too young to understand. What is more likely, I think, is that they had been so thoroughly socialized in the South of lynchings, Ku Klux Klan marches, and Jim Crew segregation that whites in front and blacks in the back no longer shocked them. It was just the way things were."

> ———— " ————
>
> *"The projects were different from what they had been in the '50s and early '60s. The difference was between low-income and no-income housing, between working families and welfare-dependent single mothers, between adolescent pranks and violent crime."*
>
> ———— " ————

As she grew older and began high school, life in the projects changed from a tight community where everyone looked out for one another to a place where drugs and poverty had taken a devastating toll on McDonald's friends and neighbors. "The projects were different from what they had been in the '50s and early '60s," she recalled. "The difference was between low-income and no-income housing, between working families and welfare-dependent single mothers, between adolescent pranks and violent crime."

For a young, sensitive girl, the projects offered formidable obstacles. As she recalled, "My challenges growing up as a project girl involved the emotional toll that actually living all the inner city urban clichés others read about takes: friends dying from violence and drugs, fear of crime, few adult role models—witnessing that kind of stuff is hard on the psyche."

EDUCATION

In 1968 McDonald began attending Erasmus Hall, considered Brooklyn's best high school. She was able to attend the highly regarded school because of the Board of Education's Open Schools program, which allowed promising students from the ghetto to attend Brooklyn's top academic schools.

The commute to Erasmus from her home was an hour each way. The ride "gave me my first taste of the blessing and curse of academic achievement,"

McDonald on her tricycle when young, playing outside the projects.

she said in her memoir. "The journey to Erasmus carried me across lines of race, class, and culture at a time when I was struggling to patch together some semblance of an adolescent self. Barely recovered from the onslaught of breasts, blemishes, and sanitary napkins, I was suddenly confronted with the first major challenge to my identity as a project girl."

Intimidated by the academic challenges and cultural differences she found at her new school, McDonald began to withdraw, and her academic performance suffered. She also felt alienated at home, where her sister teased her for her reading and her love of watching golf on television. "I was straddling contradictory worlds and not fitting in anywhere," she recalled in *Project Girl*.

Her sense of alienation led her to hang out with a hippie crowd. It wasn't long before she participated in political protests and experimented with drugs. It was the late 1960s, and significant cultural and political changes were sweeping the country. McDonald wanted to be part of it. "I became anti-Establishment, nonconformist, anarchist, revolutionary, socialist, Communist, hippie, yippie, Buddhist, Hindu, swirling dervish . . . whatever the era had to offer, I was buying," she acknowledged. "It was a heady time for a young project girl in search of a broader identity."

In 1970 McDonald graduated from Erasmus at 16 years old, but had to complete additional classes to receive an academic diploma, which was

McDonald with her family. Top row: Ann, Janet, Florence, and Willie. Bottom row: Ernest and Luke. Victor, Jean, and Kevin were not yet born.

necessary for college. Desperate to find a way to go to college, she entered Harlem Prep, a private school that offered a one-year preparatory program to give high school dropouts and underachievers the academic support they need to improve their grades and get into college. She stayed at Harlem Prep for two years.

For McDonald, this was the beginning of what would be a long-term struggle to find her identity, to escape from the projects, and to search for a career. For years, she was torn between the life she'd known in the projects and the life she was exposed to as she attended a series of prestigious schools. The experience took a serious toll on her—she struggled with depression, she succumbed to drugs, she was raped, she dealt with overpowering anger, she started setting fires. She eventually overcame all these hardships and became a respected attorney and author.

Her Time at Vassar

McDonald's first step on that path came when she was accepted in 1972 at Vassar College, north of New York City. Arriving on campus, she found that although the majority of the students in the elite college were white and privileged, there were also a number of people from various socioeconomic levels and educational backgrounds. "Vassar was mind-boggling, which was just what my stereotype-laden brain needed," she said. Yet the cultural differences between her and the rest of the student body were sometimes overwhelming. "I had left a unique subculture, a universe so distinct that we had our own mores, customs, style of dress, and even our own dialect. We were project people, a tribe apart. And I was apart from my tribe. It was terrifying."

McDonald felt a split between her new identity as a Vassar girl and her old identity as a project girl. Her yearning to stay true to her roots motivated her to fall more deeply into abusing drugs. She began to take the train into Harlem to buy heroin. With her growing drug habit, her grades suffered. Depressed and lonely, one night she attempted suicide by swallowing a bunch of pills. Luckily, the pills had no effect. However, her parents were informed and she was pulled out of college for the rest of the term. She returned to Brooklyn, where she soon realized that "it was far better to be *from* the projects than *in* the projects."

> *Attending Vassar College, McDonald felt overwhelmed by the cultural differences between her and the rest of the students. "I had left a unique subculture, a universe so distinct that we had our own mores, customs, style of dress, and even our own dialect. We were project people, a tribe apart. And I was apart from my tribe. It was terrifying."*

Falling in Love with France

McDonald returned to Vassar determined to succeed as a student. Through hard work, she did well the rest of the year. She applied to spend her junior year abroad studying in France. The experience taught her many things and allowed her to break free from the identity crisis that had negatively affected her at Vassar. "In France, I was liberated from the Vassar girl/project girl conflict," she noted. "No one judged me on specifics, and I had nothing to prove. The French saw me as just another American, though I didn't see myself that way at all."

While living in Paris, McDonald developed a deep, long-standing fascination with France. After studying abroad, she returned to Vassar for her senior year, graduating with a Bachelor of Arts (BA) degree in French literature. Unsure what to do after graduation, she had applied to two schools: to New York University (NYU) to study French literature in France and to

135

McDonald's memoir, Project Girl, *is a devastating account of her difficult early life. She's shown on the cover near the Eiffel Tower in Paris, where she eventually settled.*

Cornell University to study law. Admitted to both programs, she decided to enroll in the NYU program in French literature and return to France. "In Paris I immersed myself in the intriguing people and enveloping charm of this city said to be of light, a place that seemed to harvest a much-needed lightness in me," she recalled. After several months she decided to drop out of the graduate program. She returned to New York and enrolled in law school at Cornell.

Law School

McDonald enrolled in law school not because she had a passion for the law, but because she didn't know what else to do with her degree in French literature. During her first year in law school, she remained unsure of her decision. Her mediocre grades reflected her lack of interest in law studies, but she was able to land a summer job as a government-agency legal intern at a law firm in Manhattan.

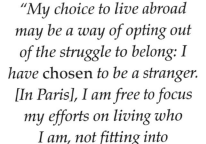

"My choice to live abroad may be a way of opting out of the struggle to belong: I have chosen to be a stranger. [In Paris], I am free to focus my efforts on living who I am, not fitting into someone else's notion of who I should be."

Shortly after her return to Cornell the next year, McDonald was raped in her dormitory by a fellow student, a man with a criminal history. He was immediately apprehended and later convicted of the crime. The incident left her distraught and unable to cope with her academic studies. "It devastates you," she explained. "It totally undermines your sense of personal integrity, of personal safety in the world, and for me it made me very afraid in general, and it also made me feel very violent, because I was enraged that I wasn't able to stop it from happening." She began psychiatric therapy, but she still struggled to cope with the rape.

That led to a difficult period for McDonald. She transferred to New York University to finish her law studies, but her pent-up rage from the rape led her to start a series of small fires on campus. She was questioned and confessed to the crimes. Once the story was reported in the paper, she was notorious. The administration banned her from campus and she was not allowed to finish her classes. As a result of the charges against her, her rapist was set free after only three years of a 12-year sentence. McDonald attempted to come to terms with her actions. "I struggled to understand what had happened," she wrote in her memoir. "I was indeed a strange hybrid of my disparate experience: a naïve Ivy League project girl whose potential for success seemed repeatedly to collide with an internal rage."

She worked as a paralegal in a Manhattan law firm and was accepted into the journalism school at Columbia University, also in New York City. She also joined the Army National Guard and was accepted into the officer training program; she was discharged when they performed a thorough background check and discovered her criminal record. She continued her psychiatric therapy, and after a few months at Columbia, she was readmitted to NYU Law School to finish her law degree.

McDonald had a difficult time at NYU. She was still haunted by the guilt from her crimes, the rape, and issues of self-identity and discrimination. However, with therapy and a renewed sense of discipline, she did well in her last two years of school. Before graduating in 1986, she already had a job offer from a prestigious law firm in New York City.

CAREER HIGHLIGHTS

Settling into her new job, McDonald was still concerned with her divided identity as a project girl and now as a highly paid attorney. Her swanky new apartment near Central Park symbolized this identity crisis. "In the projects, I was a ghost, and in my high-rise, invisible," she claims. "At first I was apologetic, as though I was doing something wrong simply by being there. I *didn't* belong. Which was precisely why I wanted to be there." She dealt with feeling like an outsider at work by virtually eliminating her past as a project girl. "Acutely aware of my nonentity status — non-white, non-male, and non-upper class — I went ahead and erased myself completely," she wrote in her memoir.

Finally, the stress became too much and McDonald took a job in Seattle. The move proved to be a much-needed step toward self-healing. "The pacific environment of the Northwest provided a perfect backdrop for peace talks between my inner warring factions," she concluded. "With time, the hubbub quieted down and I began to accept all my selves. In freeing myself of my personal stereotypes, I was able to see others more clearly."

This new sense of well-being inspired a yearning to return to Paris. She found a job at an international law firm and moved to Paris again. For McDonald, the move was liberating. "My choice to live abroad may be a way of opting out of the struggle to belong: I have *chosen* to be a stranger," she noted in her memoir. "Here, I am free to focus my efforts on living who I am, not fitting into someone else's notion of who I should be."

Becoming a Writer

McDonald had always been a writer in some form: she wrote poems as a child, short stories in college, and journals most of her adult life. "As an adult, I found refuge from the larger outside world in my journals," she contended. "They provided catharsis and comfort and were not for publication. Not that I didn't want to be a professional writer like everyone else who enjoys words, but I was certain that could never happen."

Living in Paris and working as a lawyer, McDonald began to write magazine articles. When a friend encouraged her to write about her life, she began to write *Project Girl* on weekends, at night, and during her vacations. She found it to be a profoundly cathartic experience. "From memory and journals, I pulled a story of my life, a life that up to that point I had carefully kept from view," she recalled. "It was a secret travail shared only with my closest friends. Secret because I know it to be counter-corporate, almost subversive; secret because I might fail as a writer."

Project Girl: An Inspiring Story of a Black Woman's Coming-of-Age was published in 1999 to good reviews. "In this devastating memoir," maintained reviewer Suzanne Ruta, "she argues her case with lawyerly concision, drop-dead ghetto humor, and just a touch of schoolgirl psychobabble. Because her neighbors 'equated academics with becoming corny, bookish, and ultimately white,' she was "constantly fighting off some 'phantom white girl' in herself. But graduation changed little. The corporate lawyer in a suit got dissed by street people. At her high-rent apartment building, the doormen mistook her for hired help. No wonder McDonald fled to Paris, where, freed from the American obsession with race, she wrote this stinging epitaph."

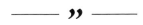

"As an adult, I found refuge from the larger outside world in my journals. They provided catharsis and comfort and were not for publication. Not that I didn't want to be a professional writer like everyone else who enjoys words, but I was certain that could never happen."

"You don't have to dig up slave narratives to read about how the lives of ordinary African Americans often contain narrow escapes, near captures, split-second decisions involving life and death, awesome courage and victories, crushing fear, violence, and defeat," reviewer Esther Iverem wrote in the *Washington Post.* "A self-described project girl from the public houses in Brooklyn who now works as a lawyer in Paris, Janet McDonald has had such a life. . . . But *Project Girl* isn't some sociological treatise on the projects or on being ghetto. Instead it is a very personal story of [a] journey that is full of heartache, tragedy, and victory. Her story proceeds at a fast pace and with fascinating turns."

For McDonald, success as a writer was thrilling. "Few ecstasies compare to the transformation from mere writer to published author," she asserted. "Good reviews, subsequent works, and larger advances are delicious as well, but the first taste of publishing a book, like the first kiss, thrills the heart like no other. Suddenly, you have a bigger voice, a voice that counts."

> "Soapboxes are for soap," McDonald argued. "I'm not into preaching, which is why I was never into reading young adult literature because it was so preachy. I wanted to show reality as it is, not as I think it should be, and from there present positive ways that reality can be addressed."

Success Inspires McDonald

After the success of *Project Girl*, McDonald began to write young adult novels directed toward black teenagers. She was determined not to preach about morality, but to honestly portray the black experience. "Soapboxes are for soap," she clarified. "I'm not into preaching, which is why I was never into reading young adult literature because it was so preachy. I wanted to show reality as it is, not as I think it should be, and from there present positive ways that reality can be addressed."

McDonald's first young adult novel, *Spellbound*, was published in 2001. The story follows the struggles of Raven Jefferson, a 15-year-old high school dropout and single mother from the projects as she competes in a spelling bee that could provide a chance for a college scholarship. Reviewers criticized the novel for strained dialogue and unbelievable plot twists, but applauded the "heart, smarts, and guts" in the story. They also asserted that McDonald succeeded in getting past the stereotypes of the project girl to present a complex and very human young woman in the character of Raven. "One of the best of the many recent stories about teens in the city projects, this first novel is read-aloud funny, even as it tells the harsh truths about how hard it is to break free," said the reviewer for *Booklist*. "What's great in this novel is the depiction of the grim reality of the neighborhood and the slick clichés of success. Best of all [McDonald] humanizes the individual people behind the stereotype of poor people who are 'project trash.'"

Chill Wind, her next young adult novel, was published in 2002. McDonald told the story of Aisha Ingram, a high-school dropout and single mother from the Brooklyn projects. When her government benefits are cut off, Aisha is forced to take responsibility for her own future and provide for her children. Along the way, she finds self-respect and a renewed hope for her future. "McDonald writes with such honesty, wit, and insight that you want to quote from every page and read much of this story aloud to share the laughter and anguish, failure and hope, fury and

Spellbound is the rarest of books, funny and moving at the same time. . . . Thank you, Ms. McDonald." —Christopher Paul Curtis, winner of the Newbery Medal for *Bud, Not Buddy*

tenderness of black project girl Aisha Ingram," said the reviewer from *Booklist.* "It's the truth of the characters and their talk (without obscenity) and the energy of the neighborhood — a neighborhood too seldom depicted in YA books — that will grab readers from everywhere."

Critics praised these first two novels not only for their humor, honesty, and insight, but also for their refreshing depictions of teenage mothers. When asked what inspired her to write about Raven and Aisha, McDonald explained that "since I grew up in the projects and know scores of Ravens and Aishas, both among friends and in my family, I know the real deal outside the negative clichés and stereotypes. We're just real people like everybody else, trying to survive and, if we're lucky, thrive — be all the way live." Writing about teenage girls appealed to McDonald. "Maybe since I had so many problems growing up and didn't have anything to read that spoke directly to me about my world I want to put something out there for other girls who might need some kind of encouragement or recognition," she maintained.

McDonald's next book, *Twists and Turns,* was published in 2003. The novel focuses on Keeba and Teesha, two sisters from a Brooklyn Heights housing

project who open a hair-braiding salon. Tenacious yet inexperienced, the young women must deal with several obstacles but remain true to their dream of being independent and successful. Critics found the book to be humorous and full of convincing and compelling details, particularly the street slang and dialogue in the novel. They described the book as an inspiring story of teens who find strength in themselves and their friendship to try to make something of their lives. According to *Booklist*, "Raucous and tender, harsh and hopeful, McDonald's latest fast-talking story about teen project girls in Brooklyn Heights focuses on the sisters, Keeba and Teesha. . . . [The] story is inspiring—not because of a slick resolution or a heavy message, but because McDonald shows how hard things are, even as she tells a story of teens who find the strength in themselves and in those around them to rebuild and carry on."

In *Brother Hood,* published in 2004, McDonald presented her first male protagonist. Nate, a street-smart boy from Harlem, earns a scholarship to a private boarding school. Torn between two worlds, he struggles to forge an identity that encompasses his two personas. Critics praised Nate as a strong and compelling character, as in this comment from *Horn Book* magazine. "Nate remains a strong, engaging character as he finds himself pulled between Harlem and the Fletcher School, his homeboys and his preppie pals. Hard-hitting yet thoughtful." Reviewers also noted the authenticity and humor of the novel. "As always with McDonald's work, it's the anger, sadness, and laugh-out-loud honesty about the contemporary scene that will hold readers," argued the critic for *Booklist*. "This is a stirring celebration of Harlem, its roots, diversity, and change."

Advice to Young Writers

McDonald has offered some interesting advice to young writers. "Every few hours get up and dance wildly," she urged. "Drink lots of water. Munch on pistachio nuts and pretzels. Do not bathe or comb hair unless outside em-

ployment is involved. Have fun. Cha-
racters are real people, only invisible.
Hang with them. Talk aloud to them.
Miss them when they're gone."

HOME AND FAMILY

McDonald, who is single, lives in
Paris, France, where she works as an
attorney and continues to write.

WRITINGS

Project Girl: An Inspiring Story of a
  Black Woman's Coming-of-Age, 1999
Spellbound, 2001
Chill Wind, 2002
Twists and Turns, 2003
Brother Hood, 2004

——— " ———

"Every few hours get
up and dance wildly,"
McDonald urges young
writers."Drink lots of water.
Munch on pistachio nuts and
pretzels. Do not bathe or
comb hair unless outside
employment is involved.
Have fun. Characters are real
people, only invisible. Hang
with them. Talk aloud to
them. Miss them when
they're gone."

——— " ———

HONORS AND AWARDS

Best Book Award (*Los Angeles Times*):
   1999, for *Project Girl*
Best Book for Young Adults (American Library Association): 2001, for
   Spellbound
Notable Children's Trade Book in the Field of Social Studies (National
   Council for Social Studies): 2002, for *Spellbound*
Coretta Scott King/John Steptoe New Talent Award (American Library
   Association): 2003, for *Chill Wind*
Books for the Teenage (New York Public Library): 2004, *Twists and Turns*

FURTHER READING

Books

Contemporary Authors, Vol. 184, 2000
Something about the Authors, Vol. 148, 2004

Periodicals

Booklist, Feb. 15, 2002, p.1026
Library Media Connection, Nov.-Dec. 2005, p.42
Literary Review, Summer 2002, p.679; Fall 2003, p.58

Newsday, Nov. 5, 2000, p.B11
O, The Oprah Magazine, Sep. 2003, p.211

Online Databases

Biography Resource Center Online, 2006, *Contemporary Authors Online,* 2003

Online Articles

http://www.kidbookpros.com/meetthepros/interviews_2003/janet_mcdonald
    (Society of Children's Book Writers and Illustrators-France, "Meet the
    Pros: Janet McDonald," 2003)
http://www.fsgkidsbooks.com/authordetails.asp?ID=McDonald
    (Farrar, Straus & Giroux Books for Young Readers, "Profile: Janet
    McDonald," undated)

ADDRESS

Janet McDonald
Farrar, Straus & Giroux
19 Union Square West
New York, NY 10003

WORLD WIDE WEB SITE

http://www.projectgirl.com

Deborah Wiles 1953-

American Children's Writer
Author of *Freedom Summer* and *Each Little Bird That Sings*

BIRTH

Deborah Wiles was born on May 7, 1953, in Mobile, Alabama. Her father is Thomas P. Edwards, an Air Force pilot, and her mother is Marie (Kilgore) Edwards. Wiles is the oldest of three children. She has a sister, Cathy, and a brother, Mike.

YOUTH

Wiles was born into a military family that moved around the country whenever her father was transferred to a new Air Force base. After living in Alabama for five years, the family moved to Hawaii, where Wiles started elementary school. When she was eight, the family moved to Camp Springs, Maryland. It was during the seven years in Maryland that she first became interested in classical music. In fourth grade, she also joined a glee club and took piano lessons. In sixth grade, her teacher Mr. Adler told her she was a good writer, something she later remembered when she decided to freelance.

Wiles attended junior high in Temple Hills, Maryland. When the family moved to Charleston, South Carolina, she attended St. Andrew's Parish High School for two years. Just before her senior year, the family moved to the Philippines, where her father was stationed at Clark Air Force Base. She graduated from Wagner High School in the Philippines, then moved back to the U.S., to Mississippi, to attend college. During all these moves over the years, Wiles would normally spend part of each summer with relatives in Louin, Mississippi.

> ———— **"** ————
>
> *As a child, Wiles said, "I read everything. I used to save my allowance until I had $1.25, and then I'd buy the next* **Nancy Drew**. *I adored* **Treasure Island** *and* **Grimm's Fairy Tales**. *I read the comics, backs of cereal boxes— I just read everything."*
>
> ———— **"** ————

Speaking of her childhood and the frequent moves across the country, Wiles explained: "I always settled in quickly, I read a lot as a child and was somewhat of a loner. I was never popular, but I always made a few very strong friendships. Friendship is important to me." In an interview posted on the Institute of Children's Literature web site, Wiles remembered that, as a child, "I read everything. I used to save my allowance until I had $1.25, and then I'd buy the next *Nancy Drew*. I adored *Treasure Island* and *Grimm's Fairy Tales.* I read the comics, backs of cereal boxes—I just read everything."

EDUCATION

Wiles graduated from Wagner High School in the Philippines in 1971. After that, she attended Jones County Junior College in Ellisville, Mississippi, for one semester, but left college to get married. She also took a creative writing class at Frederick Community College in Maryland. In 2003, she earned a Master of Fine Arts (MFA) degree in writing from Vermont College.

MARRIAGE AND FAMILY

Wiles has been married twice and has four children: Alisa, Jason, Zachary, and Hannah.

BECOMING A WRITER

After leaving college to get married, Wiles moved to the area around Washington, D.C., where she lived for the next 32 years. She raised four children, much of the time as a single mother. She also held such jobs as office assistant, school bus driver, teacher, and salesperson. For much of that time, about 25 years, she lived in Frederick, Maryland. Early on, she worked as the host of a local radio show, interviewing elderly residents about their lives. "For a few years," she remembered, "I went around Frederick County with a tape recorder collecting stories that were aired on the local radio station on Sunday mornings, and that are now archived at the local library in Frederick and in their Historical Society's library."

Here, Wiles described how she first became a writer. "I became a writer in 1976 when I was 22 years old, a single mother of two young children, the office assistant — and the only woman — in a beat-up trailer on Albemarle Street in Northwest Washington, where the construction company I worked for was building the red line of the D.C. subway system," Wiles explained. "[I] spent my lunch breaks in the Tenley Circle branch of the D.C. Public Library, learning how to write — I read every book they had in that library on how to write, and I studied the essays over and over, until I began to write [essays] on my own when I was about 26. I wrote essays as a freelancer until I discovered the beauty and wonder of children's books."

While taking a creative writing course, Wiles first became interested in writing for children, work she soon grew to love. "I loved words, and I realized, early on, that words were power, and that I had something I wanted to say. I love this job more than any job I have ever had. It suits my temperament."

After work each day, Wiles found time to write at night when her children were sleeping. She did freelance writing in her spare time, sometimes not getting paid but only receiving a writing credit. Her first published piece was about her son Zachary. Wiles explained: "I wrote a story about his graduation from preschool ('Peanut Pals,' it was called) and the local paper, the *Frederick News-Post* in Frederick, Maryland, published it. It was my first published piece and a big thrill. It ran on the op-ed page. I submitted stories to the paper for a few years, gathered clips, took them to a larger newspaper, then to a magazine, where I began to get assignments, free-

lancing. I loved this work—I could do it mostly from home, and it helped hone my skills as well."

CAREER HIGHLIGHTS

While taking a creative writing course, Wiles became interested in writing for children, work she soon grew to love. "I loved words, and I realized, early on, that words were power, and that I had something I wanted to say," she remarked. "I love this job more than any job I have ever had. It suits my temperament."

Freedom Summer

After years of freelance writing, Wiles published her first book, *Freedom Summer*, in 2001. The story is set in Mississippi in the summer of 1964—the year the Civil Rights Act of 1964 was passed into law. Before that law was passed, segregation was legal and common in the American South. Many institutions—businesses, churches, transportation facilities, and more—were exclusively white. Some Americans believed that this was unfair. They organized protests against segregation as part of the civil rights movement, which pushed for an end to racial discrimination. These efforts led to the Civil Rights Act, which outlawed discrimination on the basis of race, color, religion, sex, or national origin. This law made racial discrimination in public places illegal.

On her web site, Wiles explained her motivation for writing the story: "I was born a white child in Mobile, Alabama, and spent summers visiting my beloved Mississippi relatives. When the Civil Rights Act was passed, the town pool closed. So did the roller rink and the ice-cream parlor. Rather than lawfully giving blacks the same rights and freedoms as whites, many southern businesses chose to shut their doors in protest. . . . I couldn't get these thoughts and images out of my mind, and I wondered what it must be like to be a black child my age. . . . This story grew out of my feelings surrounding that time. It is fiction but based on real events."

In *Freedom Summer*, a picture book for young children, the story is about two young boys, one black and one white. The Civil Rights Act has just been passed into law, allowing both blacks and whites to use the same public facilities. In a small Mississippi town, however, this idea is not popular. Rather than open the public pool to both races, the city fills in the pool with asphalt and closes it for good. John and Joe, who were looking forward to swimming in the pool together, decide on a mild act of rebellion instead: they go into a local store together and buy ice pops.

"I was born a white child in Mobile, Alabama, and spent summers visiting my beloved Mississippi relatives. When the Civil Rights Act was passed, the town pool closed. So did the roller rink and the ice-cream parlor. . . . I couldn't get these thoughts and images out of my mind, and I wondered what it must be like to be a black child my age. . . . [Freedom Summer] grew out of my feelings surrounding that time. It is fiction but based on real events."

The book was widely praised by reviewers and critics. Eunice Weech, writing in the *School Library Journal*, called the story "A powerful read-aloud for introducing history or sparking discussion." Special recognition was given by the Keats Foundation and the New York Public Library, which awarded Wiles the Ezra Jack Keats New Writer Award for *Freedom Summer*.

Love, Ruby Lavender

Wiles's next book, *Love, Ruby Lavender* (2002), is a novel for middle-grade readers. It tells the story of nine-year-old Ruby and her grandmother, Miss Eula Garnet, who live in Halleluia, Mississippi. The pair spends all their time together until Miss Eula visits her son in Hawaii one summer, leaving Ruby alone. To fill the lonely days, Ruby writes a daily letter to her grandmother, befriends a new girl in town, Dove, and rehearses for the town operetta. She also comes to terms with the recent death of her grandfather. Reviewing the novel in *Booklist,* Frances Bradburn said that "Wiles has painted a picture of a time long past when communities were small and close-knit, people wrote letters, and chickens escaped only to create havoc at play practice. Yet she has also created a timeless story of life and death, the bond between grandparent and grandchild, and the reality that, regardless, 'life does go on.'" Writing in *School Library Journal,* Kirsten Martindale said that "Wiles has created an irresistible character in Ruby Lavender, the most precocious resident of Hallelulia, Mississippi. . . . A rewarding read that perfectly blends the culture and the humor of the South, [a] not-to-be-missed title."

Wiles has said that the settings for *Love, Ruby Lavender* and her later book, *Each Little Bird That Sings,* are both based on Louin, Mississippi, where she spent so many happy summers. "I've made up a fictional county, Aurora County, where my characters live," she explained. "*Love, Ruby Lavender* was the first novel to take place in Aurora Country, in the town of Halleluia. Snapfinger is 'the next town over' from Halleluia. All the names in both books are fictitious, but they represent towns in Jasper County, Mississippi, where I did so much growing up."

Wiles next wrote *One Wide Sky: A Bedtime Lullaby* (2003), a collection of verse for younger readers. The book details the many things that two squirrels and three little boys see and do in the backyard of the family house. As evening falls, both the boys and squirrels are off to sleep after their busy day. The critic for *Publishers Weekly* described the story as "a fitting tribute to the pleasures of a perfect day."

Each Little Bird That Sings

In her next book, *Each Little Bird That Sings* (2005), Wiles focused on 10-year-old Comfort Snowberger and her family. Comfort's father is an undertaker, and the family lives in the only funeral home in the small town of Snapfinger, Mississippi. Comfort has attended hundreds of funerals during her life and believes she knows something about sadness over a loved one's death. But she is unprepared for the grief she feels after the recent deaths of her Great-uncle Edisto and Great-great-aunt Florentine, which helps her to see grief in a new way. Death appears again when she is caught in a flood with her cousin, Peach. Comfort loses her beloved dog, Dismay, to the raging waters. She learns that controlling one's emotions is not as easy as it may seem.

The story is sometimes somber, focusing on death and grief. But there's also a lot of humor, and Comfort, in particular, is a funny character. The novel includes her "Top Ten Tips for First-Rate Funeral Behavior," which would be good advice for just about any funeral. Here are some of her tips:

> "During the viewing, which happens the day before the funeral, people wander up to the open casket and stare at the deceased and say things like, 'He looks so natural,' which is silly, because he DOESN'T look natural, he looks dead. But that's okay, he's supposed to be dead. But don't say, 'He looks so dead,' that's not a good idea. Some people are queasy about looking at the deceased. Don't worry about it. He doesn't mind."

> "Here's what to say to the family during the viewing, visitation, and funeral time: 'I'm so sorry.' That's all. Then move on. Don't say, 'He's gone to a better place,' or 'You must be relieved,' or 'That shirt doesn't go with those pants.'"

> "This is not a good time to remind the family that the deceased owes you money."

> "Take all arguments and fist fights outside to the parking lot."

> "Remember that death is a natural thing—it's all around us, as Edisto Snowberger always said. Don't try to hide death from kids. If Grandpa has died, don't say, 'We lost Grandpa,' because little kids

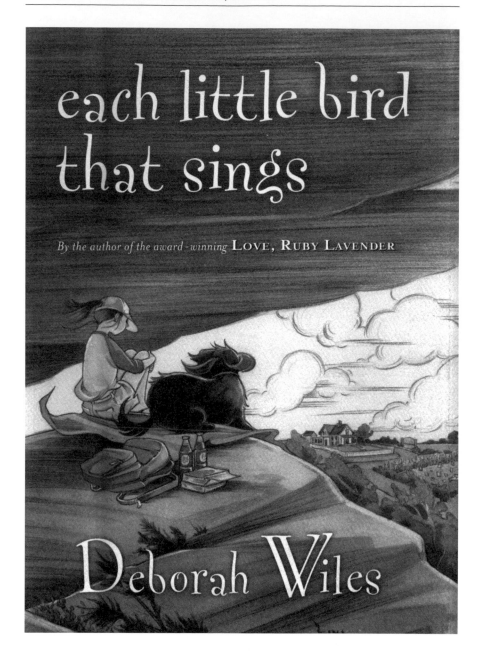

will want to know why don't you go look for him. Just say 'Grandpa died.' Don't say 'Grandpa passed' either, because we'll wonder what grade he was in. Just say he died. We get it. Kids are better at death than grown ups give them credit for."

Each Little Bird That Sings was an immediate hit with readers and reviewers. "Sensitive, funny, and occasionally impatient, Comfort is a wholly sympathetic protagonist who learns that emotions may not be as easy to control as she had assumed," Lauralyn Persson wrote in *School Library Journal*. "While the book is a bit too long and some of the Southern eccentricity wears thin, this is a deeply felt novel." The critic for *Publishers Weekly* also offered praise. "Repeating the winning formula she used in *Love, Ruby Lavender*, Wiles mixes letters, news reports, recipes, and lists such as, 'Top Ten Tips for First-Rate Funeral Behavior,' into a fine narrative, making a difficult topic go down like lemonade at a picnic. Fans of Ruby Lavender will enjoy the overlapping characters and setting, but what they'll really want is a third book—where Comfort and Ruby get together."

Wiles was deeply honored when *Each Little Bird That Sings* became a National Book Award finalist for young people's literature. The judges' citation said this: "In direct, sometimes hilarious, and often moving prose, Deborah Wiles introduces us to the remarkable and remarkably eccentric Snowberger clan, including Dismay, Funeral Dog Extraordinaire, and takes us on a journey that explores loss, love, and all the messy complications of life."

"There are three Deborah Wiles Guidelines to Writing Well: 1. Keep a notebook. Put everything in it. I put my grocery lists in my notebook, along with doodles, recipes, sayings, lists of all kinds, even writing ideas. 2. BIC—put your butt in the chair and be as messy as you need to be, but get it down. Then, 3. Revise, revise, revise."

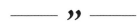

Wiles is now living in Atlanta, Georgia, and working on a novel about two girl cousins from Mississippi who make a trip to Memphis to see Elvis Presley. One of the girls is convinced that Elvis is really her father.

Advice to Young Writers

In an interview at KidsReads.com, Wiles offered the following advice to aspiring writers. "There are three Deborah Wiles Guidelines to Writing Well: 1. Keep a notebook. Put everything in it. I put my grocery lists in my notebook, along with doodles, recipes, sayings, lists of all kinds, even writing ideas. 2. BIC—put your butt in the chair and be as messy as you need to be, but get it down. Then, 3. Revise, revise, revise."

MAJOR INFLUENCES

"E. B. White has had the most profound influence on my wanting to tell stories," Wiles once said. "While I love *Charlotte's Web,* it's White's essays and letters I have read over and over for literally years, that have spoken to me deeply about what it means to tell your story. I'm also quite moved by *Delta Wedding* by Eudora Welty, *To Kill a Mockingbird* by Harper Lee, and *The Reivers* by William Faulkner."

WRITINGS

Freedom Summer, 2001
Love, Ruby Lavender, 2002
One Wide Sky: A Bedtime Lullaby, 2003
Each Little Bird That Sings, 2005

HONORS AND AWARDS

Ezra Jack Keats New Writer Award (Keats Foundation and New York Public Library): 2002, for *Freedom Summer*
Once Upon a World Children's Book Award (Simon Wiesenthal Center): 2002, for *Freedom Summer*
PEN/Phyllis Naylor Working Writer Fellowship: 2004
Golden Kite Honor Book: 2005, for *Each Little Bird That Sings*
Bank Street Fiction Award: 2005, for *Each Little Bird That Sings*
Josette Frank Award (Bank Street College): 2005, for *Each Little Bird That Sings*
Thurber House Residency in Children's Literature (Thurber House): 2005
E. B. White Read Aloud Award (Association of Booksellers for Children): 2006, for *Each Little Bird That Sings*

FURTHER READING

Books

McElmeel, Sharron R. *Children's Authors and Illustrators Too Good to Miss: Biographical Sketches and Bibliographies,* 2004

Periodicals

Booklist, May 1, 2001, p.1684; Aug. 2003, p.1991
Publishers Weekly, Jan. 27, 2003, p.257; Feb. 21, 2005, p.175
School Library Journal, Feb. 2001, p.107; Apr. 2001, p.152; Mar. 2005, p.221

Online Articles

http://www.harcourtbooks.com/AuthorInterviews/bookinterview_Wiles.asp
   (Harcourt Trade Publishers, "Interview with Deborah Wiles, Author of
   Each Little Bird That Sings," undated)
http://institutechildrenslit.com/rx/tr01/wiles.shtml
   (Institute of Children's Literature, "Mining Your Life for the Gold of
   Children's Books," Aug. 18, 2005)
http://www.kidsreads.com/authors/au-wiles-deborah.asp
   (KidsReads.com, "Author Deborah Wiles," May 11, 2005)

ADDRESS

Deborah Wiles
Harcourt Children's Books
15 East 26th Street
New York, NY 10010

WORLD WIDE WEB SITE

http://www.deborahwiles.com

Photo and Illustration Credits

Bill Amend/Photo: Andrews McMeel Publishing (p. 9). FOXTROT spot art and strip: FOXTROT copyright © 2006 Bill Amend. Used by permission of Universal Press Syndicate. All Rights Reserved (front cover, pp. 11, 12, 13, 16, 17, 20, 21). Covers: HOW COME I'M ALWAYS LUIGI? (Andrew McMeel Publishing) copyright © 2006 by Bill Amend; MY HOT DOG WENT OUT, CAN I HAVE ANOTHER? (Andrew McMeel Publishing) copyright © 2005 by Bill Amend.

Joseph Bruchac/Photo: Tom Stock (p. 24). Covers: BOWMAN'S STORE: A JOURNEY TO MYSELF (Dial Books) copyright © 1997 by Joseph Bruchac; A BOY CALLED SLOW (Paperstar/Putnam & Grosset Group) copyright © 1994 by Joseph Bruchac. Illustrations copyright © 1994 by Rocco Baviera; DOG PEOPLE (Fulcrum Kids/Fulcrum Publishing) copyright © 1995 Joseph Bruchac. Cover and interior illustrations copyright © 1995 Murv Jacob; KEEPERS OF THE EARTH (Fulcrum Publishing) copyright © 1988, 1989, 1997 Michael J. Caduto and Joseph Bruchac. Illustrations copyright © 1997 John Kahiones Fadden and Carol Wood. Cover illustration copyright © 1997 Sam English; TURKEY BROTHER AND OTHER TALES copyright © 1975 The Crossing Press; THE WINTER PEOPLE (Puffin Books/Penguin Group) copyright © Joseph Bruchac, 2002. Cover illustration copyright © James Bernardin, 2002.

Gennifer Choldenko/Photo: Penguin Young Readers Group (front cover, p. 43). Covers: AL CAPONE DOES MY SHIRTS (G.P. Putnam's Sons/Penguin Group) copyright © 2004 by Gennifer Choldenko; MOONSTRUCK (Hyperion Books for Children) text copyright © 1997 by Gennifer Choldenko. Jacket and illustrations copyright © 1997 by Paul Yalowitz; NOTES FROM A LIAR AND HER DOG (Puffin Books/Penguin Group) copyright © Gennifer Choldenko. Cover illustrations copyright © Mark Ulriksen, 2001.

Shannon Hale/Photo: Copyright © Katie Janke (p. 54). Used by permission of the publishers, Bloomsbury Children's Books (p. 54). Covers: ENNA BURNING (Bloomsbury) copyright © 2004 by Shannon Hale. Jacket art copyright © 2004 by Alison Jay; THE GOOSE GIRL (Bloomsbury) copyright © 2003 by Shannon Hale. Jacket art copyright © 2003 by Alison Jay; PRINCESS ACADEMY (Bloomsbury Children's Books) copyright © 2005 by Shannon Hale. Jacket art © 2005 by Tim Zeltner.

Carl Hiaasen/Photos: Elena Seibert (p. 66); Acey Harper/Time Life Pictures/Getty Images (p. 69); copyright © 2006 New Line Productions, Inc. All Rights Reserved (p. 75). Covers: FLUSH copyright © 2005 by Carl Hiaasen. Jacket illustration copyright © 2005 by Alfred A. Knopf; HOOT copyright © 2002 by Carl Hiaasen. Jacket copyright © 2002 Alfred A. Knopf; TEAM RODENT (Library of Contemporary Thought/Random House) copyright © 1998 by Carl Hiaasen; TOURIST SEASON (Warner Books) copyright © 1986 by Carl Hiaasen.

Will Hobbs/Photos: Jean Hobbs (front cover, p. 80); courtesy Will Hobbs (pp. 82, 88). Covers: BEARSTONE (Aladdin/Simon & Schuster) copyright © 1989 by Will Hobbs. Cover illustration copyright © 2004 by Jonathan Barkat; CROSSING THE WIRE copyright © 2006 by Will Hobbs. Jacket art copyright © 2006 by Vince Natale; FAR NORTH (Avon Books) copyright © 1996 by Will Hobbs.

Kathryn Lasky/Photos: Christoper G. Knight (front cover, pp. 94, 102). Covers: THE CAPTURE (Scholastic) text copyright © 2003 by Kathryn Lasky; I HAVE FOUR NAMES FOR MY GRANDFATHER (Little, Brown and Company) text copyright © 1976 by Kathryn Lasky Knight. Photographs copyright © 1976 by Christopher G. Knight; A JOURNEY TO THE NEW WORLD: THE DIARY OF REMEMBER PATIENCE WHIPPLE (Scholastic) copyright © 1996 by Kathryn Lasky; MEMOIRS OF A BOOKBAT (Harcourt) copyright © 1994 by Kathryn Lasky Knight. Cover illustration copyright © 1994 by Michael Steirnagle; NIGHT JOURNEY (Puffin Books/Penguin Group) text copyright © Kathryn Lasky, 1981. Illustrations copyiright © Trina Schart Hyman, 1981; SUGARING TIME (Aladdin/Simon & Schuster) text copyright © 1983 by Kathryn Lasky. Photographs copyright © 1983 by Christopher G. Knight.

Arnold Lobel/Covers: FABLES (HarperCollins Publishers) copyright © 1980 by Arnold Lobel; FROG AND TOAD ARE FRIENDS (HarperTrophy/HarperCollins Publishers) text and cover art copyright © 1970 by Arnold Lobel; HOW THE ROOSTER SAVED THE DAY (Greenwillow Books/William Morrow & Company, Inc.) text copyright © 1977 by Arnold Lobel. Illustrations copyright © 1977 by Anita Lobel; MOUSE SOUP (HarperTrophy/HarperCollins Publishers) text and cover art copyright © 1977 by Arnold Lobel; RED TAG COME BACK (Harper & Row, Publishers) text copyright © 1961 by Fred Phleger. Pictures copyright © 1961 by Arnold Lobel.

Janet McDonald/Photos: copyright © Gwen Wock (p. 129); Library of Congress (p. 130); Janet McDonald and Farrar, Straus and Giroux (pp. 133, 134). Covers: BROTHER HOOD (Frances Foster Books/Farrar, Straus and Giroux) copyright © 2004 by Janet McDonald. Jacket art copyright © 2004 by Rudy Gutierrez; PROJECT GIRL (University of California Press) copyright © 1999 by Janet McDonald; SPELLBOUND (Penguin Group) copyright © Janet McDonald, 2001. Cover illustration © copyright R. Gregory Christie, 2001.

Deborah Wiles/Photo: Fay Snowberger Stowe (p. 145). Covers: EACH LITTLE BIRD THAT SINGS (Gulliver Books/Harcourt) copyright © 2005 by Deborah Wiles. Jacket illustration copyright © 2005 by Marla Frazee; FREEDOM SUMMER (Anne Schwartz Book/Atheneum Books for Young Readers) text copyright © 2001 by Deborah Wiles. Cover and illustrations copyright © 2001 by Jerome Lagarrigue; LOVE, RUBY LAVENDER (Gulliver Books/Harcourt) copyright © 2001 by Deborah Wiles. Cover illustrations copyright © 2001 by Marla Frazee.

Cumulative General Index

This cumulative index includes names, occupations, nationalities, and ethnic and minority origins that pertain to all individuals profiled in *Biography Today* since the debut of the series in 1992.

Aaliyah . . . . Jan 02
Aaron, Hank . . . . Sport V.1
Abbey, Edward . . . . WorLdr V.1
Abdul, Paula . . . . Jan 92; Update 02
Abdul-Jabbar, Kareem . . . . Sport V.1
Aboriginal
    Freeman, Cathy . . . . Jan 01
Abzug, Bella . . . . Sep 98
activists
    Abzug, Bella . . . . Sep 98
    Arafat, Yasir . . . . Sep 94; Update 94;
      Update 95; Update 96; Update 97; Update
      98; Update 00; Update 01; Update 02
    Ashe, Arthur . . . . Sep 93
    Askins, Renee . . . . WorLdr V.1
    Aung San Suu Kyi . . . . . Apr 96; Update 98;
      Update 01; Update 02
    Banda, Hastings Kamuzu . . . . WorLdr V.2
    Bates, Daisy . . . . Apr 00
    Bellamy, Carol . . . . Jan 06
    Benjamin, Regina . . . . Science V.9
    Brower, David . . . . . WorLdr V.1; Update 01
    Burnside, Aubyn . . . . Sep 02
    Calderone, Mary S. . . . . Science V.3
    Chavez, Cesar . . . . Sep 93
    Chavis, Benjamin . . . . Jan 94; Update 94
    Cronin, John . . . . WorLdr V.3
    Dai Qing . . . . WorLdr V.3
    Dalai Lama . . . . Sep 98
    Douglas, Marjory Stoneman . . WorLdr V.1;
      Update 98
    Ebadi, Shirin . . . . Apr 04
    Edelman, Marian Wright . . . . Apr 93
    Fay, Michael . . . . Science V.9
    Foreman, Dave . . . . WorLdr V.1
    Forman, James . . . . Apr 05
    Fuller, Millard . . . . Apr 03
    Gibbs, Lois . . . . WorLdr V.1
    Haddock, Doris (Granny D) . . . . Sep 00

Huerta, Dolores . . . . Sep 03
Jackson, Jesse . . . . Sep 95; Update 01
Ka Hsaw Wa . . . . WorLdr V.3
Kaunda, Kenneth . . . . WorLdr V.2
Kenyatta, Jomo . . . . WorLdr V.2
Kielburger, Craig . . . . Jan 00
Kim Dae-jung . . . . Sep 01
LaDuke, Winona . . WorLdr V.3; Update 00
Lewis, John . . . . Jan 03
Love, Susan . . . . Science V.3
Maathai, Wangari . . . . . WorLdr V.1; Sep 05
Mandela, Nelson . . . . Jan 92; Update 94;
    Update 01
Mandela, Winnie . . . . WorLdr V.2
Mankiller, Wilma . . . . Apr 94
Martin, Bernard . . . . WorLdr V.3
Masih, Iqbal . . . . Jan 96
Menchu, Rigoberta . . . . Jan 93
Mendes, Chico . . . . WorLdr V.1
Mugabe, Robert . . . . WorLdr V.2
Marshall, Thurgood . . . . . Jan 92; Update 93
Nakamura, Leanne . . . . Apr 02
Nhat Hanh (Thich) . . . . Jan 04
Nkrumah, Kwame . . . . WorLdr V.2
Nyerere, Julius Kambarage . . . WorLdr V.2;
    Update 99
Oliver, Patsy Ruth . . . . WorLdr V.1
Parks, Rosa . . . . . Apr 92; Update 94; Apr 06
Pauling, Linus . . . . Jan 95
Poussaint, Alvin . . . . Science V.9
Saro-Wiwa, Ken . . . . WorLdr V.1
Savimbi, Jonas . . . . WorLdr V.2
Spock, Benjamin . . . . Sep 95; Update 98
Steinem, Gloria . . . . Oct 92
Steingraber, Sandra . . . . Science V.9
Teresa, Mother . . . . Apr 98
Watson, Paul . . . . WorLdr V.1
Werbach, Adam . . . . WorLdr V.1
Wolf, Hazel . . . . WorLdr V.3
Zamora, Pedro . . . . Apr 95

actors/actresses

Aaliyah . . . . Jan 02
Affleck, Ben . . . . Sep 99
Alba, Jessica. . . . . Sep 01
Allen, Tim . . . . Apr 94; Update 99
Alley, Kirstie . . . . Jul 92
Anderson, Gillian . . . . Jan 97
Aniston, Jennifer. . . . . Apr 99
Arnold, Roseanne . . . . Oct 92
Banks, Tyra . . . . PerfArt V.2
Barrymore, Drew . . . . Jan 01
Bell, Kristen . . . . Sep 05
Bergen, Candice . . . . Sep 93
Berry, Halle. . . . . Jan 95; Update 02
Bialik, Mayim . . . . Jan 94
Black, Jack . . . . Jan 05
Blanchard, Rachel. . . . . Apr 97
Bledel, Alexis . . . . Jan 03
Bloom, Orlando . . . . Sep 04
Brandis, Jonathan . . . . Sep 95
Brandy . . . . Apr 96
Brody, Adam . . . . Sep 05
Bryan, Zachery Ty . . . . Jan 97
Burke, Chris. . . . . Sep 93
Bynes, Amanda. . . . . Sep 03
Cameron, Candace. . . . . Apr 95
Campbell, Neve . . . . Apr 98
Candy, John. . . . . Sep 94
Carrey, Jim. . . . . Apr 96
Carvey, Dana . . . . Jan 93
Chan, Jackie. . . . . PerfArt V.1
Culkin, Macaulay . . . . Sep 93
Danes, Claire. Sep 97
Depp, Johnny . . . . Apr 05
Diaz, Cameron . . . . PerfArt V.3
DiCaprio, Leonardo . . . . Apr 98
Diesel, Vin . . . . Jan 03
Doherty, Shannen . . . . . Apr 92; Update 94
Duchovny, David . . . . Apr 96
Duff, Hilary . . . . Sep 02
Dunst, Kirsten . . . . PerfArt V.1
Eminem . . . . Apr 03
Eve . . . . Jan 05
Fanning, Dakota . . . . Jan 06
Fey, Tina . . . . Author V.16
Ford, Harrison. . . . . Sep 97
Garth, Jennie. Apr 96
Gellar, Sarah Michelle. . . . . Jan 99
Gilbert, Sara . . . . Apr 93
Goldberg, Whoopi . . . . Apr 94
Goodman, John . . . . Sep 95
Hanks, Tom . . . . Jan 96
Hart, Melissa Joan . . . . Jan 94
Hartnett, Josh . . . . Sep 03
Hathaway, Anne. . . . . Apr 05
Hewitt, Jennifer Love. . . . . Sep 00
Highmore, Freddie. . . . . Apr 06
Holmes, Katie . . . . Jan 00
Jones, James Earl . . . . Jan 95
Kutcher, Ashton . . . . Apr 04
Lee, Spike . . . . Apr 92
Locklear, Heather . . . . Jan 95
Lohan, Lindsay . . . . Sep 04
López, George. . . . . PerfArt V.2
Lopez, Jennifer. . . . . Jan 02
Mac, Bernie . . . . PerfArt V.1
McAdams, Rachel. . . . . Apr 06
Moore, Mandy. . . . . Jan 04
Muniz, Frankie. . . . . Jan 01
Murphy, Eddie. . . . . PerfArt V.2
Myers, Mike. . . . . PerfArt V.3
O'Donnell, Rosie . . . . . . Apr 97; Update 02
Oleynik, Larisa . . . . Sep 96
Olsen, Ashley . . . . Sep 95
Olsen, Mary Kate . . . . Sep 95
Perry, Luke. . . . . Jan 92
Phoenix, River. . . . . Apr 94
Pitt, Brad . . . . Sep 98
Portman, Natalie . . . . Sep 99
Priestley, Jason . . . . Apr 92
Prinze, Freddie, Jr. . . . . Apr 00
Radcliffe, Daniel. . . . . Jan 02
Raven . . . . Apr 04
Reagan, Ronald . . . . Sep 04
Reeve, Christopher . . . . . Jan 97; Update 02
Reeves, Keanu . . . . Jan 04
Roberts, Julia. Sep 01
Romeo, Lil' . . . . Jan 06
Ryder, Winona. . . . . Jan 93
Sandler, Adam. . . . . Jan 06
Shatner, William. . . . . Apr 95
Simpson, Ashlee. . . . . Sep 05
Sinatra, Frank. . . . . Jan 99
Smith, Will. . . . . Sep 94
Stewart, Jon . . . . Jan 06
Stewart, Patrick . . . . Jan 94
Stiles, Julia . . . . PerfArt V.2
Thiessen, Tiffani-Amber. . . . . Jan 96
Thomas, Jonathan Taylor. . . . . Apr 95
Tucker, Chris . . . . Jan 01
Usher . . . . PerfArt V.1

For cumulative places of birth and birthday indexes, please see biographytoday.com.

Vega, Alexa. Jan 04
Vidal, Christina . . . . PerfArt V.1
Washington, Denzel . . . . Jan 93; Update 02
Watson, Barry . . . . Sep 02
Watson, Emma . . . . Apr 03
Wayans, Keenen Ivory . . . . Jan 93
Welling, Tom . . . . PerfArt V.3
White, Jaleel . . . . Jan 96
Williams, Robin. . . . . Apr 92
Wilson, Mara . . . . Jan 97
Winfrey, Oprah . . . . Apr 92; Update 00;
    Business V.1
Winslet, Kate . . . . Sep 98
Witherspoon, Reese . . . . Apr 03
Wood, Elijah . . . . Apr 02
Adams, Ansel. . . . . Artist V.1
Adams, William (will.i.am)
    see Black Eyed Peas. . . . . Apr 06
Adams, Yolanda. . . . . Apr 03
Adu, Freddy . . . . Sport V.12
Affleck, Ben . . . . Sep 99
African-Americans
    see blacks
Agassi, Andre. . . . . Jul 92
Aguilera, Christina . . . . Apr 00
Aidid, Mohammed Farah . . . . . WorLdr V.2
Aikman, Troy   . . . . . . Apr 95; Update 01
Alba, Jessica . . . . Sep 01
Albanian
    Teresa, Mother . . . . Apr 98
Albright, Madeleine . . . . Apr 97
Alcindor, Lew
    see Abdul-Jabbar, Kareem. . . . . . . Sport V.1
Aldrich, George . . . . Science V.11
Alexander, Lloyd. . . . . Author V.6
Algerian
    Boulmerka, Hassiba. . . . . Sport V.1
Ali, Laila . . . . Sport V.11
Ali, Muhammad . . . . Sport V.2
Allen, Marcus. . . . . Sep 97
Allen, Tim . . . . Apr 94; Update 99
Allen, Tori. . . . . Sport V.9
Alley, Kirstie. . . . . Jul 92
Almond, David. . . . . Author V.10
Alvarez, Julia . . . . Author V.17
Alvarez, Luis W.. . . . . Science V.3
Amanpour, Christiane. . . . . Jan 01
Amend, Bill. . . . . Author V.18
Amin, Idi . . . . WorLdr V.2
Amman, Simon . . . . Sport V.8
An Na . . . . Author V.12

Anders, C.J.
    see Bennett, Cherie. . . . . Author V.9
Anderson, Brett (Donna A.)
    see Donnas. . . . . Apr 04
Anderson, Gillian. . . . . Jan 97
Anderson, Laurie Halse . . . . . . Author V.11
Anderson, Marian . . . . Jan 94
Anderson, Terry. . . . . Apr 92
André 3000
    see OutKast . . . . Sep 04
Andretti, Mario . . . . Sep 94
Andrews, Ned. . . . . Sep 94
Angelou, Maya. . . . . Apr 93
Angolan
    Savimbi, Jonas . . . . WorLdr V.2
animators
    see also cartoonists
    Hillenburg, Stephen . . . . Author V.14
    Jones, Chuck . . . . Author V.12
    Lasseter, John.. . . . . Sep 00
    Tartakovsky, Genndy . . . . Author V.11
Aniston, Jennifer. . . . . Apr 99
Annan, Kofi . . . . Jan 98; Update 01
apl.de.ap (Alan Pineda Lindo)
    see Black Eyed Peas. . . . . Apr 06
Applegate, K. A. . . . . Jan 00
Arab-American
    Nye, Naomi Shihab . . . . Author V.8
Arafat, Yasir . . . . Sep 94; Update 94;
    Update 95; Update 96; Update 97; Update
    98; Update 00; Update 01; Update 02
Arantes do Nascimento, Edson
    see Pelé. . . . . Sport V.1
architects
    Berger, Francie . . . . Sep 04
    Juster, Norton . . . . Author V.14
    Lin, Maya . . . . Sep 97
    Pei, I.M. . . . . Artist V.1
    Wright, Frank Lloyd. . . . . Artist V.1
Aristide, Jean-Bertrand . . Jan 95; Update 01
Armstrong, Billie Joe
    see Green Day . . . . Apr 06
Armstrong, Lance.. . . . . . Sep 00; Update 00;
    Update 01; Update 02
Armstrong, Robb . . . . Author V.9
Armstrong, William H.. . . . . Author V.7
Arnesen, Liv . . . . Author V.15
Arnold, Roseanne . . . . Oct 92
artists
    Adams, Ansel . . . . Artist V.1
    Barron, Robert. . . . . Science V.9

Bearden, Romare . . . . Artist V.1
Bemelmans, Ludwig . . . . Author V.16
Bennett, Olivia . . . . Sep 03
Calder, Alexander . . . . Artist V.1
Chagall, Marc . . . . Artist V.1
Chihuly, Dale . . . . Jan 06
Christo . . . . Sep 96
Feelings, Tom. . . . . Author V.16
Frankenthaler, Helen. . . . . Artist V.1
Gorey, Edward. . . . . Author V.13
GrandPré, Mary. . . . . Author V.14
Johns, Jasper . . . . Artist V.1
Lawrence, Jacob . . . . . Artist V.1; Update 01
Lin, Maya . . . . Sep 97
Lobel, Arnold . . . . Author V.18
Moore, Henry. . . . . Artist V.1
Moses, Grandma . . . . Artist V.1
Nechita, Alexandra . . . . Jan 98
Nevelson, Louise . . . . Artist V.1
O'Keeffe, Georgia . . . . Artist V.1
Parks, Gordon . . . . Artist V.1
Pinkney, Jerry . . . . Author V.2
Ringgold, Faith . . . . Author V.2
Rivera, Diego . . . . Artist V.1
Rockwell, Norman. . . . . Artist V.1
Warhol, Andy. . . . . Artist V.1
Ashanti. PerfArt V.2
Ashe, Arthur. . . . . Sep 93
Ashley, Maurice . . . . Sep 99
Asians
   An Na. . . . . Author V.12
   Aung San Suu Kyi . . . . . Apr 96; Update 98;
     Update 01; Update 02
   Chan, Jackie . . . . PerfArt V.1
   Chung, Connie. . . . . Jan 94; Update 96
   Dai Qing . . . . WorLdr V.3
   Fu Mingxia . . . . Sport V.5
   Guey, Wendy . . . . Sep 96
   Ho, David . . . . Science V.6
   Ka Hsaw Wa. . . . . WorLdr V.3
   Kim Dae-jung. . . . . Sep 01
   Kwan, Michelle. . . . . . Sport V.3; Update 02
   Lee, Jeanette . . . . Apr 03
   Lin, Maya. . . . . Sep 97
   Ma, Yo-Yo . . . . Jul 92
   Ohno, Apolo. . . . . Sport V.8
   Pak, Se Ri . . . . Sport V.4
   Park, Linda Sue . . . . Author V.12
   Pei, I.M. . . . . Artist V.1
   Shinoda, Mike (Linkin Park) . . . . Jan 04

Tan, Amy. . . . . Author V.9
Wang, An . . . . Science V.2
Wie, Michelle . . . . Sep 04
Woods, Tiger. . . . . Sport V.1; Update 00
Yamaguchi, Kristi . . . . Apr 92
Yao Ming . . . . Sep 03
Yep, Laurence . . . . Author V.5
Asimov, Isaac . . . . Jul 92
Askins, Renee . . . . WorLdr V.1
astronauts
   Collins, Eileen . . . . Science V.4
   Glenn, John . . . . Jan 99
   Harris, Bernard . . . . Science V.3
   Jemison, Mae. . . . . Oct 92
   Lovell, Jim. . . . . Jan 96
   Lucid, Shannon . . . . Science V.2
   Ochoa, Ellen . . . . Apr 01; Update 02
   Ride, Sally. . . . . Jan 92
   Whitson, Peggy. . . . . Science V.9
athletes
   see sports
Attenborough, David . . . . Science V.4
Atwater-Rhodes, Amelia . . . . . . Author V.8
Aung San Suu Kyi . . . . . Apr 96; Update 98;
   Update 01; Update 02
Australians
   Beachley, Layne . . . . Sport V.9
   Freeman, Cathy . . . . Jan 01
   Irwin, Steve . . . . Science V.7
   Norman, Greg . . . . Jan 94
   Travers, P.L. . . . . Author V.2
   Webb, Karrie . . . . Sport V.5; Update 01;
     Update 02
Austrian
   Bemelmans, Ludwig . . . . Author V.16
authors
   Abbey, Edward. . . . . WorLdr V.1
   Alexander, Lloyd. . . . . Author V.6
   Almond, David . . . . Author V.10
   Alvarez, Julia . . . . Author V.17
   An Na. . . . . Author V.12
   Anderson Laurie Halse. . . . . . . Author V.11
   Angelou, Maya . . . . Apr 93
   Applegate, K. A.. . . . . Jan 00
   Armstrong, Robb . . . . Author V.9
   Armstrong, William H.. . . . . Author V.7
   Arnesen, Liv. . . . . Author V.15
   Asimov, Isaac . . . . Jul 92
   Attenborough, David. . . . . Science V.4
   Atwater-Rhodes, Amelia . . . . . . Author V.8

For cumulative places of birth and birthday indexes, please see biographytoday.com.

Avi . . . . Jan 93
Babbitt, Natalie . . . . Jan 04
Baldwin, James . . . . Author V.2
Bauer, Joan . . . . Author V.10
Bemelmans, Ludwig . . . . Author V.16
Bennett, Cherie . . . . Author V.9
Benson, Mildred . . . . Jan 03
Berenstain, Jan . . . . Author V.2
Berenstain, Stan . . . . Author V.2
Bloor, Edward . . . . Author V.15
Blum, Deborah . . . . Science V.8
Blume, Judy . . . . Jan 92
Boyd, Candy Dawson . . . . Author V.3
Bradbury, Ray . . . . Author V.3
Brashares, Ann . . . . Author V.15
Brody, Jane . . . . Science V.2
Brooks, Gwendolyn . . . . Author V.3
Brower, David . . . . . WorLdr V.1; Update 01
Brown, Claude . . . . Author V.12
Bruchac, Joseph . . . . Author V.18
Byars, Betsy . . . . Author V.4
Cabot, Meg . . . . Author V.12
Caplan, Arthur . . . . Science V.6
Card, Orson Scott . . . . Author V.14
Carle, Eric . . . . Author V.1
Carson, Rachel . . . . WorLdr V.1
Chambers, Veronica . . . . Author V.15
Childress, Alice . . . . Author V.1
Choldenko, Gennifer . . . . Author V.18
Cleary, Beverly . . . . Apr 94
Clements, Andrew . . . . Author V.13
Colfer, Eoin . . . . Author V.13
Collier, Bryan . . . . Author V.11
Collins, Billy . . . . Author V.16
Cooney, Barbara . . . . Author V.8
Cooney, Caroline B. . . . . Author V.4
Cooper, Floyd . . . . Author V.17
Cooper, Susan . . . . Author V.17
Cormier, Robert . . . . Author V.1; Update 01
Cosby, Bill . . . . Jan 92
Coville, Bruce . . . . Author V.9
Creech, Sharon . . . . Author V.5
Crichton, Michael . . . . Author V.5
Crilley, Mark . . . . Author V.15
Cronin, John . . . . WorLdr V.3
Curtis, Christopher Paul . . . . . . Author V.4;
    Update 00
Cushman, Karen . . . . Author V.5
Dahl, Roald . . . . Author V.1
Dai Qing . . . . WorLdr V.3
Danziger, Paula . . . . Author V.6

Delany, Bessie . . . . Sep 99
Delany, Sadie . . . . Sep 99
dePaola, Tomie . . . . Author V.5
DiCamillo, Kate . . . . Author V.10
Douglas, Marjory Stoneman . . WorLdr V.1;
    Update 98
Dove, Rita . . . . Jan 94
Draper, Sharon . . . . Apr 99
Dunbar, Paul Lawrence . . . . Author V.8
Duncan, Lois . . . . Sep 93
Ellison, Ralph . . . . Author V.3
Farmer, Nancy . . . . Author V.6
Feelings, Tom . . . . Author V.16
Fey, Tina . . . . Author V.16
Feynman, Richard P. . . . . Science V.10
Filipovic, Zlata . . . . Sep 94
Fitzhugh, Louise . . . . Author V.3
Flake, Sharon . . . . Author V.13
Forman, James . . . . Apr 05
Fox, Paula . . . . Author V.15
Frank, Anne . . . . Author V.4
Freedman, Russell . . . . Author V.14
Funke, Cornelia . . . . Sep 05
Gantos, Jack . . . . Author V.10
Gates, Henry Louis, Jr. . . . . Apr 00
George, Jean Craighead . . . . . . Author V.3
Giff, Patricia Reilly . . . . Author V.7
Gorey, Edward . . . . Author V.13
Gould, Stephen Jay . . . . Science V.2;
    Update 02
Grandin, Temple . . . . Science V.3
Greenburg, Dan . . . . Author V.14
Grimes, Nikki . . . . Author V.14
Grisham, John . . . . Author V.1
Guy, Rosa . . . . Author V.9
Gwaltney, John Langston . . . . . Science V.3
Haddix, Margaret Peterson . . . Author V.11
Hakim, Joy . . . . Author V.16
Hale, Shannon . . . . Author V.18
Haley, Alex . . . . Apr 92
Hamilton, Virginia . . . . Author V.1;
    Author V.12
Handford, Martin . . . . Jan 92
Hansberry, Lorraine . . . . Author V.5
Heinlein, Robert . . . . Author V.4
Henry, Marguerite . . . . Author V.4
Herriot, James . . . . Author V.1
Hesse, Karen . . . . . . Author V.5; Update 02
Hiaasen, Carl . . . . Author V.18
Hillenbrand, Laura . . . . Author V.14

Hinton, S.E. . . . . Author V.1
Hobbs, Will . . . . Author V.18
Horvath, Polly . . . . Author V.16
Howe, James . . . . Author V.17
Hughes, Langston. . . . . Author V.7
Hurston, Zora Neale. . . . . Author V.6
Jackson, Shirley . . . . Author V.6
Jacques, Brian. . . . . Author V.5
Jenkins, Jerry B. . . . . Author V.16
Jiménez, Francisco. . . . . Author V.13
Johnson, Angela . . . . Author V.6
Jones, Diana Wynne . . . . Author V.15
Juster, Norton . . . . Author V.14
Kamler, Kenneth . . . . Science V.6
Kerr, M.E. . . . . Author V.1
King, Stephen. . . . . . Author V.1; Update 00
Konigsburg, E. L. . . . . Author V.3
Krakauer, Jon. . . . . Author V.6
Kübler-Ross, Elisabeth . . . . Science V.10
LaDuke, Winona . . WorLdr V.3; Update 00
LaHaye, Tim. . . . . Author V.16
Lansky, Bruce . . . . Author V.17
Lasky, Kathryn . . . . Author V.18
Lee, Harper. . . . . Author V.9
Lee, Stan. . . . . Author V.7; Update 02
Le Guin, Ursula K. . . . . Author V.8
L'Engle, Madeleine . . . . Jan 92; Apr 01
Leopold, Aldo. . . . . WorLdr V.3
Lester, Julius . . . . Author V.7
Levine, Gail Carson . . . . Author V.17
Lewis, C. S. . . . . Author V.3
Lindgren, Astrid . . . . Author V.13
Lionni, Leo. . . . . Author V.6
Lipsyte, Robert . . . . Author V.12
Lobel, Arnold . . . . Author V.18
Love, Susan. . . . . Science V.3
Lowry, Lois . . . . Author V.4
Lynch, Chris. . . . . Author V.13
Macaulay, David . . . . Author V.2
MacLachlan, Patricia. . . . . Author V.2
Martin, Ann M. . . . . Jan 92
Martinez, Victor. . . . . Author V.15
McCloskey, Robert . . . . Author V.15
McCully, Emily Arnold. . . Jul 92; Update 93
McDaniel, Lurlene . . . . Author V.14
McDonald, Janet. . . . . Author V.18
McKissack, Fredrick L. . . . . Author V.3
McKissack, Patricia C. . . . . Author V.3
Mead, Margaret . . . . Science V.2
Meltzer, Milton . . . . Author V.11
Morrison, Lillian . . . . Author V.12

Morrison, Toni. . . . . Jan 94
Moss, Cynthia . . . . WorLdr V.3
Mowat, Farley . . . . Author V.8
Muir, John. . . . . WorLdr V.3
Murie, Margaret. . . . . WorLdr V.1
Murie, Olaus J. . . . . WorLdr V.1
Murphy, Jim . . . . Author V.17
Myers, Walter Dean. . . . . Jan 93; Update 94
Napoli, Donna Jo. . . . . Author V.16
Naylor, Phyllis Reynolds . . . . Apr 93
Nelson, Marilyn. . . . . Author V.13
Nhat Hanh (Thich) . . . . Jan 04
Nielsen, Jerri . . . . Science V.7
Nixon, Joan Lowery . . . . Author V.1
Noor al Hussein, Queen of Jordan . . Jan 05
Nye, Naomi Shihab . . . . Author V.8
O'Dell, Scott . . . . Author V.2
Opdyke, Irene Gut. . . . . Author V.9
Paolini, Christopher . . . . Author V.16
Park, Linda Sue. . . . . Author V.12
Pascal, Francine. . . . . Author V.6
Paterson, Katherine . . . . Author V.3
Paulsen, Gary. . . . . Author V.1
Peck, Richard. . . . . Author V.10
Peet, Bill . . . . Author V.4
Peterson, Roger Tory. . . . . WorLdr V.1
Pierce, Tamora. . . . . Author V.13
Pike, Christopher . . . . Sep 96
Pinkney, Andrea Davis. . . . . . . Author V.10
Pinkwater, Daniel . . . . Author V.8
Pinsky, Robert . . . . Author V.7
Potter, Beatrix . . . . Author V.8
Poussaint, Alvin . . . . Science V.9
Prelutsky, Jack . . . . Author V.2
Pullman, Philip. . . . . Author V.9
Reid Banks, Lynne . . . . Author V.2
Rennison, Louise. . . . . Author V.10
Rice, Anne . . . . Author V.3
Rinaldi, Ann. . . . . Author V.8
Ringgold, Faith . . . . Author V.2
Rogers, Fred. . . . . PerfArt V.3
Rowan, Carl. . . . . Sep 01
Rowling, J. K. . . . . Sep 99; Update 00;
    Update 01; Update 02
Russell, Charlie. . . . . Science V.11
Ryan, Pam Muñoz . . . . Author V.12
Rylant, Cynthia . . . . Author V.1
Sachar, Louis . . . . Author V.6
Sacks, Oliver . . . . Science V.3
Salinger, J.D. . . . . Author V.2

Saro-Wiwa, Ken. . . . . WorLdr V.1
Scarry, Richard . . . . Sep 94
Scieszka, Jon. . . . . Author V.9
Sendak, Maurice . . . . Author V.2
Senghor, Léopold Sédar . . . . . WorLdr V.2
Seuss, Dr. . . . . Jan 92
Silverstein, Shel . . . . Author V.3; Update 99
Sleator, William. . . . . Author V.11
Small, David. . . . . Author V.10
Smith, Betty . . . . Author V.17
Snicket, Lemony. . . . . Author V.12
Snyder, Zilpha Keatley . . . . . . Author V.17
Sones, Sonya. . . . . Author V.11
Soto, Gary . . . . Author V.5
Speare, Elizabeth George . . . . Sep 95
Spiegelman, Art . . . . Author V.17
Spinelli, Jerry. . . . . Apr 93
Spock, Benjamin. . . . . . . Sep 95; Update 98
Steingraber, Sandra . . . . Science V.9
Stepanek, Mattie. . . . . Apr 02
Stine, R.L. . . . . Apr 94
Strasser, Todd . . . . Author V.7
Tan, Amy. . . . . Author V.9
Tarbox, Katie . . . . Author V.10
Taylor, Mildred D.. . . . Author V.1; Update 02
Thomas, Lewis . . . . Apr 94
Tolan, Stephanie S.. . . . . Author V.14
Tolkien, J.R.R. . . . . Jan 02
Travers, P.L. . . . . Author V.2
Tyson, Neil deGrasse. . . . . Science V.11
Van Allsburg, Chris . . . . Apr 92
Van Draanen, Wendelin. . . . . . Author V.11
Voigt, Cynthia. . . . . Oct 92
Vonnegut, Kurt, Jr. . . . . Author V.1
White, E.B. . . . . Author V.1
White, Ruth . . . . Author V.11
Wilder, Laura Ingalls. . . . . Author V.3
Wiles, Deborah . . . . Author V.18
Williams, Garth. . . . . Author V.2
Williams, Lori Aurelia. . . . . Author V.16
Williamson, Kevin. . . . . Author V.6
Wilson, August . . . . Author V.4
Wilson, Edward O. . . . . Science V.8
Wolff, Virginia Euwer. . . . . Author V.13
Woodson, Jacqueline. . . . . Author V.7;
  Update 01
Wrede, Patricia C.. . . . . Author V.7
Wright, Richard. . . . . Author V.5
Yep, Laurence . . . . Author V.5
Yolen, Jane. . . . . Author V.7
Zindel, Paul . . . . Author V.1; Update 02

autobiographies
  Handford, Martin . . . . Jan 92
  Iacocca, Lee . . . . Jan 92
  L'Engle, Madeleine . . . . Jan 92
  Parkinson, Jennifer. . . . . Apr 95
Avi. . . . . Jan 93
Babbitt, Bruce . . . . Jan 94
Babbitt, Natalie. . . . . Jan 04
Backstreet Boys. . . . . Jan 00
Bahrke, Shannon. . . . . Sport V.8
Bailey, Donovan . . . . Sport V.2
Baiul, Oksana. . . . . Apr 95
Baker, James . . . . Oct 92
Baldwin, James. . . . . Author V.2
Ballard, Robert. . . . . Science V.4
ballet
  see dance
Banda, Hastings Kamuzu . . . . WorLdr V.2
Banks, Tyra . . . . PerfArt V.2
Bardeen, John. . . . . Science V.1
Barkley, Charles. . . . . Apr 92; Update 02
Barr, Roseanne
  see Arnold, Roseanne . . . . Oct 92
Barron, Robert . . . . Science V.9
Barrymore, Drew. . . . . Jan 01
Barton, Hazel . . . . Science V.6
baseball
  Aaron, Hank. . . . . Sport V.1
  Beckett, Josh . . . . Sport V.11
  Bonds, Barry. . . . . Jan 03
  Fielder, Cecil . . . . Sep 93
  Griffey, Ken, Jr. . . . . Sport V.1
  Hernandez, Livan. . . . . Apr 98
  Jackson, Bo . . . . Jan 92; Update 93
  Jeter, Derek. . . . . Sport V.4
  Johnson, Randy . . . . Sport V.9
  Jordan, Michael. . . . . Jan 92; Update 93;
    Update 94; Update 95; Update 99; Update
    01
  Maddux, Greg. . . . . Sport V.3
  Mantle, Mickey . . . . Jan 96
  Martinez, Pedro . . . . Sport V.5
  McGwire, Mark . . . . Jan 99; Update 99
  Moreno, Arturo R. . . . . Business V.1
  Pujols, Albert . . . . Sport V.12
  Ramirez, Manny. . . . . Sport V.13
  Ripken, Cal, Jr. . . . . . . Sport V.1; Update 01
  Robinson, Jackie. . . . . Sport V.3
  Rodriguez, Alex . . . . Sport V.6
  Rose, Pete. . . . . Jan 92
  Ryan, Nolan. . . . . Oct 92; Update 93

Sanders, Deion . . . . Sport V.1
Schilling, Curt . . . . Sep 05
Soriano, Alfonso. . . . . Sport V.10
Sosa, Sammy . . . . Jan 99; Update 99
Williams, Ted . . . . Sport V.9
Winfield, Dave . . . . Jan 93
Basich, Tina . . . . Sport V.12
basketball
Abdul-Jabbar, Kareem. . . . . Sport V.1
Barkley, Charles . . . . Apr 92; Update 02
Bird, Larry. . . . . Jan 92; Update 98
Bird, Sue . . . . Sport V.9
Bryant, Kobe . . . . Apr 99
Carter, Vince . . . . Sport V.5; Update 01
Chamberlain, Wilt . . . . Sport V.4
Dumars, Joe. . . . . Sport V.3; Update 99
Duncan, Tim . . . . Apr 04
Ewing, Patrick . . . . Jan 95; Update 02
Ford, Cheryl . . . . Sport V.11
Garnett, Kevin . . . . Sport V.6
Hardaway, Anfernee "Penny" . . . Sport V.2
Hill, Grant. . . . . Sport V.1
Holdsclaw, Chamique.. . . . . Sep 00
Iverson, Allen . . . . Sport V.7
Jackson, Phil . . . . Sport V.10
James, LeBron. . . . . Sport V.12
Johnson, Magic . . . . Apr 92; Update 02
Jordan, Michael. . . . . . . Jan 92; Update 93;
    Update 94; Update 95; Update 99; Update
    01
Kidd, Jason . . . . Sport V.9
Lennox, Betty . . . . Sport V.13
Leslie, Lisa . . . . Jan 04
Lobo, Rebecca. . . . . Sport V.3
McGrady, Tracy . . . . Sport V.11
Nash, Steve. . . . . Jan 06
Olajuwon, Hakeem . . . . Sep 95
O'Neal, Shaquille . . . . Sep 93
Palmer, Violet . . . . Sep 05
Pippen, Scottie . . . . Oct 92
Robinson, David . . . . Sep 96
Rodman, Dennis . . . . Apr 96; Update 99
Stiles, Jackie . . . . Sport V.6
Stockton, John . . . . Sport V.3
Summitt, Pat. . . . . Sport V.3
Swoopes, Sheryl. . . . . Sport V.2
Taurasi, Diana. . . . . Sport V.10
Wallace, Ben. . . . . Jan 05
Ward, Charlie . . . . Apr 94
Weatherspoon, Teresa. . . . . Sport V.12
Yao Ming. . . . . Sep 03

Bass, Lance
  see *N Sync. Jan 01
Bates, Daisy. Apr 00
Battle, Kathleen. . . . . Jan 93
Bauer, Joan. . . . . Author V.10
Beachley, Layne. . . . . Sport V.9
Bearden, Romare. . . . . Artist V.1
beauty pageants
  Lopez, Charlotte. . . . . Apr 94
  Whitestone, Heather . . . Apr 95; Update 02
Beckett, Josh. . . . . Sport V.11
Beckham, David . . . . Jan 04
Belgian
  Clijsters, Kim. . . . . Apr 04
Bell, Kristen . . . . Sep 05
Bellamy, Carol. . . . . Jan 06
Bemelmans, Ludwig . . . . Author V.16
Ben-Ari, Miri . . . . Jan 06
Benjamin, André
  see OutKast . . . . Sep 04
Benjamin, Regina . . . . Science V.9
Bennett, Cherie . . . . Author V.9
Bennett, Olivia. . . . . Sep 03
Bennington, Chester
  see Linkin Park. . . . . Jan 04
Benson, Mildred. . . . . Jan 03
Berenstain, Jan . . . . Author V.2
Berenstain, Stan . . . . Author V.2
Bergen, Candice . . . . Sep 93
Berger, Francie . . . . Sep 04
Berners-Lee, Tim . . . . Science V.7
Berry, Halle . . . . Jan 95; Update 02
Bethe, Hans A. . . . . Science V.3
Bezos, Jeff . . . . Apr 01
Bhutto, Benazir . . . . Apr 95; Update 99;
    Update 02
Bialik, Mayim . . . . Jan 94
bicycle riding
  Armstrong, Lance. . . . . . Sep 00; Update 00;
    Update 01; Update 02
  Dunlap, Alison . . . . Sport V.7
  LeMond, Greg . . . . Sport V.1
  Mirra, Dave . . . . Sep 02
Big Boi
  see OutKast . . . . Sep 04
billiards
  Lee, Jeanette . . . . Apr 03
bin Laden, Osama . . . . Apr 02
Bird, Larry . . . . Jan 92; Update 98
Bird, Sue . . . . Sport V.9

For cumulative places of birth and birthday indexes, please see biographytoday.com.

Black, Jack . . . . Jan 05
Black, Thomas
  see Black, Jack . . . . Jan 05
Black Eyed Peas . . . . Apr 06
Blackmun, Harry . . . . Jan 00
blacks
  Aaliyah . . . . Jan 02
  Aaron, Hank . . . . Sport V.1
  Abdul-Jabbar, Kareem . . . . Sport V.1
  Adams, Yolanda . . . . Apr 03
  Adu, Freddy . . . . Sport V.12
  Aidid, Mohammed Farah . . . . . WorLdr V.2
  Ali, Laila . . . . Sport V.11
  Ali, Muhammad . . . . Sport V.2
  Allen, Marcus . . . . Sep 97
  Amin, Idi . . . . WorLdr V.2
  Anderson, Marian . . . . Jan 94
  Angelou, Maya . . . . Apr 93
  Annan, Kofi . . . . Jan 98; Update 01
  apl.de.ap (Alan Pineda Lindo) . . . . . Apr 06
  Aristide, Jean-Bertrand . . Jan 95; Update 01
  Armstrong, Robb . . . . Author V.9
  Ashanti . . . . PerfArt V.2
  Ashe, Arthur . . . . Sep 93
  Ashley, Maurice . . . . Sep 99
  Bailey, Donovan . . . . Sport V.2
  Baldwin, James . . . . Author V.2
  Banda, Hastings Kamuzu . . . . . WorLdr V.2
  Banks, Tyra . . . . PerfArt V.2
  Bates, Daisy . . . . Apr 00
  Battle, Kathleen . . . . Jan 93
  Bearden, Romare . . . . Artist V.1
  Benjamin, Regina . . . . Science V.9
  Berry, Halle . . . . Jan 95
  Blige, Mary J. . . . . Apr 02
  Bonds, Barry . . . . Jan 03
  Boyd, Candy Dawson . . . . Author V.3
  Boyz II Men . . . . Jan 96
  Bradley, Ed. Apr 94
  Brandy . . . . Apr 96
  Brooks, Gwendolyn . . . . Author V.3
  Brooks, Vincent . . . . Sep 03
  Brown, Claude . . . . Author V.12
  Brown, Ron . . . . Sep 96
  Bryant, Kobe . . . . Apr 99
  Canady, Alexa . . . . Science V.6
  Carson, Ben . . . . Science V.4
  Carter, Vince . . . . Sport V.5; Update 01
  Chamberlain, Wilt . . . . Sport V.4
  Chambers, Veronica . . . . Author V.15

Champagne, Larry III . . . . Apr 96
Chavis, Benjamin . . . . Jan 94; Update 94
Childress, Alice . . . . Author V.1
Collier, Bryan . . . . Author V.11
Combs, Sean (Puff Daddy) . . . . Apr 98
Coolio . . . . Sep 96
Cooper, Floyd . . . . Author V.17
Cosby, Bill . . . . Jan 92
Cruz, Celia . . . . Apr 04
Culpepper, Daunte . . . . Sport V.13
Curtis, Christopher Paul . . . . . . Author V.4;
  Update 00
Dawson, Matel, Jr. . . . . Jan 04
Dayne, Ron . . . . Apr 00
Delany, Bessie . . . . Sep 99
Delany, Sadie . . . . Sep 99
Destiny's Child . . . . Apr 01
Devers, Gail . . . . Sport V.2
Dove, Rita . . . . Jan 94
Draper, Sharon . . . . Apr 99
Dumars, Joe . . . . Sport V.3; Update 99
Dunbar, Paul Lawrence . . . . Author V.8
Duncan, Tim . . . . Apr 04
Edelman, Marian Wright . . . . Apr 93
Elliott, Missy . . . . PerfArt V.3
Ellison, Ralph . . . . Author V.3
Eve . . . . Jan 05
Ewing, Patrick . . . . Jan 95; Update 02
Farrakhan, Louis . . . . Jan 97
Feelings, Tom . . . . Author V.16
Felix, Allyson . . . . Sport V.10
Fielder, Cecil . . . . Sep 93
Fitzgerald, Ella . . . . Jan 97
Flake, Sharon . . . . Author V.13
Flowers, Vonetta . . . . Sport V.8
Ford, Cheryl . . . . Sport V.11
Forman, James . . . . Apr 05
Franklin, Aretha . . . . Apr 01
Freeman, Cathy . . . . Jan 01
Garnett, Kevin . . . . Sport V.6
Gates, Henry Louis, Jr. . . . . Apr 00
Gayle, Helene . . . . Science V.8
George, Eddie . . . . Sport V.6
Gillespie, Dizzy . . . . Apr 93
Glover, Savion . . . . Apr 99
Goldberg, Whoopi . . . . Apr 94
Gonzalez, Tony . . . . Sport V.11
Graves, Earl . . . . Business V.1
Griffey, Ken, Jr. . . . . Sport V.1
Grimes, Nikki . . . . Author V.14
Gumbel, Bryant . . . . Apr 97

Guy, Jasmine . . . . Sep 93
Guy, Rosa . . . . Author V.9
Gwaltney, John Langston . . . . . Science V.3
Haley, Alex . . . . Apr 92
Hamilton, Virginia . . . . Author V.1;
    Author V.12
Hammer . . . . Jan 92
Hansberry, Lorraine . . . . Author V.5
Hardaway, Anfernee "Penny" . . . Sport V.2
Harris, Bernard . . . . Science V.3
Hayden, Carla . . . . Sep 04
Hayes, Tyrone . . . . Science V.10
Hernandez, Livan . . . . Apr 98
Hill, Anita . . . . Jan 93
Hill, Grant . . . . Sport V.1
Hill, Lauryn . . . . Sep 99
Holdsclaw, Chamique . . . . Sep 00
Holmes, Priest . . . . Apr 05
Honoré, Russel . . . . Jan 06
Hoskins, Michele . . . . Business V.1
Houston, Whitney . . . . Sep 94
Howard, Tim . . . . Apr 06
Hughes, Langston . . . . Author V.7
Hunter-Gault, Charlayne . . . . Jan 00
Hurston, Zora Neale . . . . Author V.6
Ice-T . . . . Apr 93
Iverson, Allen . . . . Sport V.7
Jackson, Bo . . . . Jan 92; Update 93
Jackson, Jesse . . . . Sep 95; Update 01
Jackson, Shirley Ann . . . . Science V.2
Jakes, T.D. Jan 05
James, LeBron . . . . Sport V.12
Jamison, Judith . . . . Jan 96
Jemison, Mae . . . . Oct 92
Jeter, Derek . . . . Sport V.4
Johnson, Angela . . . . Author V.6
Johnson, John . . . . Jan 97
Johnson, Keyshawn . . . . Sport V.10
Johnson, Lonnie . . . . Science V.4
Johnson, Magic . . . . Apr 92; Update 02
Johnson, Michael . . . . Jan 97; Update 00
Jones, James Earl . . . . Jan 95
Jones, Marion . . . . Sport V.5
Jones, Quincy . . . . PerfArt V.2
Jordan, Barbara . . . . Apr 96
Jordan, Michael . . . . Jan 92; Update 93;
    Update 94; Update 95; Update 99; Update
    01
Joyner-Kersee, Jackie . . . . Oct 92; Update
    96; Update 97; Update 98
Kaunda, Kenneth . . . . WorLdr V.2

Kenyatta, Jomo . . . . WorLdr V.2
Kidd, Jason . . . . Sport V.9
Koff, Clea . . . . Science V.11
Lawrence, Jacob . . . . . Artist V.1; Update 01
Lee, Spike . . . . Apr 92
Lennox, Betty . . . . Sport V.13
Leslie, Lisa . . . . Jan 04
Lester, Julius . . . . Author V.7
Lewis, Carl . . . . Sep 96; Update 97
Lewis, John . . . . Jan 03
Long, Irene D. . . . . Jan 04
Maathai, Wangari . . . . . WorLdr V.1; Sep 05
Mac, Bernie . . . . PerfArt V.1
Mandela, Nelson . . . . Jan 92; Update 94;
    Update 01
Mandela, Winnie . . . . WorLdr V.2
Marsalis, Wynton . . . . Apr 92
Marshall, Thurgood . . . . . Jan 92; Update 93
Martinez, Pedro . . . . Sport V.5
Maxwell, Jody-Anne . . . . Sep 98
McCarty, Oseola . . . . Jan 99; Update 99
McDonald, Janet . . . . Author V.18
McGrady, Tracy . . . . Sport V.11
McGruder, Aaron . . . . Author V.10
McKissack, Fredrick L. . . . . Author V.3
McKissack, Patricia C. . . . . Author V.3
McNabb, Donovan . . . . Apr 03
McNair, Steve . . . . Sport V.11
Mitchell-Raptakis, Karen . . . . Jan 05
Mobutu Sese Seko . . . . WorLdr V.2;
    Update 97
Morgan, Garrett . . . . Science V.2
Morrison, Sam . . . . Sep 97
Morrison, Toni . . . . Jan 94
Moss, Randy . . . . Sport V.4
Mugabe, Robert . . . . WorLdr V.2
Murphy, Eddie . . . . PerfArt V.2
Myers, Walter Dean . . . . . Jan 93; Update 94
Ndeti, Cosmas . . . . Sep 95
Nelly . . . . Sep 03
Nelson, Marilyn . . . . Author V.13
Nkrumah, Kwame . . . . WorLdr V.2
Nyerere, Julius Kambarage . . . WorLdr V.2;
    Update 99
Olajuwon, Hakeem . . . . Sep 95
Oliver, Patsy Ruth . . . . WorLdr V.1
O'Neal, Shaquille . . . . Sep 93
OutKast . . . . Sep 04
Palmer, Violet . . . . Sep 05
Parks, Gordon . . . . Artist V.1
Parks, Rosa . . . . . Apr 92; Update 94; Apr 06

For cumulative places of birth and birthday indexes, please see biographytoday.com.

Payton, Walter . . . . Jan 00
Pelé . . . . Sport V.1
Pinkney, Andrea Davis . . . . . . Author V.10
Pinkney, Jerry . . . . Author V.2
Pippen, Scottie . . . . Oct 92
Poussaint, Alvin . . . . Science V.9
Powell, Colin . . . . Jan 92; Update 93;
    Update 95; Update 01
Queen Latifah . . . . Apr 92
Raven . . . . Apr 04
Rice, Condoleezza . . . . Apr 02
Rice, Jerry . . . . Apr 93
Ringgold, Faith . . . . Author V.2
Roba, Fatuma . . . . Sport V.3
Robinson, David . . . . Sep 96
Robinson, Jackie . . . . Sport V.3
Rodman, Dennis . . . . Apr 96; Update 99
Romeo, Lil' . . . . Jan 06
Rowan, Carl . . . . Sep 01
Rudolph, Wilma . . . . Apr 95
Salt 'N' Pepa . . . . Apr 95
Sanders, Barry . . . . Sep 95; Update 99
Sanders, Deion . . . . Sport V.1
Sapp, Warren . . . . Sport V.5
Saro-Wiwa, Ken . . . . WorLdr V.1
Satcher, David . . . . Sep 98
Savimbi, Jonas . . . . WorLdr V.2
Schwikert, Tasha . . . . Sport V.7
Scurry, Briana . . . . Jan 00
Senghor, Léopold Sédar . . . . . . WorLdr V.2
Shabazz, Betty . . . . Apr 98
Shakur, Tupac . . . . Apr 97
Simmons, Russell . . . . Apr 06
Simmons, Ruth . . . . Sep 02
Smith, Emmitt . . . . Sep 94
Smith, Will . . . . Sep 94
Soriano, Alfonso . . . . Sport V.10
Sosa, Sammy . . . . Jan 99; Update 99
Stanford, John . . . . Sep 99
Stewart, Kordell . . . . Sep 98
Strahan, Michael . . . . Sport V.12
Swoopes, Sheryl . . . . Sport V.2
Tarvin, Herbert . . . . Apr 97
Taylor, Mildred D. . . Author V.1; Update 02
Thomas, Clarence . . . . Jan 92
Tubman, William V. S. . . . . WorLdr V.2
Tucker, Chris . . . . Jan 01
Tyson, Neil deGrasse . . . . Science V.11
Usher . . . . PerfArt V.1
Vick, Michael . . . . Sport V.9
Wallace, Ben . . . . Jan 05

Ward, Charlie . . . . Apr 94
Ward, Lloyd D. . . . . Jan 01
Washington, Denzel . . . . Jan 93; Update 02
Watley, Natasha . . . . Sport V.11
Wayans, Keenen Ivory . . . . Jan 93
Weatherspoon, Teresa . . . . Sport V.12
White, Jaleel . . . . Jan 96
White, Reggie . . . . Jan 98
WilderBrathwaite, Gloria . . . . . . Science V.7
will.i.am (William Adams) . . . . Apr 06
Williams, Lori Aurelia . . . . Author V.16
Williams, Serena . . . . Sport V.4; Update 00;
    Update 02
Williams, Venus . . . . Jan 99; Update 00;
    Update 01; Update 02
Willingham, Tyrone . . . . Sep 02
Wilson, August . . . . Author V.4
Winans, CeCe . . . . Apr 00
Winfield, Dave . . . . Jan 93
Winfrey, Oprah . . . . Apr 92; Update 00;
    Business V.1
Woods, Tiger . . . . Sport V.1; Update 00;
    Sport V.6
Woodson, Jacqueline . . . . Author V.7;
    Update 01
Wright, Richard . . . . Author V.5
Blair, Bonnie . . . . Apr 94; Update 95
Blair, Tony . . . . Apr 04
Blanchard, Rachel . . . . Apr 97
Bledel, Alexis . . . . Jan 03
Bleiler, Gretchen . . . . Sport V.13
Blige, Mary J. . . . . Apr 02
Bloom, Orlando . . . . Sep 04
Bloor, Edward . . . . Author V.15
Blum, Deborah . . . . Science V.8
Blume, Judy . . . . Jan 92
BMX
    see bicycle riding
bobsledding
    Flowers, Vonetta . . . . Sport V.8
Bonds, Barry . . . . Jan 03
Borgman, Jim . . . . Author V.15
Bosnian
    Filipovic, Zlata . . . . Sep 94
Boulmerka, Hassiba . . . . Sport V.1
Bourdon, Rob
    see Linkin Park . . . . Jan 04
Bourke-White, Margaret . . . . Artist V.1
Boutros-Ghali, Boutros . . . . Apr 93;
    Update 98

boxing
Ali, Laila . . . . Sport V.11
Ali, Muhammad . . . . Sport V.2
Boyd, Candy Dawson . . . . Author V.3
Boyle, Ryan . . . . Sport V.10
Boyz II Men . . . . Jan 96
Bradbury, Ray . . . . Author V.3
Bradley, Ed . . . . Apr 94
Brady, Tom . . . . Sport V.7
Branch, Michelle . . . . PerfArt V.3
Brandis, Jonathan . . . . Sep 95
Brandy . . . . Apr 96
Brashares, Ann . . . . Author V.15
Brazilians
da Silva, Fabiola . . . . Sport V.9
Mendes, Chico . . . . WorLdr V.1
Pelé . . . . Sport V.1
Breathed, Berke . . . . Jan 92
Brin, Sergey . . . . Sep 05
Brody, Adam . . . . Sep 05
Brody, Jane . . . . Science V.2
Brooks, Garth . . . . Oct 92
Brooks, Gwendolyn . . . . Author V.3
Brooks, Vincent . . . . Sep 03
Brower, David . . . . . WorLdr V.1; Update 01
Brown, Claude . . . . Author V.12
Brown, Ron . . . . Sep 96
Bruchac, Joseph . . . . Author V.18
Brundtland, Gro Harlem . . . . . . Science V.3
Bryan, Zachery Ty . . . . Jan 97
Bryant, Kobe . . . . Apr 99
Buffett, Warren . . . . Business V.1
Bulgarian
Christo . . . . Sep 96
Burger, Warren . . . . Sep 95
Burke, Chris . . . . Sep 93
Burmese
Aung San Suu Kyi . . . . . Apr 96; Update 98;
Update 01; Update 02
Ka Hsaw Wa . . . . WorLdr V.3
Burns, Ken . . . . Jan 95
Burnside, Aubyn . . . . Sep 02
Burrell, Stanley Kirk
see Hammer . . . . Jan 92
Bush, Barbara . . . . Jan 92
Bush, George . . . . Jan 92
Bush, George W. . . . . Sep 00; Update 00;
Update 01; Update 02
Bush, Laura . . . . Apr 03
business
Barron, Robert . . . . Science V.9
Berger, Francie . . . . Sep 04

Bezos, Jeff . . . . Apr 01
Brashares, Ann . . . . Author V.15
Brin, Sergey . . . . Sep 05
Brown, Ron . . . . Sep 96
Buffett, Warren . . . . Business V.1
Capolino, Peter . . . . Business V.1
Case, Steve . . . . Science V.5
Chavez, Julz . . . . Sep 02
Cheney, Dick . . . . Jan 02
Combs, Sean (Puff Daddy) . . . . Apr 98
Dell, Michael . . . . Business V.1
Diemer, Walter . . . . Apr 98
Fields, Debbi . . . . Jan 96
Fiorina, Carly . . . . Sep 01; Update 01;
Update 02
Fox, Vicente . . . . Apr 03
Fuller, Millard . . . . Apr 03
Gates, Bill . . . . Apr 93; Update 98;
Update 00; Science V.5; Update 01
Graves, Earl . . . . Business V.1
Groppe, Laura . . . . Science V.5
Handler, Ruth . . . . Apr 98; Update 02
Hoskins, Michele . . . . Business V.1
Iacocca, Lee A. . . . . Jan 92
Jobs, Steven . . . . Jan 92; Science V.5
Johnson, John . . . . Jan 97
Johnson, Lonnie . . . . Science V.4
Joy, Bill . . . . Science V.10
Kamen, Dean . . . . Science V.11
Kapell, Dave . . . . Science V.8
Kurzweil, Raymond . . . . Science V.2
Kwolek, Stephanie . . . . Science V.10
Land, Edwin . . . . Science V.1
Mars, Forrest Sr. . . . . Science V.4
McGrath, Judy . . . . Business V.1
Mitchell-Raptakis, Karen . . . . Jan 05
Mohajer, Dineh . . . . Jan 02
Moreno, Arturo R. . . . . Business V.1
Morgan, Garrett . . . . Science V.2
Morita, Akio . . . . Science V.4
Page, Larry . . . . Sep 05
Perot, H. Ross . . . . Apr 92; Update 93
Rowland, Pleasant T. . . . . Business V.1
Romero, John . . . . Science V.8
Simmons, Russell . . . . Apr 06
Stachowski, Richie . . . . Science V.3
Stewart, Martha . . . . Business V.1
Swanson, Janese . . . . Science V.4
Thomas, Dave . . . . Apr 96; Update 02
Tompkins, Douglas . . . . WorLdr V.3

For cumulative places of birth and birthday indexes, please see biographytoday.com.

Trump, Donald . . . . Apr 05
Wang, An . . . . Science V.2
Ward, Lloyd D.. . . . . Jan 01
Whitman, Meg . . . . Sep 03
Winfrey, Oprah. . . . . Business V.1
Wright, Will. . . . . Apr 04
Butcher, Susan. . . . . Sport V.1
Byars, Betsy . . . . Author V.4
Bynes, Amanda . . . . Sep 03
Cabot, Meg . . . . Author V.12
Caldecott Medal
 Cooney, Barbara . . . . , Author V.8
 Lobel, Arnold . . . . Author V.18
 Macauley, David . . . . Author V.2
 McCully, Emily Arnold. . . Jul 92; Update 93
 Myers, Walter Dean. . . . . Jan 93; Update 94
 Sendak, Maurice . . . . Author V.2
 Small, David. . . . . Author V.10
 Van Allsburg, Chris . . . . Apr 92
Calder, Alexander. . . . . Artist V.1
Calderone, Mary S. . . . . Science V.3
Cameron, Candace. . . . . Apr 95
Campbell, Neve. . . . . Apr 98
Canadians
 Bailey, Donovan. . . . . Sport V.2
 Blanchard, Rachel. . . . . Apr 97
 Campbell, Neve . . . . Apr 98
 Candy, John. . . . . Sep 94
 Carrey, Jim. . . . . Apr 96
 Dion, Celine . . . . Sep 97
 Galdikas, Biruté. . . . . Science V.4
 Giguère, Jean-Sébastien . . . . Sport V.10
 Gretzky, Wayne . . . . Jan 92; Update 93;
 Update 99
 Howe, Gordie. . . . . Sport V.2
 Jennings, Peter . . . . Jul 92
 Johnston, Lynn . . . . Jan 99
 Kielburger, Craig . . . . Jan 00
 lang, k.d. Sep 93
 Lavigne, Avril . . . . PerfArt V.2
 Lemieux, Mario. . . . . Jul 92; Update 93
 Martin, Bernard . . . . WorLdr V.3
 McAdams, Rachel. . . . . Apr 06
 Messier, Mark . . . . Apr 96
 Morissette, Alanis. . . . . Apr 97
 Mowat, Farley . . . . Author V.8
 Myers, Mike. . . . . PerfArt V.3
 Nash, Steve. . . . . Jan 06
 Priestley, Jason . . . . Apr 92
 Reeves, Keanu . . . . Jan 04
 Roy, Patrick. . . . . Sport V.7

Russell, Charlie . . . . Science V.11
Sakic, Joe. . . . . Sport V.6
Shatner, William. . . . . Apr 95
Twain, Shania . . . . Apr 99
Vernon, Mike . . . . Jan 98; Update 02
Watson, Paul . . . . WorLdr V.1
Wolf, Hazel. . . . . WorLdr V.3
Yzerman, Steve. . . . . Sport V.2
Canady, Alexa . . . . Science V.6
Candy, John . . . . Sep 94
Cantore, Jim . . . . Science V.9
Caplan, Arthur. . . . . Science V.6
Capolino, Peter. . . . . Business V.1
Capriati, Jennifer. . . . . Sport V.6
car racing
 Andretti, Mario. . . . . Sep 94
 Earnhardt, Dale. . . . . Apr 01
 Earnhardt, Dale, Jr.. . . . . Sport V.12
 Gordon, Jeff. . . . . Apr 99
 Muldowney, Shirley. . . . . Sport V.7
 Newman, Ryan . . . . Sport V.11
 Patrick, Danica . . . . Apr 06
 Petty, Richard . . . . Sport V.2
 Stewart, Tony . . . . Sport V.9
Card, Orson Scott. . . . . Author V.14
Carey, Mariah. . . . . Apr 96
Carle, Eric. . . . . Author V.1
Carmona, Richard . . . . Science V.8
Carpenter, Mary Chapin . . . . Sep 94
Carrabba, Chris . . . . Apr 05
Carrey, Jim . . . . Apr 96
Carson, Ben . . . . Science V.4
Carson, Rachel . . . . WorLdr V.1
Carter, Aaron . . . . Sep 02
Carter, Chris . . . . Author V.4
Carter, Jimmy . . . . Apr 95; Update 02
Carter, Nick
 see Backstreet Boys. . . . . Jan 00
Carter, Vince. . . . . Sport V.5; Update 01
cartoonists
 see also animators
 Amend, Bill . . . . Author V.18
 Armstrong, Robb . . . . Author V.9
 Borgman, Jim. . . . . Author V.15
 Breathed, Berke . . . . Jan 92
 Crilley, Mark . . . . Author V.15
 Davis, Jim. . . . . Author V.1
 Groening, Matt . . . . Jan 92
 Guisewite, Cathy . . . . Sep 93
 Hillenburg, Stephen . . . . Author V.14

Johnston, Lynn . . . . Jan 99
Jones, Chuck . . . . Author V.12
Larson, Gary . . . . Author V.1
Lee, Stan. . . . . Author V.7; Update 02
McGruder, Aaron . . . . Author V.10
Schulz, Charles . . . . Author V.2; Update 00
Scott, Jerry . . . . Author V.15
Spiegelman, Art . . . . Author V.17
Tartakovsky, Genndy . . . . Author V.11
Watterson, Bill . . . . Jan 92
Carvey, Dana . . . . Jan 93
Case, Steve . . . . Science V.5
Castellano, Torry (Donna C.)
see Donnas . . . . Apr 04
Castro, Fidel . . . . Jul 92; Update 94
Chagall, Marc. . . . . Artist V.1
Chamberlain, Wilt . . . . Sport V.4
Chambers, Veronica . . . . Author V.15
Champagne, Larry III . . . . Apr 96
Chan, Jackie. . . . . PerfArt V.1
Chan Kwong Sang
see Chan, Jackie . . . . PerfArt V.1
Chasez, JC
see *N Sync. Jan 01
Chastain, Brandi . . . . . Sport V.4; Update 00
Chavez, Cesar. . . . . Sep 93
Chavez, Julz . . . . Sep 02
Chavis, Benjamin . . . . Jan 94; Update 94
Cheney, Dick. . . . . Jan 02
chess
Ashley, Maurice . . . . Sep 99
Chihuly, Dale . . . . Jan 06
Childress, Alice . . . . Author V.1
Chinese
Chan, Jackie. . . . . PerfArt V.1
Dai Qing . . . . WorLdr V.3
Fu Mingxia . . . . Sport V.5
Pei, I.M. . . . . Artist V.1
Wang, An . . . . Science V.2
Yao Ming . . . . Sep 03
Yuen Wo-Ping. . . . . PerfArt V.3
Choldenko, Gennifer . . . . Author V.18
choreography
see dance
Christo . . . . Sep 96
Chung, Connie . . . . Jan 94; Update 95;
Update 96
Cisneros, Henry . . . . Sep 93
civil rights movement
Chavis, Benjamin. . . . . . . Jan 94; Update 94
Edelman, Marian Wright. . . . . Apr 93

Jackson, Jesse. . . . . Sep 95; Update 01
Lewis, John. . . . . Jan 03
Marshall, Thurgood. . . . . Jan 92; Update 93
Parks, Rosa. . . . . Apr 92; Update 94; Apr 06
Shabazz, Betty. . . . . Apr 98
Clark, Kelly . . . . Sport V.8
Clarkson, Kelly. . . . . Jan 03
Clay, Cassius Marcellus, Jr.
see Ali, Muhammad . . . . Sport V.2
Cleary, Beverly. . . . . Apr 94
Clements, Andrew. . . . . Author V.13
Clijsters, Kim . . . . Apr 04
Clinton, Bill . . . . Jul 92; Update 94;
Update 95; Update 96; Update 97; Update 98;
Update 99; Update 00; Update 01
Clinton, Chelsea . . . . Apr 96; Update 97;
Update 01
Clinton, Hillary Rodham . . . . Apr 93;
Update 94; Update 95; Update 96; Update
99; Update 00; Update 01
Cobain, Kurt. . . . . Sep 94
Cohen, Adam Ezra. . . . . Apr 97
Cohen, Sasha . . . . Sport V.12
Colfer, Eoin . . . . Author V.13
Collier, Bryan . . . . Author V.11
Collins, Billy . . . . Author V.16
Collins, Eileen . . . . Science V.4
Collins, Francis . . . . Science V.6
Columbian
Ocampo, Adriana C. . . . . Science V.8
Shakira . . . . PerfArt V.1
Combs, Benji
see Madden, Benji . . . . PerfArt V.3
Combs, Joel
see Madden, Joel . . . . PerfArt V.3
Combs, Sean (Puff Daddy) . . . . Apr 98
comedians
Allen, Tim . . . . Apr 94; Update 99
Arnold, Roseanne. . . . . Oct 92
Candy, John. . . . . Sep 94
Carrey, Jim. . . . . Apr 96
Carvey, Dana . . . . Jan 93
Cosby, Bill. . . . . Jan 92
Fey, Tina . . . . Author V.16
Goldberg, Whoopi . . . . Apr 94
Leno, Jay . . . . Jul 92
Letterman, David. . . . . Jan 95
López, George. . . . . PerfArt V.2
Mac, Bernie . . . . PerfArt V.1
Murphy, Eddie. . . . . PerfArt V.2
Myers, Mike. . . . . PerfArt V.3

O'Donnell, Rosie . . . . . . Apr 97; Update 02
Sandler, Adam . . . . Jan 06
Seinfeld, Jerry . . . . Oct 92; Update 98
Stewart, Jon . . . . Jan 06
Tucker, Chris . . . . Jan 01
Wayans, Keenen Ivory . . . . Jan 93
Williams, Robin. . . . . Apr 92
comic strips
see cartoonists
computers
Berners-Lee, Tim . . . . Science V.7
Bezos, Jeff. . . . . Apr 01
Case, Steve . . . . Science V.5
Cray, Seymour . . . . Science V.2
Dell, Michael . . . . Business V.1
Engelbart, Douglas. . . . . Science V.5
Fanning, Shawn . . . Science V.5; Update 02
Fiorina, Carly . . . . Sep 01; Update 01;
   Update 02
Flannery, Sarah. . . . . Science V.5
Gates, Bill . . . . Apr 93; Update 98;
   Update 00; Science V.5; Update 01
Groppe, Laura. . . . . Science V.5
Hopper, Grace Murray. . . . . . . Science V.5
Jobs, Steven . . . . Jan 92; Science V.5
Joy, Bill . . . . Science V.10
Kurzweil, Raymond . . . . Science V.2
Miller, Rand. . . . . Science V.5
Miller, Robyn. . . . . Science V.5
Miyamoto, Shigeru. . . . . Science V.5
Perot, H. Ross . . . . Apr 92
Romero, John . . . . Science V.8
Torvalds, Linus . . . . Science V.11
Wang, An . . . . Science V.2
Wozniak, Steve. . . . . Science V.5
Wright, Will. . . . . Apr 04
Congress
see representatives
see senators
conservationists
see environmentalists
Cool, Tré (Frank Edwin Wright III)
see Green Day . . . . Apr 06
Coolio. . . . . Sep 96
Cooney, Barbara. . . . . Author V.8
Cooney, Caroline B.. . . . . Author V.4
Cooper, Floyd . . . . Author V.17
Cooper, Susan . . . . Author V.17
Córdova, France. . . . . Science V.7
Cormier, Robert . . . . Author V.1; Update 01
Cosby, Bill . . . . Jan 92

Coughlin, Natalie . . . . Sport V.10
Cousteau, Jacques. . . . . . . Jan 93; Update 97
Covel, Toby Keith
see Keith, Toby. . . . . Jan 05
Coville, Bruce. . . . . Author V.9
Cox, Lynne . . . . Sport V.13
Crawford, Cindy . . . . Apr 93
Cray, Seymour . . . . Science V.2
Creech, Sharon . . . . Author V.5
Crichton, Michael. . . . . Author V.5
Crilley, Mark. . . . . Author V.15
Cronin, John. . . . . WorLdr V.3
Cruz, Celia. . . . . Apr 04
Cubans
Castro, Fidel. . . . . Jul 92; Update 94
Cruz, Celia. . . . . Apr 04
Estefan, Gloria. . . . . Jul 92
Fuentes, Daisy . . . . Jan 94
Hernandez, Livan. . . . . Apr 98
Zamora, Pedro . . . . Apr 95
Culkin, Macaulay . . . . Sep 93
Culpepper, Daunte. . . . . Sport V.13
Curtis, Christopher Paul . . . . . . Author V.4;
   Update 00
Cushman, Karen. . . . . Author V.5
Czechoslovakians
Hasek, Dominik . . . . Sport V.3
Hingis, Martina . . . . Sport V.2
Jagr, Jaromir . . . . Sport V.5
Navratilova, Martina . . . . Jan 93; Update 94
da Silva, Fabiola . . . . Sport V.9
Dae-jung, Kim
see Kim Dae-jung . . . . Sep 01
Dahl, Roald . . . . Author V.1
Dai Qing . . . . WorLdr V.3
Dakides, Tara. . . . . Sport V.7
Dalai Lama . . . . Sep 98
Daly, Carson . . . . Apr 00
dance
Abdul, Paula. . . . . Jan 92; Update 02
de Mille, Agnes . . . . Jan 95
Estefan, Gloria. . . . . Jul 92
Farrell, Suzanne. . . . . PerfArt V.1
Glover, Savion. . . . . Apr 99
Hammer . . . . Jan 92
Jamison, Judith. . . . . Jan 96
Kistler, Darci. . . . . Jan 93
Nureyev, Rudolf . . . . Apr 93
Tharp, Twyla . . . . PerfArt V.3
Danes, Claire . . . . Sep 97
Daniel, Beth . . . . Sport V.1

Danziger, Paula . . . . Author V.6
da Silva, Fabiola . . . . Sport V.9
Davenport, Lindsay . . . . Sport V.5
Davis, Jim. . . . . Author V.1
Dawson, Matel, Jr. . . . . Jan 04
Dayne, Ron . . . . Apr 00
de Klerk, F.W.. . . . . Apr 94; Update 94
Delany, Bessie . . . . Sep 99
Delany, Sadie. . . . . Sep 99
Dell, Michael . . . . Business V.1
Delson, Brad
  see Linkin Park . . . . Jan 04
DeMayo, Neda . . . . Apr 06
de Mille, Agnes. . . . . Jan 95
Democratic Party
  Brown, Ron . . . . Sep 96
  Carter, Jimmy . . . . Apr 95; Update 02
  Clinton, Bill. . . . . Jul 92; Update 94;
    Update 95; Update 96; Update 97; Update
    98; Update 99; Update 00; Update 01
  Gore, Al. . . . . Jan 93; Update 96; Update 97;
    Update 98; Update 99; Update 00; Update
    01
  Lewis, John. Jan 03
dentist
  Delany, Bessie. . . . . Sep 99
Denton, Sandi
  see Salt 'N' Pepa . . . . Apr 95
dePaola, Tomie. . . . . Author V.5
Depp, Johnny . . . . Apr 05
Destiny's Child . . . . Apr 01
Devers, Gail . . . . Sport V.2
Diana, Princess of Wales . . . . Jul 92;
  Update 96; Update 97; Jan 98
Diaz, Cameron . . . . PerfArt V.3
DiCamillo, Kate . . . . Author V.10
DiCaprio, Leonardo . . . . Apr 98
Diemer, Walter. . . . . Apr 98
Diesel, Vin . . . . Jan 03
Dion, Celine . . . . Sep 97
diplomats
  Albright, Madeleine . . . . Apr 97
  Annan, Kofi . . . . Jan 98; Update 01
  Boutros-Ghali, Boutros. . . . . Apr 93;
    Update 98
  Rowan, Carl. . . . . Sep 01
directors
  Burns, Ken . . . . Jan 95
  Carter, Chris. . . . . Author V.4
  Chan, Jackie. . . . . PerfArt V.1

  Crichton, Michael . . . . Author V.5
  Farrell, Suzanne. . . . . PerfArt V.1
  Jackson, Peter . . . . PerfArt V.2
  Jones, Chuck . . . . Author V.12
  Lasseter, John.. . . . . Sep 00
  Lee, Spike . . . . Oct 92
  Lucas, George . . . . Apr 97; Update 02
  Parks, Gordon . . . . Artist V.1
  Spielberg, Steven . . . . . . Jan 94; Update 94;
    Update 95
  Taymor, Julie . . . . PerfArt V.1
  Warhol, Andy. . . . . Artist V.1
  Wayans, Keenen Ivory . . . . Jan 93
  Whedon, Joss . . . . Author V.9
  Williamson, Kevin. . . . . Author V.6
  Yuen Wo-Ping. . . . . PerfArt V.3
Dirnt, Mike (Michael Pritchard)
  see Green Day . . . . Apr 06
disabled
  Burke, Chris. . . . . Sep 93
  Chihuly, Dale . . . . Jan 06
  Dole, Bob . . . . Jan 96
  Driscoll, Jean . . . . Sep 97
  Glennie, Evelyn. . . . . PerfArt V.3
  Grandin, Temple . . . . Science V.3
  Gwaltney, John Langston . . . . . Science V.3
  Hamilton, Bethany . . . . Apr 05
  Hawking, Stephen . . . . Apr 92
  Hillenbrand, Laura . . . . Author V.14
  Howard, Tim. . . . . Apr 06
  Parkinson, Jennifer. . . . . Apr 95
  Perlman, Itzhak . . . . Jan 95
  Reeve, Christopher . . . . . Jan 97; Update 02
  Runyan, Marla. . . . . Apr 02
  Stepanek, Mattie. . . . . Apr 02
  Whitestone, Heather . . . Apr 95; Update 02
diving
  Fu Mingxia . . . . Sport V.5
  Streeter, Tanya . . . . Sport V.11
Dixie Chicks . . . . PerfArt V.1
doctors
  Benjamin, Regina . . . . Science V.9
  Brundtland, Gro Harlem . . . . . . Science V.3
  Calderone, Mary S.. . . . . Science V.3
  Canady, Alexa. . . . . Science V.6
  Carmona, Richard . . . . Science V.8
  Carson, Ben. . . . . Science V.4
  Collins, Francis . . . . Science V.6
  Farmer, Paul, Jr. . . . . Science V.11
  Fauci, Anthony S.. . . . . Science V.7
  Gayle, Helene . . . . Science V.8

Gerberding, Julie . . . . Science V.10
Greer, Pedro José, Jr.. . . . . Science V.10
Harris, Bernard . . . . Science V.3
Healy, Bernadine . . . Science V.1; Update 01
Heimlich, Henry. . . . . Science V.6
Ho, David . . . . Science V.6
Jemison, Mae. . . . . Oct 92
Kamler, Kenneth . . . . Science V.6
Kübler-Ross, Elisabeth . . . . Science V.10
Long, Irene D. . . . . Jan 04
Love, Susan. . . . . Science V.3
Nielsen, Jerri . . . . Science V.7
Novello, Antonia . . . . Apr 92
Pippig, Uta . . . . Sport V.1
Poussaint, Alvin . . . . Science V.9
Richardson, Dot . . . . . Sport V.2; Update 00
Sabin, Albert . . . . Science V.1
Sacks, Oliver . . . . Science V.3
Salk, Jonas . . . . Jan 94; Update 95
Satcher, David . . . . Sep 98
Spelman, Lucy . . . . Science V.6
Spock, Benjamin . . . . Sep 95; Update 98
WilderBrathwaite, Gloria. . . . . . Science V.7
Doherty, Shannen . . . . . . Apr 92; Update 94
Dole, Bob . . . . Jan 96; Update 96
Dole, Elizabeth . . . . Jul 92; Update 96;
Update 99
Domingo, Placido . . . . Sep 95
Dominicans
Alvarez, Julia . . . . Author V.17
Martinez, Pedro . . . . Sport V.5
Pujols, Albert . . . . Sport V.12
Ramirez, Manny. . . . . Sport V.13
Soriano, Alfonso. . . . . Sport V.10
Sosa, Sammy . . . . Jan 99; Update 99
Donnas. . . . . Apr 04
Donovan, Marion . . . . Science V.9
Dorough, Howie
see Backstreet Boys. . . . . Jan 00
Douglas, Marjory Stoneman. . WorLdr V.1;
Update 98
Dove, Rita. . . . . Jan 94
Dragila, Stacy. . . . . Sport V.6
Draper, Sharon. . . . . Apr 99
Driscoll, Jean . . . . Sep 97
Duchovny, David . . . . Apr 96
Duff, Hilary . . . . Sep 02
Duke, David . . . . Apr 92
Dumars, Joe. . . . . Sport V.3; Update 99
Dumitriu, Ioana . . . . Science V.3

Dunbar, Paul Lawrence . . . . Author V.8
Duncan, Lois. . . . . Sep 93
Duncan, Tim. . . . . Apr 04
Dunlap, Alison . . . . Sport V.7
Dunst, Kirsten . . . . PerfArt V.1
Dutch
Lionni, Leo. . . . . Author V.6
Earle, Sylvia . . . . Science V.1
Earnhardt, Dale . . . . Apr 01
Earnhardt, Dale, Jr, ... Sport V.12
Ebadi, Shirin. . . . . Apr 04
Edelman, Marian Wright. . . . . Apr 93
educators
Armstrong, William H.. . . . . Author V.7
Arnesen, Liv. . . . . Author V.15
Calderone, Mary S.. . . . . Science V.3
Córdova, France . . . . Science V.7
Delany, Sadie . . . . Sep 99
Draper, Sharon . . . . Apr 99
Forman, Michele . . . . Jan 03
Gates, Henry Louis, Jr. . . . . Apr 00
Giff, Patricia Reilly. . . . . Author V.7
Jiménez, Francisco. . . . . Author V.13
Napoli, Donna Jo. . . . . Author V.16
Poussaint, Alvin . . . . Science V.9
Rodriguez, Gloria . . . . Apr 05
Simmons, Ruth . . . . Sep 02
Stanford, John. . . . . Sep 99
Suzuki, Shinichi . . . . Sep 98
Egyptians
Boutros-Ghali, Boutros . . . . Apr 93;
Update 98
Sadat, Anwar . . . . WorLdr V.2
Elion, Getrude . . . . Science V.6
Ellerbee, Linda. . . . . Apr 94
Elliott, Missy. . . . . PerfArt V.3
Ellison, Ralph . . . . Author V.3
Elway, John. . . . . Sport V.2; Update 99
Eminem . . . . Apr 03
Engelbart, Douglas . . . . Science V.5
English
Almond, David . . . . Author V.10
Amanpour, Christiane . . . . Jan 01
Attenborough, David. . . . . Science V.4
Barton, Hazel . . . . Science V.6
Beckham, David. . . . . Jan 04
Berners-Lee, Tim . . . . Science V.7
Blair, Tony . . . . Apr 04
Bloom, Orlando . . . . Sep 04
Cooper, Susan . . . . Author V.17
Dahl, Roald . . . . Author V.1

Diana, Princess of Wales. . . . . Jul 92;
   Update 96; Update 97; Jan 98
Goodall, Jane. . . . . . Science V.1; Update 02
Handford, Martin . . . . Jan 92
Hargreaves, Alison . . . . Jan 96
Hawking, Stephen . . . . Apr 92
Herriot, James . . . . Author V.1
Highmore, Freddie . . . . Apr 06
Jacques, Brian. . . . . Author V.5
Jones, Diana Wynne . . . . Author V.15
Koff, Clea. . . . . Science V.11
Leakey, Louis . . . . Science V.1
Leakey, Mary. . . . . Science V.1
Lewis, C. S. . . . . Author V.3
MacArthur, Ellen . . . . Sport V.11
Macaulay, David . . . . Author V.2
Moore, Henry. . . . . Artist V.1
Potter, Beatrix . . . . Author V.8
Pullman, Philip. . . . . Author V.9
Radcliffe, Daniel. . . . . Jan 02
Reid Banks, Lynne . . . . Author V.2
Rennison, Louise. . . . . Author V.10
Rowling, J. K. . . . . Sep 99; Update 00;
   Update 01; Update 02
Sacks, Oliver . . . . Science V.3
Stewart, Patrick . . . . Jan 94
Stone, Joss. . . . . Jan 06
Streeter, Tanya . . . . Sport V.11
Tolkien, J.R.R. . . . . Jan 02
Watson, Emma . . . . Apr 03
Winslet, Kate . . . . Sep 98
environmentalists
Abbey, Edward. . . . . WorLdr V.1
Adams, Ansel . . . . Artist V.1
Askins, Renee. . . . . WorLdr V.1
Babbitt, Bruce. . . . . Jan 94
Brower, David. . . . . WorLdr V.1; Update 01
Brundtland, Gro Harlem . . . . . Science V.3
Carson, Rachel . . . . WorLdr V.1
Cousteau, Jacques . . . . Jan 93
Cronin, John. . . . . WorLdr V.3
Dai Qing . . . . WorLdr V.3
DeMayo, Neda . . . . Apr 06
Douglas, Marjory Stoneman . . WorLdr V.1;
   Update 98
Earle, Sylvia. . . . . Science V.1
Fay, Michael . . . . Science V.9
Foreman, Dave. . . . . WorLdr V.1
Gibbs, Lois . . . . WorLdr V.1
Irwin, Steve . . . . Science V.7
Ka Hsaw Wa. . . . . WorLdr V.3

LaDuke, Winona . . WorLdr V.3; Update 00
Leopold, Aldo. . . . . WorLdr V.3
Maathai, Wangari . . . . WorLdr V.1
Martin, Bernard . . . . WorLdr V.3
Mendes, Chico . . . . WorLdr V.1
Mittermeier, Russell A. . . . . WorLdr V.1
Moss, Cynthia . . . . WorLdr V.3
Mowat, Farley . . . . Author V.8
Muir, John. . . . . WorLdr V.3
Murie, Margaret. . . . . WorLdr V.1
Murie, Olaus J. . . . . WorLdr V.1
Nakamura, Leanne. . . . . Apr 02
Nelson, Gaylord. . . . . WorLdr V.3
Oliver, Patsy Ruth . . . . WorLdr V.1
Patrick, Ruth . . . . Science V.3
Peterson, Roger Tory . . . . WorLdr V.1
Saro-Wiwa, Ken. . . . . WorLdr V.1
Steingraber, Sandra . . . . Science V.9
Tompkins, Douglas . . . . WorLdr V.3
Watson, Paul . . . . WorLdr V.1
Werbach, Adam. . . . . WorLdr V.1
Wolf, Hazel. . . . . WorLdr V.3
Erdös, Paul . . . . Science V.2
Estefan, Gloria . . . . Jul 92
Ethiopians
  Haile Selassie . . . . WorLdr V.2
  Roba, Fatuma . . . . Sport V.3
Evans, Janet . . . . Jan 95; Update 96
Eve . . . . Jan 05
Evert, Chris. . . . . Sport V.1
Ewing, Patrick . . . . Jan 95; Update 02
Fanning, Dakota. . . . . Jan 06
Fanning, Shawn . . . . Science V.5; Update 02
Farmer, Nancy. . . . . Author V.6
Farmer, Paul, Jr. . . . . Science V.11
Farrakhan, Louis. . . . . Jan 97
Farrell, Dave
  see Linkin Park. . . . . Jan 04
Farrell, Suzanne . . . . PerfArt V.1
Fatone, Joey
  see *N Sync. . . . . Jan 01
Fauci, Anthony S. . . . . Science V.7
Favre, Brett . . . . Sport V.2
Fay, Michael . . . . Science V.9
Fedorov, Sergei. . . . . Apr 94; Update 94
Feelings, Tom . . . . Author V.16
Felix, Allyson. . . . . Sport V.10
Fergie (Ferguson, Stacy)
  see Black Eyed Peas . . . . Apr 06
Ferguson, Stacy (Fergie)
  see Black Eyed Peas . . . . Apr 06

Fernandez, Lisa . . . . Sport V.5
Fey, Tina . . . . Author V.16
Feynman, Richard P. . . . . Science V.10
Ficker, Roberta Sue
   see Farrell, Suzanne . . . . PerfArt V.1
Fielder, Cecil . . . . Sep 93
Fields, Debbi . . . . Jan 96
Fijian
   Singh, Vijay . . . . Sport V.13
Filipino
   apl.de.ap (Alan Pineda Lindo) . . . . . Apr 06
Filipovic, Zlata . . . . Sep 94
film critic
   Siskel, Gene . . . . Sep 99
Finch, Jennie . . . . Jan 05
Finnish
   Torvalds, Linus . . . . Science V.11
Fiorina, Carly . . . . Sep 01; Update 01;
   Update 02
First Ladies of the United States
   Bush, Barbara . . . . Jan 92
   Bush, Laura . . . . Apr 03
   Clinton, Hillary Rodham. . . . . Apr 93;
   Update 94; Update 95; Update 96; Update
   99; Update 00; Update 01
fishing
   Yelas, Jay . . . . Sport V.9
Fitzgerald, Ella . . . . Jan 97
Fitzhugh, Louise . . . . Author V.3
Flake, Sharon . . . . Author V.13
Flannery, Sarah . . . . Science V.5
Flowers, Vonetta . . . . Sport V.8
football
   Aikman, Troy. . . . . Apr 95; Update 01
   Allen, Marcus . . . . Sep 97
   Brady, Tom . . . . Sport V.7
   Culpepper, Daunte . . . . Sport V.13
   Dayne, Ron . . . . Apr 00
   Elway, John . . . . Sport V.2; Update 99
   Favre, Brett . . . . Sport V.2
   George, Eddie . . . . Sport V.6
   Gonzalez, Tony . . . . Sport V.11
   Griese, Brian. . . . . Jan 02
   Harbaugh, Jim . . . . Sport V.3
   Holmes, Priest. . . . . Apr 05
   Jackson, Bo . . . . Jan 92; Update 93
   Johnson, Jimmy. . . . . Jan 98
   Johnson, Keyshawn . . . . Sport V.10
   Madden, John . . . . Sep 97
   Manning, Peyton. . . . . Sep 00
   Marino, Dan . . . . Apr 93; Update 00

McNabb, Donovan . . . . Apr 03
McNair, Steve . . . . Sport V.11
Montana, Joe . . . . Jan 95; Update 95
Moss, Randy . . . . Sport V.4
Payton, Walter . . . . Jan 00
Rice, Jerry. . . . . Apr 93
Sanders, Barry . . . . Sep 95; Update 99
Sanders, Deion . . . . Sport V.1
Sapp, Warren . . . . Sport V.5
Shula, Don. Apr 96
Smith, Emmitt. . . . . Sep 94
Stewart, Kordell . . . . Sep 98
Strahan, Michael . . . . Sport V.12
Urlacher, Brian . . . . Sep 04
Vick, Michael . . . . Sport V.9
Ward, Charlie . . . . Apr 94
Warner, Kurt. . . . . Sport V.4
Weinke, Chris . . . . Apr 01
White, Reggie. . . . . Jan 98
Willingham, Tyrone . . . . Sep 02
Young, Steve . . . . Jan 94; Update 00
Ford, Cheryl . . . . Sport V.11
Ford, Harrison . . . . Sep 97
Ford, Maya (Donna F.)
   see Donnas . . . . Apr 04
Foreman, Dave . . . . WorLdr V.1
Forman, James . . . . Apr 05
Forman, Michele. . . . . Jan 03
Fossey, Dian . . . . Science V.1
Foudy, Julie . . . . Sport V.13
Fox, Paula. . . . . Author V.15
Fox, Vicente. . . . . Apr 03
Frank, Anne. . . . . Author V.4
Frankenthaler, Helen . . . . Artist V.1
Franklin, Aretha. . . . . Apr 01
Freedman, Russell . . . . Author V.14
Freeman, Cathy . . . . Jan 01
French
   Cousteau, Jacques . . . . . . Jan 93; Update 97
   Marceau, Marcel . . . . PerfArt V.2
Fresh Prince
   see Smith, Will. . . . . Sep 94
Friday, Dallas. . . . . Sport V.10
Fu Mingxia . . . . Sport V.5
Fuentes, Daisy. . . . . Jan 94
Fuller, Millard . . . . Apr 03
Funk, Mary Wallace
   see Funk, Wally. . . . . Jan 05
Funk, Wally . . . . Jan 05
Funke, Cornelia . . . . Sep 05
Galdikas, Biruté. . . . . Science V.4

Galeczka, Chris . . . . Apr 96
Gantos, Jack. . . . . Author V.10
Garcia, Jerry . . . . Jan 96
Garcia, Sergio. . . . . Sport V.7
Garnett, Kevin . . . . Sport V.6
Garth, Jennie. . . . . Apr 96
Gates, Bill . . . . Apr 93; Update 98;
    Update 00; Science V.5; Update 01
Gates, Henry Louis, Jr. . . . . Apr 00
Gayle, Helene . . . . Science V.8
Geisel, Theodor Seuss
    see Seuss, Dr. . . . . Jan 92
Gellar, Sarah Michelle . . . . Jan 99
Geography Bee, National
    Galeczka, Chris. . . . . Apr 96
George, Eddie . . . . Sport V.6
George, Jean Craighead . . . . Author V.3
Gerberding, Julie . . . . Science V.10
Germans
    Bethe, Hans A. . . . . Science V.3
    Frank, Anne . . . . Author V.4
    Funke, Cornelia. . . . . Sep 05
    Graf, Steffi. . . . . Jan 92; Update 01
    Otto, Sylke . . . . Sport V.8
    Pippig, Uta . . . . Sport V.1
Ghanaians
    Adu, Freddy . . . . Sport V.12
    Annan, Kofi . . . . Jan 98; Update 01
    Nkrumah, Kwame . . . . WorLdr V.2
Gibbs, Lois . . . . WorLdr V.1
Giff, Patricia Reilly . . . . Author V.7
Giguère, Jean-Sébastien . . . . . . Sport V.10
Gilbert, Sara . . . . Apr 93
Gilbert, Walter . . . . Science V.2
Gillespie, Dizzy . . . . Apr 93
Gilman, Billy . . . . Apr 02
Gingrich, Newt . . . . Apr 95; Update 99
Ginsburg, Ruth Bader . . . . Jan 94
Giuliani, Rudolph . . . . Sep 02
Glenn, John . . . . Jan 99
Glennie, Evelyn . . . . PerfArt V.3
Glover, Savion . . . . Apr 99
Goldberg, Whoopi. . . . . Apr 94
golf
    Daniel, Beth . . . . Sport V.1
    Garcia, Sergio . . . . Sport V.7
    Nicklaus, Jack . . . . Sport V.2
    Norman, Greg . . . . Jan 94
    Pak, Se Ri . . . . Sport V.4
    Singh, Vijay. . . . . Sport V.13
    Sorenstam, Annika . . . . Sport V.6

Webb, Karrie . . . . Sport V.5; Update 01;
    Update 02
Wie, Michelle . . . . Sep 04
Woods, Tiger . . . . Sport V.1; Update 00;
    Sport V.6
Gomez, Jamie (Taboo)
    see Black Eyed Peas. . . . . Apr 06
Gonzalez, Tony . . . . Sport V.11
Good Charlotte
    see Madden, Benji and
    Madden, Joel . . . . PerfArt V.3
Goodall, Jane . . . . . . Science V.1; Update 02
Goodman, John . . . . Sep 95
Gorbachev, Mikhail. . . . . Jan 92; Update 96
Gordon, Jeff . . . . Apr 99
Gore, Al . . . . Jan 93; Update 96;
    Update 97; Update 98; Update 99; Update 00;
    Update 01
Gorey, Edward . . . . Author V.13
Gould, Stephen Jay . . . . Science V.2;
    Update 02
governors
    Babbitt, Bruce. . . . . Jan 94
    Bush, George W. . . . . . . Sep 00; Update 00;
        Update 01; Update 02
    Carter, Jimmy . . . . Apr 95; Update 02
    Clinton, Bill. . . . . Jul 92; Update 94;
        Update 95; Update 96; Update 97; Update
        98; Update 99; Update 00; Update 01
    Nelson, Gaylord. . . . . WorLdr V.3
    Reagan, Ronald . . . . Sep 04
    Ventura, Jesse . . . . Apr 99; Update 02
Graf, Steffi . . . . Jan 92; Update 01
Granato, Cammi . . . . Sport V.8
Grandin, Temple. . . . . Science V.3
GrandPré, Mary . . . . Author V.14
Granny D
    see Haddock, Doris. . . . . Sep 00
Grant, Amy . . . . Jan 95
Graves, Earl. . . . . Business V.1
Green Day . . . . Apr 06
Greenburg, Dan . . . . Author V.14
Greer, Pedro José, Jr. . . . . Science V.10
Gretzky, Wayne . . . . Jan 92; Update 93;
    Update 99
Griese, Brian . . . . Jan 02
Griffey, Ken, Jr. . . . . Sport V.1
Griffith Joyner, Florence . . . . Sport V.1;
    Update 98
Grimes, Nikki. . . . . Author V.14

For cumulative places of birth and birthday indexes, please see biographytoday.com.

Grisham, John . . . . Author V.1
Groening, Matt . . . . Jan 92
Groppe, Laura . . . . Science V.5
Guatemalan
   Menchu, Rigoberta . . . . Jan 93
Guey, Wendy . . . . Sep 96
Guisewite, Cathy . . . . Sep 93
Gumbel, Bryant . . . . Apr 97
Guy, Jasmine . . . . Sep 93
Guy, Rosa . . . . Author V.9
Gwaltney, John Langston . . . . . Science V.3
Gyatso, Tenzin
   see Dalai Lama . . . . Sep 98
gymnastics
   Miller, Shannon . . . . Sep 94; Update 96
   Moceanu, Dominique . . . . Jan 98
   Patterson, Carly . . . . Sport V.12
   Schwikert, Tasha . . . . Sport V.7
   Zmeskal, Kim . . . . Jan 94
Haddix, Margaret Peterson . . . Author V.11
Haddock, Doris . . . . Sep 00
Hahn, Joe
   see Linkin Park . . . . Jan 04
Haile Selassie . . . . WorLdr V.2
Haitian
   Aristide, Jean-Bertrand . . Jan 95; Update 01
Hakim, Joy . . . . Author V.16
Halaby, Lisa
   see Noor al Hussein, Queen
     of Jordan . . . . Jan 05
Hale, Shannon . . . . Author V.18
Haley, Alex . . . . Apr 92
Hamilton, Bethany . . . . Apr 05
Hamilton, Laird . . . . Sport V.13
Hamilton, Virginia . . . . Author V.1;
   Author V.12
Hamm, Mia . . . . Sport V.2; Update 00
Hammer . . . . Jan 92
Hampton, David . . . . Apr 99
Handford, Martin . . . . Jan 92
Handler, Daniel
   see Snicket, Lemony . . . . Author V.12
Handler, Ruth . . . . Apr 98; Update 02
Hanh, Thich Nhat
   see Nhat Hanh (Thich) . . . . Jan 04
Hanks, Tom . . . . Jan 96
Hansberry, Lorraine . . . . Author V.5
Hanson . . . . Jan 98
Hanson, Ike
   see Hanson . . . . Jan 98
Hanson, Taylor
   see Hanson . . . . Jan 98

Hanson, Zac
   see Hanson . . . . Jan 98
Harbaugh, Jim . . . . Sport V.3
Hardaway, Anfernee "Penny" . . . Sport V.2
Harding, Tonya . . . . Sep 94
Hargreaves, Alison . . . . Jan 96
Harris, Bernard . . . . Science V.3
Hart, Melissa Joan . . . . Jan 94
Hartnett, Josh . . . . Sep 03
Hasek, Dominik . . . . Sport V.3
Hassan II . . . . WorLdr V.2; Update 99
Hathaway, Anne . . . . Apr 05
Haughton, Aaliyah Dana
   see Aaliyah . . . . Jan 02
Hawk, Tony . . . . Apr 01
Hawking, Stephen . . . . Apr 92
Hayden, Carla . . . . Sep 04
Hayes, Tyrone . . . . Science V.10
Haynes, Cornell, Jr.
   see Nelly . . . . Sep 03
Healy, Bernadine . . . . Science V.1; Update 01
Heimlich, Henry . . . . Science V.6
Heinlein, Robert . . . . Author V.4
Hendrickson, Sue . . . . Science V.7
Henry, Marguerite . . . . Author V.4
Hernandez, Livan . . . . Apr 98
Herriot, James . . . . Author V.1
Hesse, Karen . . . . Author V.5; Update 02
Hewitt, Jennifer Love . . . . Sep 00
Hiaasen, Carl . . . . Author V.18
Highmore, Freddie . . . . Apr 06
Hill, Anita . . . . Jan 93
Hill, Faith . . . . Sep 01
Hill, Grant . . . . Sport V.1
Hill, Lauryn . . . . Sep 99
Hillary, Sir Edmund . . . . Sep 96
Hillenbrand, Laura . . . . Author V.14
Hillenburg, Stephen . . . . Author V.14
Hingis, Martina . . . . Sport V.2
Hinton, S.E. . . . . Author V.1
Hispanics
   Aguilera, Christina . . . . Apr 00
   Alba, Jessica . . . . Sep 01
   Alvarez, Julia . . . . Author V.17
   Alvarez, Luis W. . . . . Science V.3
   Bledel, Alexis . . . . Jan 03
   Carmona, Richard . . . . Science V.8
   Castro, Fidel . . . . Jul 92; Update 94
   Chambers, Veronica . . . . Author V.15
   Chavez, Cesar . . . . Sep 93

Chavez, Julz . . . . Sep 02
Cisneros, Henry . . . . Sep 93
Córdova, France . . . . Science V.7
Cruz, Celia. Apr 04
Diaz, Cameron . . . . PerfArt V.3
Domingo, Placido. . . . . Sep 95
Estefan, Gloria. . . . . Jul 92
Fernandez, Lisa . . . . Sport V.5
Fox, Vicente. . . . . Apr 03
Fuentes, Daisy . . . . Jan 94
Garcia, Sergio . . . . Sport V.7
Gonzalez, Tony . . . . Sport V.11
Greer, Pedro José, Jr.. . . . . Science V.10
Hernandez, Livan. . . . . Sep 93
Huerta, Dolores . . . . Sep 03
Iglesias, Enrique. . . . . Jan 03
Jiménez, Francisco. . . . . Author V.13
Lopez, Charlotte. . . . . Apr 94
Lopez, Jennifer. . . . . Jan 02
López, George. . . . . PerfArt V.2
Martin, Ricky . . . . Jan 00
Martinez, Pedro . . . . Sport V.5
Martinez, Victor. . . . . Author V.15
Mendes, Chico . . . . WorLdr V.1
Moreno, Arturo R. . . . . Business V.1
Muniz, Frankie. . . . . Jan 01
Novello, Antonia . . . . Apr 92
Ocampo, Adriana C. . . . . Science V.8
Ochoa, Ellen . . . . Apr 01; Update 02
Ochoa, Severo . . . . Jan 94
Pele . . . . Sport V.1
Prinze, Freddie, Jr. . . . . Apr 00
Pujols, Albert . . . . Sport V.12
Ramirez, Manny. . . . . Sport V.13
Ramos, Jorge . . . . Apr 06
Rivera, Diego . . . . Artist V.1
Rodriguez, Alex . . . . Sport V.6
Rodriguez, Eloy. . . . . Science V.2
Rodriguez, Gloria . . . . Apr 05
Ryan, Pam Muñoz . . . . Author V.12
Sanchez, Ricardo . . . . Sep 04
Sanchez Vicario, Arantxa . . . . Sport V.1
Selena . . . . Jan 96
Shakira. . . . . PerfArt V.1
Soriano, Alfonso. . . . . Sport V.10
Soto, Gary . . . . Author V.5
Taboo (Jamie Gomez) . . . . Apr 06
Toro, Natalia. . . . . Sep 99
Vega, Alexa. . . . . Jan 04
Vidal, Christina . . . . PerfArt V.1
Villa, Brenda. . . . . Jan 06

Villa-Komaroff, Lydia . . . . Science V.6
Zamora, Pedro . . . . Apr 95
Ho, David . . . . Science V.6
Hobbs, Will. . . . . Author V.18
hockey
Fedorov, Sergei . . . . Apr 94; Update 94
Giguère, Jean-Sébastien . . . . Sport V.10
Granato, Cammi. . . . . Sport V.8
Gretzky, Wayne . . . . Jan 92; Update 93;
   Update 99
Hasek, Dominik . . . . Sport V.3
Howe, Gordie. . . . . Sport V.2
Jagr, Jaromir . . . . Sport V.5
Lemieux, Mario. . . . . Jul 92; Update 93
Lidstrom, Nicklas . . . . Sep 03
Messier, Mark . . . . Apr 96
Roy, Patrick. . . . . Sport V.7
Sakic, Joe . . . . Sport V.6
Vernon, Mike . . . . Jan 98; Update 02
Yzerman, Steve. . . . . Sport V.7
Hogan, Hulk . . . . Apr 92
Holdsclaw, Chamique. . . . . Sep 00
Holmes, Katie . . . . Jan 00
Holmes, Priest . . . . Apr 05
Honoré, Russel . . . . Jan 06
Hooper, Geoff . . . . Jan 94
Hopper, Grace Murray . . . . Science V.5
Horner, Jack . . . . Science V.1
horse racing
Krone, Julie . . . . Jan 95; Update 00
Horvath, Polly. . . . . Author V.16
Hoskins, Michele. . . . . Business V.1
House, Donna. . . . . Science V.11
House of Representatives
   see representatives
Houston, Whitney . . . . Sep 94
Howard, Tim . . . . Apr 06
Howe, Gordie. . . . . Sport V.2
Howe, James . . . . Author V.17
Huerta, Dolores . . . . Sep 03
Hughes, Langston . . . . Author V.7
Hughes, Sarah. . . . . Jan 03
Hungarians
   Erdös, Paul . . . . Science V.2
   Seles, Monica. . . . . Jan 96
   Teller, Edward. . . . . Science V.9
Hunter-Gault, Charlayne . . . . Jan 00
Hurston, Zora Neale. . . . . Author V.6
Hussein, King. . . . . Apr 99
Hussein, Saddam . . . . Jul 92; Update 96;
   Update 01; Update 02
Iacocca, Lee A.. . . . . Jan 92

Ice-T . . . . Apr 93
Iglesias, Enrique . . . . Jan 03
illustrators
Bemelmans, Ludwig . . . . Author V.16
Berenstain, Jan. . . . . Author V.2
Berenstain, Stan. . . . . Author V.2
Carle, Eric. . . . . Author V.1
Collier, Bryan. . . . . Author V.11
Cooney, Barbara . . . . Author V.8
Cooper, Floyd . . . . Author V.17
Crilley, Mark . . . . Author V.15
dePaola, Tomie . . . . Author V.5
Feelings, Tom. . . . . Author V.16
Fitzhugh, Louise . . . . Author V.3
George, Jean Craighead . . . . Author V.3
Gorey, Edward. . . . . Author V.13
GrandPré, Mary. . . . . Author V.14
Handford, Martin . . . . Jan 92
Konigsburg, E. L. . . . . Author V.3
Lionni, Leo. . . . . Author V.6
Lobel, Arnold . . . . Author V.18
Macaulay, David . . . . Author V.2
McCloskey, Robert . . . . Author V.15
McCully, Emily Arnold. . Apr 92; Update 93
Peet, Bill . . . . Author V.4
Pinkney, Jerry . . . . Author V.2
Pinkwater, Daniel . . . . Author V.8
Potter, Beatrix . . . . Author V.8
Ringgold, Faith . . . . Author V.2
Rockwell, Norman. . . . . Artist V.1
Scarry, Richard . . . . Sep 94
Sendak, Maurice . . . . Author V.2
Seuss, Dr. . . . . Jan 92
Silverstein, Shel . . . . Author V.3; Update 99
Small, David. . . . . Author V.10
Van Allsburg, Chris . . . . Apr 92
Williams, Garth . . . . Author V.2
Indian
Wadhwa, Meenakshi . . . . Science V.11
in-line skating
see skating (in-line). . . . . Sport V.9
Internet
Berners-Lee, Tim . . . . Science V.7
Bezos, Jeff. Apr 01
Brin, Sergey. . . . . Sep 05
Case, Steve . . . . Science V.5
Fanning, Shawn . . . Science V.5; Update 02
Flannery, Sarah. . . . . Science V.5
Groppe, Laura. . . . . Science V.5
Page, Larry. . . . . Sep 05
Tarbox, Katie . . . . Author V.10
Whitman, Meg . . . . Sep 03

inventors
Alvarez, Luis W. . . . . Science V.3
Berners-Lee, Tim . . . . Science V.7
Brin, Sergey. . . . . Sep 05
Cousteau, Jacques . . . . . . Jan 93; Update 97
Diemer, Walter . . . . Apr 98
Donovan, Marion . . . . Science V.9
Engelbart, Douglas . . . . Science V.5
Fanning, Shawn . . . Science V.5; Update 02
Grandin, Temple . . . . Science V.3
Hampton, David. . . . . Apr 99
Handler, Ruth . . . . Apr 98; Update 02
Heimlich, Henry. . . . . Science V.6
Johnson, Lonnie . . . . Science V.4
Kamen, Dean . . . . Science V.11
Kapell, Dave . . . . Science V.8
Kurzweil, Raymond . . . . Science V.2
Kwolek, Stephanie . . . . Science V.10
Land, Edwin . . . . Science V.1
Lemelson, Jerome. . . . . Science V.3
Mars, Forrest Sr. . . . . Science V.4
Morgan, Garrett . . . . Science V.2
Ochoa, Ellen . . . . Apr 01; Update 02
Page, Larry. . . . . Sep 05
Patterson, Ryan. . . . . Science V.7
Stachowski, Richie . . . . Science V.3
Swanson, Janese. . . . . Science V.4
Wang, An . . . . Science V.2
Warrick, Earl . . . . Science V.8
Wozniak, Steve. . . . . Science V.5
Iranian
Ebadi, Shirin . . . . Apr 04
Iraqi
Hussein, Saddam. . . . . . . Jul 92; Update 96;
  Update 01; Update 02
Irish
Colfer, Eoin . . . . Author V.13
Flannery, Sarah. . . . . Science V.5
Lewis, C. S. . . . . Author V.3
Robinson, Mary. . . . . Sep 93
Irwin, Steve. . . . . Science V.7
Israelis
Ben-Ari, Miri . . . . Jan 06
Perlman, Itzhak . . . . Jan 95
Portman, Natalie . . . . Sep 99
Rabin, Yitzhak . . . . Oct 92; Update 93;
  Update 94; Update 95
Italians
Andretti, Mario . . . . Sep 94
Krim, Mathilde . . . . Science V.1
Levi-Montalcini, Rita . . . . Science V.1
Iverson, Allen. . . . . Sport V.7

Ivey, Artis, Jr.
  see Coolio . . . . Sep 96
Jackson, Bo . . . . Jan 92; Update 93
Jackson, Jesse . . . . Sep 95; Update 01
Jackson, Peter . . . . PerfArt V.2
Jackson, Phil . . . . Sport V.10
Jackson, Shirley . . . . Author V.6
Jackson, Shirley Ann . . . . Science V.2
Jacques, Brian . . . . Author V.5
Jagr, Jaromir . . . . Sport V.5
Jakes, T.D. . . . . Jan 05
Jamaicans
  Ashley, Maurice . . . . Sep 99
  Bailey, Donovan . . . . Sport V.2
  Denton, Sandi
    see Salt 'N' Pepa . . . . Apr 95
  Ewing, Patrick . . . . Jan 95; Update 02
  Maxwell, Jody-Anne . . . . Sep 98
James, Cheryl
  see Salt 'N' Pepa . . . . Apr 95
James, LeBron . . . . Sport V.12
Jamison, Judith . . . . Jan 96
Jansen, Dan . . . . Apr 94
Japanese
  Miyamoto, Shigeru . . . . Science V.5
  Morita, Akio . . . . Science V.4
  Suzuki, Shinichi . . . . Sep 98
  Uchida, Mitsuko . . . . Apr 99
Javacheff, Christo V.
  see Christo . . . . Sep 96
Jeffers, Eve
  see Eve . . . . Jan 05
Jemison, Mae . . . . Oct 92
Jenkins, Jerry B. . . . . Author V.16
Jennings, Peter . . . . Jul 92
Jeter, Derek . . . . Sport V.4
Jewel . . . . Sep 98
Jiménez, Francisco . . . . Author V.13
Jobs, Steven . . . . Jan 92; Science V.5
jockey
  Krone, Julie . . . . Jan 95; Update 00
John Paul II . . . . Oct 92; Update 94;
  Update 95; Sep 05
Johns, Jasper . . . . Artist V.1
Johnson, Angela . . . . Author V.6
Johnson, Jimmy . . . . Jan 98
Johnson, Johanna . . . . Apr 00
Johnson, John . . . . Jan 97
Johnson, Keyshawn . . . . Sport V.10
Johnson, Lonnie . . . . Science V.4

Johnson, Magic . . . . Apr 92; Update 02
Johnson, Michael . . . . . . Jan 97; Update 00
Johnson, Randy . . . . Sport V.9
Johnston, Lynn . . . . Jan 99
Jones, Chuck . . . . Author V.12
Jones, Diana Wynne . . . . Author V.15
Jones, James Earl . . . . Jan 95
Jones, Marion . . . . Sport V.5
Jones, Norah . . . . PerfArt V.2
Jones, Quincy . . . . PerfArt V.2
Jordan, Barbara . . . . Apr 96
Jordan, Michael . . . . Jan 92; Update 93;
  Update 94; Update 95; Update 99; Update 01
Jordanian
  Hussein, King . . . . Apr 99
journalists
  Amanpour, Christiane . . . . Jan 01
  Anderson, Terry . . . . Apr 92
  Benson, Mildred . . . . Jan 03
  Blum, Deborah . . . . Science V.8
  Bradley, Ed . . . . Apr 94
  Brody, Jane . . . . Science V.2
  Chung, Connie . . . . Jan 94; Update 95;
    Update 96
  Dai Qing . . . . WorLdr V.3
  Ellerbee, Linda . . . . Apr 94
  Hiaasen, Carl . . . . Author V.18
  Hunter-Gault, Charlayne . . . . Jan 00
  Jennings, Peter . . . . Jul 92
  Krakauer, Jon . . . . Author V.6
  Lipsyte, Robert . . . . Author V.12
  Pauley, Jane . . . . Oct 92
  Ramos, Jorge . . . . Apr 06
  Roberts, Cokie . . . . Apr 95
  Rowan, Carl . . . . Sep 01
  Soren, Tabitha . . . . Jan 97
  Steinem, Gloria . . . . Oct 92
  Walters, Barbara . . . . Sep 94
Joy, Bill . . . . Science V.10
Joyner-Kersee, Jackie . . . . . . Oct 92; Update
  96; Update 97; Update 98
Jung, Kim Dae
  see Kim Dae-jung . . . . Sep 01
Juster, Norton . . . . Author V.14
Ka Hsaw Wa . . . . WorLdr V.3
Kaddafi, Muammar
  see Qaddafi, Muammar . . . . Apr 97
Kamen, Dean . . . . Science V.11
Kamler, Kenneth . . . . Science V.6

For cumulative places of birth and birthday indexes, please see biographytoday.com.

Kapell, Dave .... Science V.8
Kaunda, Kenneth .... WorLdr V.2
Keene, Carolyne
   see Benson, Mildred .... Jan 03
Keith, Toby .... Jan 05
Kenyans
   Kenyatta, Jomo .... WorLdr V.2
   Maathai, Wangari ..... WorLdr V.1; Sep 05
   Ndeti, Cosmas .... Sep 95
Kenyatta, Jomo .... WorLdr V.2
Kenyon, Cynthia .... Science V.11
Kerr, M.E. .... Author V.1
Kerrigan, Nancy .... Apr 94
Kidd, Jason .... Sport V.9
Kielburger, Craig .... Jan 00
Kiessling, Laura L. .... Science V.9
Kilcher, Jewel
   see Jewel .... Sep 98
Kim Dae-jung .... Sep 01
King, Mary-Claire .... Science V.10
King, Stephen ...... Author V.1; Update 00
Kiraly, Karch .... Sport V.4
Kirkpatrick, Chris
   see *N Sync .... Jan 01
Kistler, Darci .... Jan 93
Klug, Chris .... Sport V.8
Knowles, Beyoncé
   see Destiny's Child .... Apr 01
Koff, Clea .... Science V.11
Konigsburg, E. L. .... Author V.3
Korean
   An Na .... Author V.12
   Kim Dae-jung .... Sep 01
   Pak, Se Ri .... Sport V.4
Krakauer, Jon .... Author V.6
Kratt, Chris .... Science V.10
Kratt, Martin .... Science V.10
Krauss, Alison .... Apr 05
Krim, Mathilde .... Science V.1
Krone, Julie .... Jan 95; Update 00
Kübler-Ross, Elisabeth .... Science V.10
Kurzweil, Raymond .... Science V.2
Kutcher, Ashton .... Apr 04
Kwan, Michelle ...... Sport V.3; Update 02
Kwolek, Stephanie .... Science V.10
lacrosse
   Boyle, Ryan .... Sport V.10
Laden, Osama bin
   see bin Laden, Osama .... Apr 02
LaDuke, Winona ... WorLdr V.3; Update 00

LaHaye, Tim .... Author V.16
Lalas, Alexi .... Sep 94
Lama, Dalai
   see Dalai Lama .... Sep 98
Land, Edwin .... Science V.1
lang, k.d. .... Sep 93
Lansky, Bruce .... Author V.17
Larson, Gary .... Author V.1
Lasky, Kathryn .... Author V.18
Lasseter, John .... Sep 00
Latino/Latina
   see Hispanics
Lavigne, Avril .... PerfArt V.2
Lawrence, Jacob ...... Artist V.1; Update 01
lawyers
   Abzug, Bella .... Sep 98
   Babbitt, Bruce .... Jan 94
   Boutros-Ghali, Boutros .. Apr 93; Update 98
   Clinton, Hillary Rodham .... Apr 93
   Ebadi, Shirin .... Apr 04
   Giuliani, Rudolph .... Sep 02
   Grisham, John .... Author V.1
   Reno, Janet .... Sep 93
   Schroeder, Pat .... Jan 97
Leakey, Louis .... Science V.1
Leakey, Mary .... Science V.1
Lee, Harper .... Author V.9
Lee, Jeanette .... Apr 03
Lee, Spike .... Apr 92
Lee, Stan .... Author V.7; Update 02
Le Guin, Ursula K. .... Author V.8
Leibovitz, Annie .... Sep 96
Lemelson, Jerome .... Science V.3
Lemieux, Mario .... Jul 92; Update 93
LeMond, Greg .... Sport V.1
L'Engle, Madeleine .... Jan 92; Apr 01
Lennox, Betty .... Sport V.13
Leno, Jay .... Jul 92
Leopold, Aldo .... WorLdr V.3
Leslie, Lisa .... Jan 04
Lester, Julius .... Author V.7
Letterman, David .... Jan 95
Levi-Montalcini, Rita .... Science V.1
Levine, Gail Carson .... Author V.17
Lewis, C. S. .... Author V.3
Lewis, Carl .... Sep 96; Update 97
Lewis, John .... Jan 03
Lewis, Shari .... Jan 99
Liberian
   Tubman, William V. S. .... WorLdr V.2

librarians
Avi .... Jan 93
Bush, Laura .... Apr 03
Cleary, Beverly .... Apr 94
Hayden, Carla .... Sep 04
Morrison, Lillian .... Author V.12
Morrison, Sam .... Sep 97
Rylant, Cynthia .... Author V.1
Libyan
Qaddafi, Muammar .... Apr 97
Lidstrom, Nicklas .... Sep 03
Lil' Romeo
see Romeo, Lil' .... Jan 06
Limbaugh, Rush .... Sep 95; Update 02
Lin, Maya .... Sep 97
Lindgren, Astrid .... Author V.13
Lindo, Alan Pineda (apl.de.ap)
see Black Eyed Peas .... Apr 06
Linkin Park .... Jan 04
Lionni, Leo .... Author V.6
Lipinski, Tara .... Apr 98
Lipsyte, Robert .... Author V.12
Lisanti, Mariangela .... Sep 01
Lithuanian
Galdikas, Biruté .... Science V.4
Littrell, Brian
see Backstreet Boys .... Jan 00
Lobel, Arnold .... Author V.18
Lobo, Rebecca .... Sport V.3
Locklear, Heather .... Jan 95
Lohan, Lindsay .... Sep 04
Long, Irene D. .... Jan 04
Lopez, Charlotte .... Apr 94
López, George .... PerfArt V.2
Lopez, Jennifer .... Jan 02
Love, Susan .... Science V.3
Lovell, Jim .... Jan 96
Lowe, Alex .... Sport V.4
Lowman, Meg .... Science V.4
Lowry, Lois .... Author V.4
Lucas, George .... Apr 97; Update 02
Lucid, Shannon .... Science V.2
luge
Otto, Sylke .... Sport V.8
Lynch, Chris .... Author V.13
Ma, Yo-Yo .... Jul 92
Maathai, Wangari ..... WorLdr V.1; Sep 05
Mac, Bernie .... PerfArt V.1
MacArthur, Ellen .... Sport V.11
Macaulay, David .... Author V.2

MacLachlan, Patricia .... Author V.2
Madden, Benji .... PerfArt V.3
Madden, Joel .... PerfArt V.3
Madden, John .... Sep 97
Maddux, Greg .... Sport V.3
Maguire, Martie
see Dixie Chicks .... PerfArt V.1
Maines, Natalie
see Dixie Chicks .... PerfArt V.1
Malawian
Banda, Hastings Kamuzu .... WorLdr V.2
Mandela, Nelson .... Jan 92; Update 94;
Update 01
Mandela, Winnie .... WorLdr V.2
Mangel, Marcel
see Marceau, Marcel .... PerfArt V.2
Mankiller, Wilma .... Apr 94
Manning, Peyton .... Sep 00
Mantle, Mickey .... Jan 96
Marceau, Marcel .... PerfArt V.2
Margulis, Lynn .... Sep 96
Marino, Dan .... Apr 93; Update 00
Marrow, Tracy
see Ice-T .... Apr 93
Mars, Forrest Sr. .... Science V.4
Marsalis, Wynton .... Apr 92
Marshall, Thurgood ..... Jan 92; Update 93
Martin, Ann M. .... Jan 92
Martin, Bernard .... WorLdr V.3
Martin, Ricky .... Jan 00
Martinez, Pedro .... Sport V.5
Martinez, Victor .... Author V.15
Masih, Iqbal .... Jan 96
mathematicians
Dumitriu, Ioana .... Science V.3
Erdös, Paul .... Science V.2
Flannery, Sarah .... Science V.5
Hopper, Grace Murray .... Science V.5
Nash, John Forbes, Jr. .... Science V.7
Mathers, Marshall III
see Eminem .... Apr 03
Mathis, Clint .... Apr 03
Mathison, Melissa .... Author V.4
Maxwell, Jody-Anne .... Sep 98
Mayer, John .... Apr 04
McAdams, Rachel .... Apr 06
McCain, John .... Apr 00
McCarty, Oseola .... Jan 99; Update 99
McCary, Michael
see Boyz II Men .... Jan 96

McClintock, Barbara . . . . Oct 92
McCloskey, Robert . . . . Author V.15
McCully, Emily Arnold . . Jul 92; Update 93
McDaniel, Lurlene. . . . . Author V.14
McDonald, Janet . . . . Author V.18
McEntire, Reba. . . . . Sep 95
McGrady, Tracy. . . . . Sport V.11
McGrath, Judy . . . . Business V.1
McGruder, Aaron. . . . . Author V.10
McGwire, Mark . . . . Jan 99; Update 99
McKissack, Fredrick L. . . . . Author V.3
McKissack, Patricia C. . . . . Author V.3
McLean, A. J.
    see Backstreet Boys. . . . . Jan 00
McNabb, Donovan . . . . Apr 03
McNair, Steve . . . . Sport V.11
McNutt, Marcia . . . . Science V.11
Mead, Margaret . . . . Science V.2
Meaker, Marijane
    see Kerr, M.E. . . . . Author V.1
Mebarak Ripoll, Shakira Isabel
    see Shakira . . . . PerfArt V.1
Meltzer, Milton. . . . . Author V.11
Menchu, Rigoberta. . . . . Jan 93
Mendes, Chico . . . . WorLdr V.1
Messier, Mark . . . . Apr 96
Mexicans
    Fox, Vicente. . . . . Apr 03
    Jiménez, Francisco. . . . . Author V.13
    Ramos, Jorge . . . . Apr 06
    Rivera, Diego . . . . Artist V.1
    Santana, Carlos. . . . . Sep 05
Milbrett, Tiffeny . . . . Sport V.10
military service
– Israel
    Rabin, Yitzhak . . . . Oct 92
– Libya
    Qaddafi, Muammar . . . . Apr 97
– Somalia
    Aidid, Mohammed Farah . . . WorLdr V.2
– Uganda
    Amin, Idi . . . . WorLdr V.2
– United States
    Brooks, Vincent . . . . Sep 03
    Honoré, Russel. . . . . Jan 06
    Hopper, Grace Murray . . . . . . Science V.5
    McCain, John. . . . . Apr 00
    Powell, Colin . . . . Jan 92; Update 93;
        Update 95; Update 01
    Sanchez, Ricardo . . . . Sep 04
    Schwarzkopf, H. Norman . . . . Jan 92
    Stanford, John . . . . Sep 99

– Zaire
    Mobutu Sese Seko . . . . WorLdr V.2
Miller, Percy Romeo
    see Romeo, Lil' . . . . Jan 06
Miller, Rand . . . . Science V.5
Miller, Robyn. . . . . Science V.5
Miller, Shannon. . . . . Sep 94; Update 96
Milosevic, Slobodan . . . Sep 99; Update 00;
    Update 01; Update 02
mime
    Marceau, Marcel . . . . PerfArt V.2
Mirra, Dave . . . . Sep 02
Mister Rogers
    see Rogers, Fred. . . . . PerfArt V.3
Mitchell-Raptakis, Karen . . . . Jan 05
Mittermeier, Russell A. . . . . . . WorLdr V.1
Miyamoto, Shigeru . . . . Science V.5
Mobutu Sese Seko . . WorLdr V.2; Update 97
Moceanu, Dominique . . . . Jan 98
models
    Banks, Tyra . . . . PerfArt V.2
    Crawford, Cindy. . . . . Apr 93
Mohajer, Dineh. . . . . Jan 02
Monroe, Bill . . . . Sep 97
Montana, Joe . . . . Jan 95; Update 95
Moore, Henry. . . . . Artist V.1
Moore, Mandy. . . . . Jan 04
Moreno, Arturo R. . . . . Business V.1
Morgan, Garrett . . . . Science V.2
Morissette, Alanis . . . . Apr 97
Morita, Akio . . . . Science V.4
Moroccan
    Hassan II . . . . WorLdr V.2; Update 99
Morris, Nathan
    see Boyz II Men. . . . . Jan 96
Morris, Wanya
    see Boyz II Men. . . . . Jan 96
Morrison, Lillian . . . . Author V.12
Morrison, Samuel . . . . Sep 97
Morrison, Toni . . . . Jan 94
Moseley, Jonny . . . . Sport V.8
Moses, Grandma. . . . . Artist V.1
Moss, Cynthia . . . . WorLdr V.3
Moss, Randy. . . . . Sport V.4
Mother Teresa
    see Teresa, Mother . . . . Apr 98
mountain climbing
    Hargreaves, Alison . . . . Jan 96
    Hillary, Sir Edmund . . . . Sep 96
    Kamler, Kenneth . . . . Science V.6
    Krakauer, Jon. . . . . Author V.6
    Lowe, Alex . . . . Sport V.4

movies
  see actors/actresses
  see animators
  see directors
  see film critic
  see producers
  see screenwriters
Mowat, Farley . . . . Author V.8
Mugabe, Robert . . . . WorLdr V.2
Muir, John . . . . WorLdr V.3
Muldowney, Shirley . . . . Sport V.7
Muniz, Frankie . . . . Jan 01
Murie, Margaret . . . . WorLdr V.1
Murie, Olaus J. . . . . WorLdr V.1
Murphy, Eddie . . . . PerfArt V.2
Murphy, Jim . . . . Author V.17
Murray, Ty . . . . Sport V.7
music
  Aaliyah . . . . Jan 02
  Abdul, Paula . . . . Jan 92; Update 02
  Adams, Yolanda . . . . Apr 03
  Aguilera, Christina . . . . Apr 00
  Anderson, Marian . . . . Jan 94
  Ashanti . . . . PerfArt V.2
  Backstreet Boys . . . . Jan 00
  Battle, Kathleen . . . . Jan 93
  Ben-Ari, Miri . . . . Jan 06
  Black, Jack . . . . Jan 05
  Black Eyed Peas . . . . Apr 06
  Blige, Mary J. . . . . Apr 02
  Boyz II Men . . . . Jan 96
  Branch, Michelle . . . . PerfArt V.3
  Brandy . . . . Apr 96
  Brooks, Garth . . . . Oct 92
  Carey, Mariah . . . . Apr 96
  Carpenter, Mary Chapin . . . . Sep 94
  Carrabba, Chris . . . . Apr 05
  Carter, Aaron . . . . Sep 02
  Clarkson, Kelly . . . . Jan 03
  Cobain, Kurt . . . . Sep 94
  Combs, Sean (Puff Daddy) . . . . Apr 98
  Coolio . . . . Sep 96
  Cruz, Celia . . . . Apr 04
  Destiny's Child . . . . Apr 01
  Dion, Celine . . . . Sep 97
  Dixie Chicks . . . . PerfArt V.1
  Domingo, Placido . . . . Sep 95
  Donnas . . . . Apr 04
  Elliott, Missy . . . . PerfArt V.3
  Eminem . . . . Apr 03

Estefan, Gloria . . . . Jul 92
Eve . . . . Jan 05
Fitzgerald, Ella . . . . Jan 97
Franklin, Aretha . . . . Apr 01
Garcia, Jerry . . . . Jan 96
Gillespie, Dizzy . . . . Apr 93
Gilman, Billy . . . . Apr 02
Glennie, Evelyn . . . . PerfArt V.3
Grant, Amy . . . . Jan 95
Green Day . . . . Apr 06
Guy, Jasmine . . . . Sep 93
Hammer . . . . Jan 92
Hanson . . . . Jan 98
Hill, Faith . . . . Sep 01
Hill, Lauryn . . . . Sep 99
Houston, Whitney . . . . Sep 94
Ice-T . . . . Apr 93
Iglesias, Enrique . . . . Jan 03
Jewel . . . . Sep 98
Johnson, Johanna . . . . Apr 00
Jones, Norah . . . . PerfArt V.2
Jones, Quincy . . . . PerfArt V.2
Keith, Toby . . . . Jan 05
Krauss, Alison . . . . Apr 05
lang, k.d. . . . . Sep 93
Lavigne, Avril . . . . PerfArt V.2
Linkin Park . . . . Jan 04
Lopez, Jennifer . . . . Jan 02
Ma, Yo-Yo . . . . Jul 92
Madden, Benji . . . . PerfArt V.3
Madden, Joel . . . . PerfArt V.3
Marsalis, Wynton . . . . Apr 92
Martin, Ricky . . . . Jan 00
Mayer, John . . . . Apr 04
McGrath, Judy . . . . Business V.1
McEntire, Reba . . . . Sep 95
Monroe, Bill . . . . Sep 97
Moore, Mandy . . . . Jan 04
Morissette, Alanis . . . . Apr 97
*N Sync . . . . Jan 01
Nelly . . . . Sep 03
OutKast . . . . Sep 04
Perlman, Itzhak . . . . Jan 95
Queen Latifah . . . . Apr 92
Raven . . . . Apr 04
Rimes, LeAnn . . . . Jan 98
Romeo, Lil' . . . . Jan 06
Salt 'N' Pepa . . . . Apr 95
Santana, Carlos . . . . Sep 05
Selena . . . . Jan 96

For cumulative places of birth and birthday indexes, please see biographytoday.com.

Shakira . . . . PerfArt V.1
Shakur, Tupac . . . . Apr 97
Simmons, Russell . . . . Apr 06
Simpson, Ashlee . . . . Sep 05
Sinatra, Frank . . . . Jan 99
Smith, Will . . . . Sep 94
Spears, Britney . . . . Jan 01
Stefani, Gwen . . . . Sep 03
Stern, Isaac . . . . PerfArt V.1
Stone, Joss . . . . Jan 06
Suzuki, Shinichi . . . . Sep 98
Twain, Shania . . . . Apr 99
Uchida, Mitsuko . . . . Apr 99
Usher . . . . PerfArt V.1
Vidal, Christina . . . . PerfArt V.1
Winans, CeCe . . . . Apr 00
Myers, Mike . . . . PerfArt V.3
Myers, Walter Dean . . . . . Jan 93; Update 94
***N Sync** . . . . Jan 01
Nakamura, Leanne . . . . Apr 02
Napoli, Donna Jo . . . . Author V.16
Nash, John Forbes, Jr. . . . . Science V.7
Nash, Steve . . . . Jan 06
Native Americans
  Bruchac, Joseph . . . . Author V.18
  Fergie (Stacy Ferguson) . . . . Apr 06
  House, Donna . . . . Science V.11
  LaDuke, Winona . . WorLdr V.3; Update 00
  Mankiller, Wilma . . . . Apr 94
  Menchu, Rigoberta . . . . Jan 93
Navratilova, Martina . . . . Jan 93; Update 94
Naylor, Phyllis Reynolds . . . . Apr 93
Ndeti, Cosmas . . . . Sep 95
Nechita, Alexandra . . . . Jan 98
Nelly . . . . Sep 03
Nelson, Gaylord . . . . WorLdr V.3
Nelson, Marilyn . . . . Author V.13
Nevelson, Louise . . . . Artist V.1
New Zealanders
  Hillary, Sir Edmund . . . . Sep 96
  Jackson, Peter . . . . PerfArt V.2
Newbery Medal
  Alexander, Lloyd . . . . Author V.6
  Armstrong, William H . . . . Author V.7
  Cleary, Beverly . . . . Apr 94
  Creech, Sharon . . . . Author V.5
  Curtis, Christopher Paul . . . . . . Author V.4;
    Update 00
  Cushman, Karen . . . . Author V.5
  Freedman, Russell . . . . Author V.14
  George, Jean Craighead . . . . Author V.3

Hamilton, Virginia . . . . Author V.1;
  Author V.12
Hesse, Karen . . . . . . Author V.5; Update 02
Konigsburg, E. L . . . . Author V.3
L'Engle, Madeleine . . . . Jan 92; Apr 01
MacLachlan, Patricia . . . . Author V.2
Naylor, Phyllis Reynolds . . . . Apr 93
O'Dell, Scott . . . . Author V.2
Paterson, Katherine . . . . Author V.3
Peck, Richard . . . . Author V.10
Rylant, Cynthia . . . . Author V.1
Sachar, Louis . . . . Author V.6
Speare, Elizabeth George . . . . Sep 95
Spinelli, Jerry . . . . Apr 93
Taylor, Mildred D . . . Author V.1; Update 02
Voight, Cynthia . . . . Oct 92
Newman, Ryan . . . . Sport V.11
Newsom, Lee Ann . . . . Science V.11
Nhat Hanh (Thich) . . . . Jan 04
Nicklaus, Jack . . . . Sport V.2
Nielsen, Jerri . . . . Science V.7
Nigerians
  Olajuwon, Hakeem . . . . Sep 95
  Saro-Wiwa, Ken . . . . WorLdr V.1
Nixon, Joan Lowery . . . . Author V.1
Nixon, Richard . . . . Sep 94
Nkrumah, Kwame . . . . WorLdr V.2
Nobel Prize
  Alvarez, Luis W. . . . . Science V.3
  Aung San Suu Kyi . . . . . Apr 96; Update 98;
    Update 01; Update 02
  Bardeen, John . . . . Science V.1
  Bethe, Hans A. . . . . Science V.3
  Dalai Lama . . . . Sep 98
  de Klerk, F.W. . . . . Apr 94
  Ebadi, Shirin . . . . Apr 04
  Elion, Gertrude . . . . Science V.6
  Feynman, Ricahrd . . . . Science V.10
  Gilbert, Walter . . . . Science V.2
  Gorbachev, Mikhail . . . . Jan 92
  Kim Dae-jung . . . . Sep 01
  Levi-Montalcini, Rita . . . . Science V.1
  Maathai, Wangari . . . . Sep 05
  Mandela, Nelson . . . . . . Jan 92; Update 94;
    Update 01
  McClintock, Barbara . . . . Oct 92
  Menchu, Rigoberta . . . . Jan 93
  Morrison, Toni . . . . Jan 94
  Nash, John Forbes, Jr. . . . . Science V.7
  Ochoa, Severo . . . . Jan 94
  Pauling, Linus . . . . Jan 95
  Sadat, Anwar . . . . WorLdr V.2

Teresa, Mother . . . . Apr 98
Watson, James D. . . . . Science V.1
Noor al Hussein, Queen of Jordan . . Jan 05
Norman, Greg . . . . Jan 94
Norwegians
 Arnesen, Liv. . . . . Author V.15
 Brundtland, Gro Harlem . . . . . . Science V.3
Norwood, Brandy
 see Brandy . . . . Apr 96
Novello, Antonia . . . . Apr 92; Update 93
*N Sync . . . . Jan 01
Nureyev, Rudolf . . . . Apr 93
Nye, Bill . . . . Science V.2
Nye, Naomi Shihab . . . . Author V.8
Nyerere, Julius Kambarage . . . WorLdr V.2;
 Update 99
Ocampo, Adriana C. . . . . Science V.8
Ochoa, Ellen . . . . Apr 01; Update 02
Ochoa, Severo . . . . Jan 94
O'Connor, Sandra Day . . . . Jul 92
O'Dell, Scott . . . . Author V.2
O'Donnell, Rosie . . . . Apr 97; Update 02
Ohno, Apolo . . . . Sport V.8
O'Keeffe, Georgia . . . . Artist V.1
Olajuwon, Hakeem . . . . Sep 95
Oleynik, Larisa . . . . Sep 96
Oliver, Patsy Ruth . . . . WorLdr V.1
Olsen, Ashley . . . . Sep 95
Olsen, Mary Kate . . . . Sep 95
Olympics
 Ali, Muhammad . . . . Sport V.2
 Ammann, Simon . . . . Sport V.8
 Armstrong, Lance . . . . . . Sep 00; Update 00;
  Update 01; Update 02
 Bahrke, Shannon . . . . Sport V.8
 Bailey, Donovan . . . . Sport V.2
 Baiul, Oksana . . . . Apr 95
 Bird, Larry . . . . Jan 92; Update 98
 Blair, Bonnie . . . . Apr 94
 Boulmerka, Hassiba . . . . Sport V.1
 Capriati, Jennifer . . . . Sport V.6
 Carter, Vince . . . . Sport V.5; Update 01
 Chastain, Brandi . . . . . Sport V.4; Update 00
 Clark, Kelly . . . . Sport V.8
 Cohen, Sasha . . . . Sport V.12
 Davenport, Lindsay . . . . Sport V.5
 Devers, Gail . . . . Sport V.2
 Dragila, Stacy . . . . Sport V.6
 Dunlap, Alison . . . . Sport V.7
 Evans, Janet . . . . Jan 95; Update 96
 Ewing, Patrick . . . . Jan 95; Update 02

 Fernandez, Lisa . . . . Sport V.5
 Finch, Jennie . . . . Jan 05
 Flowers, Vonetta . . . . Sport V.8
 Foudy, Julie . . . . Sport V.13
 Freeman, Cathy . . . . Jan 01
 Fu Mingxia . . . . Sport V.5
 Garnett, Kevin . . . . Sport V.6
 Granato, Cammi . . . . Sport V.8
 Griffith Joyner, Florence . . . . Sport V.1;
  Update 98
 Hamm, Mia . . . . Sport V.2; Update 00
 Harding, Tonya . . . . Sep 94
 Hasek, Dominik . . . . Sport V.3
 Hill, Grant . . . . Sport V.1
 Hughes, Sarah . . . . Jan 03
 James, LeBron . . . . Sport V.12
 Jansen, Dan . . . . Apr 94
 Johnson, Michael . . . . Jan 97; Update 00
 Jones, Marion . . . . Sport V.5
 Joyner-Kersee, Jackie . . . . . . Oct 92; Update
  96; Update 97; Update 98
 Kerrigan, Nancy . . . . Apr 94
 Klug, Chris . . . . Sport V.8
 Kwan, Michelle . . . . . . Sport V.3; Update 02
 Leslie, Lisa . . . . Jan 04
 Lewis, Carl . . . . Sep 96
 Lipinski, Tara . . . . Apr 98
 Lobo, Rebecca . . . . Sport V.3
 Milbrett, Tiffeny . . . . Sport V.10
 Miller, Shannon . . . . Sep 94; Update 96
 Moceanu, Dominique . . . . Jan 98
 Moseley, Jonny . . . . Sport V.8
 Ohno, Apolo . . . . Sport V.8
 Otto, Sylke . . . . Sport V.8
 Patterson, Carly . . . . Sport V.12
 Phelps, Michael . . . . Sport V.13
 Pippig, Uta . . . . Sport V.1
 Richardson, Dot . . . . . Sport V.2; Update 00
 Roba, Fatuma . . . . Sport V.3
 Robinson, David . . . . Sep 96
 Roy, Patrick . . . . Sport V.7
 Rudolph, Wilma . . . . Apr 95
 Runyan, Marla . . . . Apr 02
 Sakic, Joe . . . . Sport V.6
 Sanborn, Ryne . . . . Sport V.8
 Sanchez Vicario, Arantxa . . . . Sport V.1
 Schwikert, Tasha . . . . Sport V.7
 Scurry, Briana . . . . Jan 00
 Shea, Jim, Jr. . . . . Sport V.8
 Stockton, John . . . . Sport V.3

For cumulative places of birth and birthday indexes, please see biographytoday.com.

Street, Picabo . . . . Sport V.3
Summitt, Pat. . . . . Sport V.3
Swoopes, Sheryl. . . . . Sport V.2
Thompson, Jenny. . . . . Sport V.5
Van Dyken, Amy . . . . Sport V.3; Update 00
Villa, Brenda. . . . . Jan 06
Walsh, Kerri . . . . Sport V.13
Weatherspoon, Teresa. . . . . Sport V.12
Williams, Serena . . . . Sport V.4; Update 00;
   Update 02
Williams, Venus . . . . Jan 99; Update 00;
   Update 01; Update 02
Yamaguchi, Kristi . . . . Apr 92
Zmeskal, Kim. . . . . Jan 94
O'Neal, Shaquille . . . . Sep 93
Opdyke, Irene Gut . . . . Author V.9
Oppenheimer, J. Robert. . . . . . . Science V.1
Otto, Sylke . . . . Sport V.8
OutKast . . . . Sep 04
Page, Larry. Sep 05
painters
   see artists
Pak, Se Ri . . . . Sport V.4
Pakistanis
   Bhutto, Benazir . . . . Apr 95; Update 99
   Masih, Iqbal . . . . Jan 96
Palestinian
   Arafat, Yasir. . . . . Sep 94; Update 94;
      Update 95; Update 96; Update 97; Update
      98; Update 00; Update 01; Update 02
Palmer, Violet. . . . . Sep 05
Panamanian
   Chambers, Veronica . . . . Author V.15
Paolini, Christopher. . . . . Author V.16
Park, Linda Sue . . . . Author V.12
Parkinson, Jennifer. . . . . Apr 95
Parks, Gordon . . . . Artist V.1
Parks, Rosa . . . . . Apr 92; Update 94; Apr 06
Pascal, Francine . . . . Author V.6
Paterson, Katherine . . . . Author V.3
Patrick, Danica. . . . . Apr 06
Patrick, Ruth. . . . . Science V.3
Patterson, Carly . . . . Sport V.12
Patterson, Ryan . . . . Science V.7
Patton, Antwan
   see OutKast . . . . Sep 04
Pauley, Jane. . . . . Oct 92
Pauling, Linus . . . . Jan 95
Paulsen, Gary . . . . Author V.1
Payton, Walter. . . . . Jan 00

Pearman, Raven-Symone
   see Raven. Apr 04
Peck, Richard . . . . Author V.10
Peet, Bill . . . . Author V.4
Pei, I.M. . . . . Artist V.1
Pelé. . . . . Sport V.1
Perlman, Itzhak. . . . . Jan 95
Perot, H. Ross. . . . . Apr 92; Update 93;
   Update 95; Update 96
Perry, Luke. . . . . Jan 92
Peterson, Roger Troy . . . . WorLdr V.1
Petty, Richard. . . . . Sport V.2
Phelps, Michael. . . . . Sport V.13
philanthropists
   Dawson, Matel, Jr. . . . . Jan 04
   McCarty, Oseola. . . . . . . Jan 99; Update 99
   Rowland, Pleasant T. . . . . Business V.1
philosopher
   Caplan, Arthur . . . . Science V.6
Phoenix, River . . . . Apr 94
photographers
   Adams, Ansel. . . . . Artist V.1
   Bourke-White, Margaret. . . . . . . Artist V.1
   Land, Edwin . . . . Science V.1
   Leibovitz, Annie . . . . Sep 96
   Parks, Gordon . . . . Artist V.1
Pierce, Tamora . . . . Author V.13
Pike, Christopher. . . . . Sep 96
pilots
   Funk, Wally . . . . Jan 05
   Van Meter, Vicki . . . . Jan 95
Pine, Elizabeth Michele . . . . Jan 94
Pinkney, Andrea Davis. . . . . . . Author V.10
Pinkney, Jerry . . . . Author V.2
Pinkwater, Daniel . . . . Author V.8
Pinsky, Robert . . . . Author V.7
Pippen, Scottie . . . . Oct 92
Pippig, Uta . . . . Sport V.1
Pitt, Brad . . . . Sep 98
playwrights
   Bennett, Cherie. . . . . Author V.9
   Bruchac, Joseph. . . . . Author V.18
   Hansberry, Lorraine . . . . Author V.5
   Hughes, Langston. . . . . Author V.7
   Smith, Betty . . . . Author V.17
   Wilson, August . . . . Author 98
poets
   Alvarez, Julia . . . . Author V.17
   Brooks, Gwendolyn . . . . Author V.3

Bruchac, Joseph. . . . . Author V.18
Collins, Billy . . . . Author V.16
Dove, Rita. Jan 94
Dunbar, Paul Lawrence . . . . . . Author V.8
Grimes, Nikki . . . . Author V.14
Hughes, Langston. . . . . Author V.7
Jewel . . . . Sep 98
Lansky, Bruce . . . . Author V.17
Martinez, Victor. . . . . Author V.15
Morrison, Lillian . . . . Author V.12
Nelson, Marilyn. . . . . Author V.13
Nye, Naomi Shihab . . . . Author V.8
Pinsky, Robert . . . . Author V.7
Prelutsky, Jack . . . . Author V.2
Senghor, Léopold Sédar . . . . . WorLdr V.2
Silverstein, Shel . . . . Author V.3; Update 99
Sones, Sonya . . . . Author V.11
Soto, Gary . . . . Author V.5
Stepanek, Mattie. . . . . Apr 02
Polish
John Paul II. . . . . Oct 92; Update 94;
    Update 95; Sep 05
Opdyke, Irene Gut. . . . . Author V.9
political leaders
Abzug, Bella . . . . Sep 98
Amin, Idi . . . . WorLdr V.2
Annan, Kofi . . . . Jan 98; Update 01
Arafat, Yasir. . . . . Sep 94; Update 94;
    Update 95; Update 96; Update 97; Update
    98; Update 00; Update 01; Update 02
Aristide, Jean-Bertrand . . Jan 95; Update 01
Babbitt, Bruce. . . . . Jan 94
Baker, James . . . . Oct 92
Banda, Hastings Kamuzu . . . . WorLdr V.2
Bellamy, Carol . . . . Jan 06
Bhutto, Benazir. . . . . Apr 95; Update 99;
    Update 02
Blair, Tony . . . . Apr 04
Boutros-Ghali, Boutros. . Apr 93; Update 98
Brundtland, Gro Harlem . . . . . . Science V.3
Bush, George . . . . Jan 92
Bush, George W.. . . . . . . Sep 00; Update 00;
    Update 01; Update 02
Carter, Jimmy . . . . Apr 95; Update 02
Castro, Fidel. . . . . Jul 92; Update 94
Cheney, Dick . . . . Jan 02
Cisneros, Henry . . . . Sep 93
Clinton, Bill. . . . . Jul 92; Update 94;
    Update 95; Update 96; Update 97; Update
    98; Update 99; Update 00; Update 01

Clinton, Hillary Rodham. . . . . Apr 93;
    Update 94; Update 95; Update 96; Update
    99; Update 00; Update 01
de Klerk, F.W. . . . . Apr 94; Update 94
Dole, Bob . . . . Jan 96; Update 96
Duke, David . . . . Apr 92
Fox, Vicente. Apr 03
Gingrich, Newt . . . . Apr 95; Update 99
Giuliani, Rudolph . . . . Sep 02
Glenn, John . . . . Jan 99
Gorbachev, Mikhail . . . . . Jan 92; Update 94;
    Update 96
Gore, Al . . . . . Jan 93; Update 96; Update 97;
    Update 98; Update 99; Update 00; Update
    01
Hussein, King . . . . Apr 99
Hussein, Saddam. . . . . . . Jul 92; Update 96;
    Update 01; Update 02
Jackson, Jesse. . . . . Sep 95; Update 01
Jordan, Barbara . . . . Apr 96
Kaunda, Kenneth . . . . WorLdr V.2
Kenyatta, Jomo . . . . WorLdr V.2
Kim Dae-jung . . . . Sep 01
Lewis, John. Jan 03
Mandela, Nelson. . . . . . . Jan 92; Update 94;
    Update 01
McCain, John . . . . Apr 00
Milosevic, Slobodan . . . Sep 99; Update 00;
    Update 01; Update 02
Mobutu Sese Seko . . WorLdr V.2; Update 97
Mugabe, Robert . . . . WorLdr V.2
Nelson, Gaylord. . . . . WorLdr V.3
Nixon, Richard . . . . Sep 94
Nkrumah, Kwame . . . . WorLdr V.2
Nyerere, Julius Kambarage . . . WorLdr V.2;
    Update 99
Perot, H. Ross. . . . . Apr 92; Update 93;
    Update 95; Update 96
Rabin, Yitzhak . . . . Oct 92; Update 93;
    Update 94; Update 95
Reagan, Ronald . . . . Sep 04
Rice, Condoleezza. . . . . Apr 02
Robinson, Mary. . . . . Sep 93
Sadat, Anwar . . . . WorLdr V.2
Savimbi, Jonas . . . . WorLdr V.2
Schroeder, Pat . . . . Jan 97
Senghor, Léopold Sédar . . . . . WorLdr V.2
Tubman, William V. S. . . . . WorLdr V.2
Ventura, Jesse . . . . Apr 99; Update 02
Yeltsin, Boris. . . . . Apr 92; Update 93;
    Update 95; Update 96; Update 98; Update
    00

For cumulative places of birth and birthday indexes, please see biographytoday.com.

Pope of the Roman Catholic Church
John Paul II . . . . Oct 92; Update 94;
Update 95; Sep 05
Portman, Natalie . . . . Sep 99
Potter, Beatrix . . . . Author V.8
Poussaint, Alvin. . . . . Science V.9
Powell, Colin . . . . Jan 92; Update 93;
Update 95; Update 01
Prelutsky, Jack . . . . Author V.2
presidents
– **Cuba**
Castro, Fidel . . . . Jul 92; Update 94
– **Egypt**
Sadat, Anwar . . . . WorLdr V.2
– **Ghana**
Nkrumah, Kwame . . . . WorLdr V.2
– **Haiti**
Aristide, Jean-Bertrand . . . . Jan 95;
Update 01
– **Iraq**
Hussein, Saddam . . . . . Jul 92; Update 96;
Update 01
– **Ireland**
Robinson, Mary . . . . Sep 93
– **Kenya**
Kenyatta, Jomo . . . . WorLdr V.2
– **Liberia**
Tubman, William V. S. . . . . . WorLdr V.2
– **Malawi**
Banda, Hastings Kamuzu . . . WorLdr V.2
– **Republic of South Africa**
de Klerk, F.W. . . . . Apr 94; Update 9
Mandela, Nelson . . . . . Jan 92; Update 94;
Update 01
– **Republic of Tanzania**
Nyerere, Julius Kambarage . . WorLdr V.2;
Update 99
– **Russian Federation**
Yeltsin, Boris . . . . Apr 92; Update 93;
Update 95; Update 96; Update 98; Update
00
– **Senegal**
Senghor, Léopold Sédar . . . . WorLdr V.2
– **South Korea**
Kim Dae-jung . . . . Sep 01
– **Soviet Union**
Gorbachev, Mikhail . . . . Jan 92
– **Uganda**
Amin, Idi . . . . WorLdr V.2

– **United States**
Bush, George . . . . Jan 92
Bush, George W. . . . . . Sep 00; Update 00;
Update 01; Update 02
Carter, Jimmy . . . . Apr 95; Update 02
Clinton, Bill . . . . Jul 92; Update 94;
Update 95; Update 96; Update 97; Update
98; Update 99; Update 00; Update 01
Nixon, Richard . . . . Sep 94
Reagan, Ronald . . . . Sep 04
– **Yugoslavia**
Milosevic, Slobodan . . . . Sep 99; Update
00; Update 01; Update 02
– **Zaire**
Mobutu Sese Seko . . . . WorLdr V.2;
Update 97
– **Zambia**
Kaunda, Kenneth . . . . WorLdr V.2
– **Zimbabwe**
Mugabe, Robert . . . . WorLdr V.2
Priestley, Jason . . . . Apr 92
prime ministers
– **Israel**
Rabin, Yitzhak . . . . Oct 92; Update 93;
Update 94; Update 95
– **Norway**
Brundtland, Gro Harlem . . . . Science V.3
– **Pakistan**
Bhutto, Benazir . . . . . . Apr 95; Update 99;
Update 02
– **United Kingdom**
Blair, Tony . . . . Apr 04
Prinze, Freddie, Jr. . . . . Apr 00
Pritchard, Michael (Mike Dirnt)
see Green Day . . . . Apr 06
Probst, Jeff . . . . Jan 01
producers
Barrymore, Drew . . . . Jan 01
Carter, Chris . . . . Author V.4
Chan, Jackie . . . . PerfArt V.1
Combs, Sean (Puff Daddy) . . . . Apr 98
Cousteau, Jacques . . . . Jan 93
Groppe, Laura . . . . Science V.5
Hillenburg, Stephen . . . . Author V.14
Jackson, Peter . . . . PerfArt V.2
Jones, Chuck . . . . Author V.12
Jones, Quincy . . . . PerfArt V.2
Kutcher, Ashton . . . . Apr 04
Lucas, George . . . . Apr 97; Update 02
Rogers, Fred . . . . PerfArt V.3

Spielberg, Steven . . . . Jan 94
Whedon, Joss . . . . Author V.9
Williamson, Kevin . . . . Author V.6
Winfrey, Oprah . . . . Business V.1
Puerto Ricans
see also Hispanics
Lopez, Charlotte . . . . Apr 94
Martin, Ricky . . . . Jan 00
Novello, Antonia . . . . Apr 92
Puff Daddy
see Combs, Sean (Puff Daddy) . . . . . Apr 98
Puffy
see Combs, Sean (Puff Daddy) . . . . . Apr 98
Pujols, Albert . . . . Sport V.12
Pullman, Philip . . . . Author V.9
Qaddafi, Muammar . . . . Apr 97
Qing, Dai
see Dai Qing . . . . WorLdr V.3
Queen Latifah . . . . Apr 92
Quesada, Vicente Fox
see Fox, Vicente . . . . Apr 03
Quintanilla, Selena
see Selena . . . . Jan 96
Rabin, Yitzhak . . . . Oct 92; Update 93;
Update 94; Update 95
Radcliffe, Daniel . . . . Jan 02
radio
Hunter-Gault, Charlayne . . . . Jan 00
Limbaugh, Rush . . . . Sep 95; Update 02
Roberts, Cokie . . . . Apr 95
Ramirez, Manny . . . . Sport V.13
Ramos, Jorge . . . . Apr 06
rappers
see music
Raven . . . . Apr 04
Raymond, Usher, IV
see Usher . . . . PerfArt V.1
Reagan, Ronald . . . . Sep 04
Reeve, Christopher . . . . . . Jan 97; Update 02
Reeves, Keanu . . . . Jan 04
referee
Palmer, Violet . . . . Sep 05
Reid Banks, Lynne . . . . Author V.2
religious leaders
Aristide, Jean-Bertrand . . Jan 95; Update 01
Chavis, Benjamin . . . . Jan 94; Update 94
Dalai Lama . . . . Sep 98
Farrakhan, Louis . . . . Jan 97
Jackson, Jesse . . . . Sep 95; Update 01
Jakes, T.D. . . . . Jan 05

John Paul II . . . . Oct 92; Update 94;
Update 95; Sep 05
Nhat Hanh (Thich) . . . . Jan 04
Teresa, Mother . . . . Apr 98
Rennison, Louise . . . . Author V.10
Reno, Janet . . . . Sep 93; Update 98
representatives
Abzug, Bella . . . . Sep 98
Cheney, Dick . . . . Jan 02
Gingrich, Newt . . . . Apr 95; Update 99
Jordan, Barbara . . . . Apr 96
Lewis, John . . . . Jan 03
Schroeder, Pat . . . . Jan 97
Republican Party
Baker, James . . . . Oct 92
Bush, George . . . . Jan 92
Bush, George W. . . . . Sep 00; Update 00;
Update 01; Update 02
Cheney, Dick . . . . Jan 02
Gingrich, Newt . . . . Apr 95; Update 99
Giuliani, Rudolph . . . . Sep 02
Nixon, Richard . . . . Sep 94
Reagan, Ronald . . . . Sep 04
Rice, Anne . . . . Author V.3
Rice, Condoleezza . . . . Apr 02
Rice, Jerry . . . . Apr 93
Richardson, Dot . . . . . . Sport V.2; Update 00
Richardson, Kevin
see Backstreet Boys . . . . Jan 00
Ride, Sally . . . . Jan 92
Riley, Dawn . . . . Sport V.4
Rimes, LeAnn . . . . Jan 98
Rinaldi, Ann . . . . Author V.8
Ringgold, Faith . . . . Author V.2
Ripken, Cal, Jr. . . . . Sport V.1; Update 01
Risca, Viviana . . . . Sep 00
Rivera, Diego . . . . Artist V.1
Roba, Fatuma . . . . Sport V.3
Roberts, Cokie . . . . Apr 95
Roberts, Julia . . . . Sep 01
Robertson, Allison (Donna R.)
see Donnas . . . . Apr 04
Robinson, David . . . . Sep 96
Robinson, Jackie . . . . Sport V.3
Robinson, Mary . . . . Sep 93
Robison, Emily
see Dixie Chicks . . . . PerfArt V.1
rock climbing
Allen, Tori . . . . Sport V.9
Rockwell, Norman . . . . Artist V.1
Roddick, Andy . . . . Jan 03

For cumulative places of birth and birthday indexes, please see biographytoday.com.

rodeo
Murray, Ty . . . . Sport V.7
Rodman, Dennis . . . . Apr 96; Update 99
Rodriguez, Alex . . . . Sport V.6
Rodriguez, Eloy . . . . Science V.2
Rodriguez, Gloria . . . . Apr 05
Rogers, Fred . . . . PerfArt V.3
Romanians
Dumitriu, Ioana . . . . Science V.3
Nechita, Alexandra . . . . Jan 98
Risca, Viviana . . . . Sep 00
Romeo, Lil' . . . . Jan 06
Romero, John . . . . Science V.8
Roper, Dee Dee
see Salt 'N' Pepa . . . . Apr 95
Rosa, Emily . . . . Sep 98
Rose, Pete . . . . Jan 92
Rowan, Carl . . . . Sep 01
Rowland, Kelly
see Destiny's Child . . . . Apr 01
Rowland, Pleasant T. . . . . Business V.1
Rowling, J. K. . . . . Sep 99; Update 00;
Update 01; Update 02
Roy, Patrick . . . . Sport V.7
royalty
Diana, Princess of Wales . . . . Jul 92;
Update 96; Update 97; Jan 98
Haile Selassie . . . . WorLdr V.2
Hassan II . . . . WorLdr V.2; Update 99
Hussein, King . . . . Apr 99
Noor al Hussein, Queen of Jordan . . Jan 05
Rubin, Jamie . . . . Science V.8
Rudolph, Wilma . . . . Apr 95
running
Bailey, Donovan . . . . Sport V.2
Boulmerka, Hassiba . . . . Sport V.1
Felix, Allyson . . . . Sport V.10
Freeman, Cathy . . . . Jan 01
Griffith Joyner, Florence . . . . Sport V.1;
Update 98
Johnson, Michael . . . . Jan 97; Update 00
Jones, Marion . . . . Sport V.5
Lewis, Carl . . . . Sep 96; Update 97
Ndeti, Cosmas . . . . Sep 95
Pippig, Uta . . . . Sport V.1
Roba, Fatuma . . . . Sport V.3
Rudolph, Wilma . . . . Apr 95
Runyan, Marla . . . . Apr 02
Webb, Alan . . . . Sep 01
Runyan, Marla . . . . Apr 02
Russell, Charlie . . . . Science V.11

Russians
Brin, Sergey . . . . Sep 05
Chagall, Marc . . . . Artist V.1
Fedorov, Sergei . . . . Apr 94; Update 94
Gorbachev, Mikhail . . . . . Jan 92; Update 96
Nevelson, Louise . . . . Artist V.1
Sharapova, Maria . . . . Sep 05
Tartakovsky, Genndy . . . . Author V.11
Yeltsin, Boris . . . . Apr 92; Update 93;
Update 95; Update 96; Update 98; Update 00
Ryan, Nolan . . . . Oct 92; Update 93
Ryan, Pam Muñoz . . . . Author V.12
Ryder, Winona . . . . Jan 93
Rylant, Cynthia . . . . Author V.1
Sabin, Albert . . . . Science V.1
Sachar, Louis . . . . Author V.6
Sacks, Oliver . . . . Science V.3
Sadat, Anwar . . . . WorLdr V.2
Sagan, Carl . . . . Science V.1
sailing
MacArthur, Ellen . . . . Sport V.11
Riley, Dawn . . . . Sport V.4
Sakic, Joe . . . . Sport V.6
Salinger, J.D. . . . . Author V.2
Salk, Jonas . . . . Jan 94; Update 95
Salt 'N' Pepa . . . . Apr 95
Sampras, Pete . . . . Jan 97; Update 02
Sanborn, Ryne . . . . Sport V.8
Sanchez, Ricardo . . . . Sep 04
Sanchez Vicario, Arantxa . . . . Sport V.1
Sanders, Barry . . . . Sep 95; Update 99
Sanders, Deion . . . . Sport V.1
Sandler, Adam . . . . Jan 06
Santana, Carlos . . . . Sep 05
Sapp, Warren . . . . Sport V.5
Saro-Wiwa, Ken . . . . WorLdr V.1
Satcher, David . . . . Sep 98
Saudi
bin Laden, Osama . . . . Apr 02
Savimbi, Jonas . . . . WorLdr V.2
Scalia, Antonin . . . . Jan 05
Scarry, Richard . . . . Sep 94
Schilling, Curt . . . . Sep 05
Schroeder, Pat . . . . Jan 97
Schulz, Charles M . . Author V.2; Update 00
Schwarzkopf, H. Norman . . . . Jan 92
Schwikert, Tasha . . . . Sport V.7
science competitions
Cohen, Adam Ezra . . . . Apr 97
Lisanti, Mariangela . . . . Sep 01

Patterson, Ryan. . . . . Science V.7
Pine, Elizabeth Michele. . . . . Jan 94
Risca, Viviana. . . . . Sep 00
Rosa, Emily . . . . Sep 98
Rubin, Jamie . . . . Science V.8
Toro, Natalia. . . . . Sep 99
Vasan, Nina. . . . . Science V.7
scientists
Alvarez, Luis W. . . . . Science V.3
Asimov, Isaac . . . . Jul 92
Askins, Renee. . . . . WorLdr V.1
Attenborough, David. . . . . Science V.4
Ballard, Robert . . . . Science V.4
Bardeen, John . . . . Science V.1
Barton, Hazel . . . . Science V.6
Berners-Lee, Tim . . . . Science V.7
Bethe, Hans A. . . . . Science V.3
Brundtland, Gro Harlem . . . . . . Science V.3
Calderone, Mary S.. . . . . Science V.3
Carson, Ben. . . . . Science V.4
Carson, Rachel . . . . WorLdr V.1
Collins, Francis . . . . Science V.6
Córdova, France . . . . Science V.7
Cray, Seymour . . . . Science V.2
Earle, Sylvia. . . . . Science V.1
Elion, Gertrude . . . . Science V.6
Engelbart, Douglas. . . . . Science V.5
Farmer, Paul, Jr. . . . . Science V.11
Fauci, Anthony S.. . . . . Science V.7
Fay, Michael . . . . Science V.9
Feynman, Richard P.. . . . . Science V.10
Fossey, Dian . . . . Science V.1
Galdikas, Biruté. . . . . Science V.4
Gayle, Helene . . . . Science V.8
Gilbert, Walter . . . . Science V.2
Goodall, Jane. . . . . . Science V.1; Update 02
Gould, Stephen Jay . . . . Science V.2;
   Update 02
Grandin, Temple . . . . Science V.3
Gwaltney, John Langston . . . . . Science V.3
Harris, Bernard . . . . Science V.3
Hawking, Stephen . . . . Apr 92
Hayes, Tyrone . . . . Science V.10
Healy, Bernadine . . . Science V.1; Update 01
Hendrickson, Sue. . . . . Science V.7
Ho, David . . . . Science V.6
Horner, Jack . . . . Science V.1
House, Donna . . . . Science V.11
Jackson, Shirley Ann . . . . Science V.2
Jemison, Mae. . . . . Oct 92
Kenyon, Cynthia. . . . . Science V.11
Kiessling, Laura L. . . . . Science V.9

King, Mary-Claire . . . . Science V.10
Koff, Clea. . . . . Science V.11
Krim, Mathilde . . . . Science V.1
Kübler-Ross, Elisabeth . . . . Science V.10
Kurzweil, Raymond . . . . Science V.2
Kwolek, Stephanie . . . . Science V.10
Leakey, Louis . . . . Science V.1
Leakey, Mary. . . . . Science V.1
Levi-Montalcini, Rita . . . . Science V.1
Long, Irene D. . . . . Jan 04
Love, Susan. . . . . Science V.3
Lowman, Meg. . . . . Science V.4
Lucid, Shannon . . . . Science V.2
Margulis, Lynn . . . . Sep 96
McClintock, Barbara. . . . . Oct 92
McNutt, Marcia. . . . . Science V.11
Mead, Margaret . . . . Science V.2
Mittermeier, Russell A. . . . . WorLdr V.1
Moss, Cynthia . . . . WorLdr V.3
Newsom, Lee Ann . . . . Science V.11
Ocampo, Adriana C. . . . . Science V.8
Ochoa, Severo . . . . Jan 94
Oppenheimer, J. Robert. . . . . . . Science V.1
Patrick, Ruth . . . . Science V.3
Pauling, Linus . . . . Jan 95
Ride, Sally. . . . . Jan 92
Rodriguez, Eloy. . . . . Science V.2
Sabin, Albert . . . . Science V.1
Sacks, Oliver . . . . Science V.3
Sagan, Carl . . . . Science V.1
Salk, Jonas . . . . Jan 94; Update 95
Satcher, David . . . . Sep 98
Spelke, Elizabeth. . . . . Science V.10
Steingraber, Sandra . . . . Science V.9
Tarter, Jill . . . . Science V.8
Teller, Edward. . . . . Science V.9
Thomas, Lewis . . . . Apr 94
Tuttle, Merlin. . . . . Apr 97
Tyson, Neil deGrasse. . . . . Science V.11
Villa-Komaroff, Lydia . . . . Science V.6
Wadhwa, Meenakshi. . . . . Science V.11
Warrick, Earl . . . . Science V.8
Watson, James D. . . . . Science V.1
Whitson, Peggy. . . . . Science V.9
Wilson, Edward O. . . . . Science V.8
Scieszka, Jon. . . . . Author V.9
Scott, Jerry . . . . Author V.15
Scottish
Glennie, Evelyn. . . . . PerfArt V.3
Muir, John. . . . . WorLdr V.3

screenwriters
  Affleck, Ben. . . . . Sep 99
  Carter, Chris. . . . . Author V.4
  Crichton, Michael . . . . Author V.5
  Jackson, Peter . . . . PerfArt V.2
  Mathison, Melissa. . . . . Author V.4
  Peet, Bill . . . . Author V.4
  Whedon, Joss . . . . Author V.9
  Williamson, Kevin. . . . . Author V.6
sculptors
  see artists
Scurry, Briana . . . . Jan 00
Sealfon, Rebecca . . . . Sep 97
Seinfeld, Jerry. . . . . Oct 92; Update 98
Selena . . . . Jan 96
Seles, Monica. . . . . Jan 96
senators
  Clinton, Hillary Rodham. . . . . Apr 93;
    Update 94; Update 95; Update 96; Update
    99; Update 00; Update 01
  Dole, Bob . . . . Jan 96; Update 96
  Glenn, John . . . . Jan 99
  Gore, Al . . . . . Jan 93; Update 96; Update 97;
    Update 98; Update 99; Update 00; Update
    01
  McCain, John . . . . Apr 00
  Nelson, Gaylord. . . . . WorLdr V.3
  Nixon, Richard . . . . Sep 94
Sendak, Maurice. . . . . Author V.2
Senegalese
  Senghor, Léopold Sédar . . . . . . WorLdr V.2
Senghor, Léopold Sédar . . . . . . WorLdr V.2
Serbian
  Milosevic, Slobodan . . . Sep 99; Update 00;
    Update 01; Update 02
Seuss, Dr. . . . . Jan 92
Shabazz, Betty . . . . Apr 98
Shakira . . . . PerfArt V.1
Shakur, Tupac . . . . Apr 97
Sharapova, Maria. . . . . Sep 05
Shatner, William . . . . Apr 95
Shea, Jim, Jr.. . . . . Sport V.8
Shinoda, Mike
  see Linkin Park. . . . . Jan 04
Shula, Don . . . . Apr 96
Silva, Fabiola da
  see da Silva, Fabiola . . . . Sport V.9
Silverstein, Shel . . . . Author V.3; Update 99
Simmons, Russell . . . . Apr 06
Simmons, Ruth . . . . Sep 02
Simpson, Ashlee . . . . Sep 05

Sinatra, Frank . . . . Jan 99
singers
  see music
Singh, Vijay . . . . Sport V.13
Siskel, Gene . . . . Sep 99
skateboarding
  Hawk, Tony. . . . . Apr 01
skating (ice)
  Baiul, Oksana . . . . Apr 95
  Blair, Bonnie . . . . Apr 94; Update 95
  Cohen, Sasha . . . . Sport V.12
  Harding, Tonya. . . . . Sep 94
  Hughes, Sarah . . . . Jan 03
  Jansen, Dan. . . . . Apr 94
  Kerrigan, Nancy . . . . Apr 94
  Kwan, Michelle. . . . . . Sport V.3; Update 02
  Lipinski, Tara. . . . . Apr 98
  Ohno, Apolo. . . . . Sport V.8
  Yamaguchi, Kristi . . . . Apr 92
skating (in-line)
  da Silva, Fabiola . . . . Sport V.9
skeleton
  Shea, Jim, Jr. . . . . Sport V.8
skiing
  Amman, Simon . . . . Sport V.8
  Arnesen, Liv. . . . . Author V.15
  Bahrke, Shannon . . . . Sport V.8
  Moseley, Jonny. . . . . Sport V.8
  Street, Picabo . . . . Sport V.3
Sleator, William . . . . Author V.11
sled-dog racing
  Butcher, Susan . . . . Sport V.1
  Zirkle, Aliy. . . . . Sport V.6
Small, David . . . . Author V.10
Smith, Betty . . . . Author V.17
Smith, Emmitt . . . . Sep 94
Smith, Will . . . . Sep 94
Smyers, Karen . . . . Sport V.4
Snicket, Lemony. . . . . Author V.12
snowboarding
  Basich, Tina. . . . . Sport V.12
  Bleiler, Gretchen. . . . . Sport V.13
  Clark, Kelly . . . . Sport V.8
  Dakides, Tara . . . . Sport V.7
  Klug, Chris . . . . Sport V.8
Snyder, Zilpha Keatley . . . . . . Author V.17
soccer
  Adu, Freddy . . . . Sport V.12
  Beckham, David. . . . . Jan 04
  Chastain, Brandi. . . . . Sport V.4; Update 00
  Foudy, Julie . . . . Sport V.13

Hamm, Mia. . . . . Sport V.2; Update 00
Howard, Tim. . . . . Apr 06
Lalas, Alexi . . . . Sep 94
Mathis, Clint . . . . Apr 03
Milbrett, Tiffeny . . . . Sport V.10
Pelé . . . . Sport V.1
Scurry, Briana. . . . . Jan 00
softball
Fernandez, Lisa . . . . Sport V.5
Finch, Jennie. . . . . Jan 05
Richardson, Dot . . . . . Sport V.2; Update 00
Watley, Natasha. . . . . Sport V.11
Somalian
Aidid, Mohammed Farah . . . . . WorLdr V.2
Sones, Sonya. . . . . Author V.11
Soren, Tabitha. . . . . Jan 97
Sorenstam, Annika. . . . . Sport V.6
Soriano, Alfonso . . . . Sport V.10
Sosa, Sammy . . . . Jan 99; Update 99
Soto, Gary . . . . Author V.5
South Africans
de Klerk, F.W. . . . . Apr 94; Update 94
Mandela, Nelson. . . . . . . Jan 92; Update 94;
Update 01
Mandela, Winnie . . . . WorLdr V.2
South Korean
Pak, Se Ri . . . . Sport V.4
Spaniards
Domingo, Placido. . . . . Sep 95
Garcia, Sergio . . . . Sport V.7
Iglesias, Enrique. . . . . Jan 03
Sanchez Vicario, Arantxa . . . . Sport V.1
Speare, Elizabeth George. . . . . Sep 95
Spears, Britney . . . . Jan 01
Spelke, Elizabeth . . . . Science V.10
spelling bee competition
Andrews, Ned. . . . . Sep 94
Guey, Wendy . . . . Sep 96
Hooper, Geoff . . . . Jan 94
Maxwell, Jody-Anne . . . . Sep 98
Sealfon, Rebecca. . . . . Sep 97
Thampy, George. . . . . Sep 00
Spelman, Lucy . . . . Science V.6
Spencer, Diana
see Diana, Princess of Wales. . . . . Jul 92;
Update 96; Update 97; Jan 98
Spiegelman, Art . . . . Author V.17
Spielberg, Steven. . . . . . . Jan 94; Update 94;
Update 95
Spinelli, Jerry . . . . Apr 93
Spock, Dr. Benjamin. . . . Sep 95; Update 98

sports
Aaron, Hank. . . . . Sport V.1
Abdul-Jabbar, Kareem. . . . . Sport V.1
Adu, Freddy . . . . Sport V.12
Agassi, Andre . . . . Jul 92
Aikman, Troy. . . . . Apr 95; Update 01
Ali, Laila . . . . Sport V.11
Ali, Muhammad. . . . . Sport V.2
Allen, Marcus . . . . Sep 97
Allen, Tori . . . . Sport V.9
Ammann, Simon . . . . Sport V.8
Andretti, Mario. . . . . Sep 94
Armstrong, Lance. . . . . . Sep 00; Update 00;
Update 01; Update 02
Ashe, Arthur . . . . Sep 93
Bahrke, Shannon . . . . Sport V.8
Bailey, Donovan. . . . . Sport V.2
Baiul, Oksana . . . . Apr 95
Barkley, Charles . . . . Apr 92; Update 02
Basich, Tina. . . . . Sport V.12
Beachley, Layne . . . . Sport V.9
Beckett, Josh . . . . Sport V.11
Beckham, David. . . . . Jan 04
Bird, Larry. . . . . Jan 92; Update 98
Bird, Sue . . . . Sport V.9
Blair, Bonnie . . . . Apr 94
Bleiler, Gretchen. . . . . Sport V.13
Bonds, Barry. . . . . Jan 03
Boulmerka, Hassiba. . . . . Sport V.1
Boyle, Ryan . . . . Sport V.10
Brady, Tom . . . . Sport V.7
Bryant, Kobe . . . . Apr 99
Butcher, Susan . . . . Sport V.1
Capolino, Peter. . . . . Business V.1
Capriati, Jennifer . . . . Sport V.6
Carter, Vince . . . . Sport V.5; Update 01
Chamberlain, Wilt . . . . Sport V.4
Chastain, Brandi. . . . . Sport V.4; Update 00
Clark, Kelly . . . . Sport V.8
Clijsters, Kim. . . . . Apr 04
Cohen, Sasha . . . . Sport V.12
Coughlin, Natalie. . . . . Sport V.10
Cox, Lynne . . . . Sport V.13
Culpepper, Daunte . . . . Sport V.13
Dakides, Tara . . . . Sport V.7
Daniel, Beth . . . . Sport V.1
da Silva, Fabiola . . . . Sport V.9
Davenport, Lindsay . . . . Sport V.5
Dayne, Ron . . . . Apr 00
Devers, Gail . . . . Sport V.2
Dragila, Stacy . . . . Sport V.6

Driscoll, Jean . . . . Sep 97
Dumars, Joe . . . . Sport V.3; Update 99
Duncan, Tim . . . . Apr 04
Dunlap, Alison . . . . Sport V.7
Earnhardt, Dale . . . . Apr 01
Earnhardt, Dale, Jr. . . . . Sport V.12
Elway, John . . . . Sport V.2; Update 99
Evans, Janet . . . . Jan 95
Evert, Chris . . . . Sport V.1
Ewing, Patrick . . . . Jan 95; Update 02
Favre, Brett . . . . Sport V.2
Fedorov, Sergei . . . . Apr 94; Update 94
Felix, Allyson . . . . Sport V.10
Fernandez, Lisa . . . . Sport V.5
Finch, Jennie . . . . Jan 05
Flowers, Vonetta . . . . Sport V.8
Ford, Cheryl . . . . Sport V.11
Foudy, Julie . . . . Sport V.13
Freeman, Cathy . . . . Jan 01
Friday, Dallas . . . . Sport V.10
Fu Mingxia . . . . Sport V.5
Garcia, Sergio . . . . Sport V.7
Garnett, Kevin . . . . Sport V.6
George, Eddie . . . . Sport V.6
Giguère, Jean-Sébastien . . . . Sport V.10
Gonzalez, Tony . . . . Sport V.11
Gordon, Jeff . . . . Apr 99
Graf, Steffi . . . . Jan 92; Update 01
Granato, Cammi . . . . Sport V.8
Gretzky, Wayne . . . . Jan 92; Update 93;
    Update 99
Griese, Brian . . . . Jan 02
Griffey, Ken, Jr. . . . . Sport V.1
Griffith Joyner, Florence . . . . Sport V.1;
    Update 98
Hamilton, Bethany . . . . Apr 05
Hamilton, Laird . . . . Sport V.13
Hamm, Mia . . . . Sport V.2; Update 00
Harbaugh, Jim . . . . Sport V.3
Hardaway, Anfernee "Penny" . . . Sport V.2
Harding, Tonya . . . . Sep 94
Hasek, Dominik . . . . Sport V.3
Hawk, Tony . . . . Apr 01
Hernandez, Livan . . . . Apr 98
Hill, Grant . . . . Sport V.1
Hingis, Martina . . . . Sport V.2
Hogan, Hulk . . . . Apr 92
Holdsclaw, Chamique . . . . Sep 00
Holmes, Priest . . . . Apr 05
Howard, Tim . . . . Apr 06
Howe, Gordie . . . . Sport V.2

Hughes, Sarah . . . . Jan 03
Iverson, Allen . . . . Sport V.7
Jackson, Bo . . . . Jan 92; Update 93
Jackson, Phil . . . . Sport V.10
Jagr, Jaromir . . . . Sport V.5
James, LeBron . . . . Sport V.12
Jansen, Dan . . . . Apr 94
Jeter, Derek . . . . Sport V.4
Johnson, Jimmy . . . . Jan 98
Johnson, Keyshawn . . . . Sport V.10
Johnson, Magic . . . . Apr 92; Update 02
Johnson, Michael . . . . . . Jan 97; Update 00
Johnson, Randy . . . . Sport V.9
Jones, Marion . . . . Sport V.5
Jordan, Michael . . . . Jan 92; Update 93;
    Update 94; Update 95; Update 99; Update
    01
Joyner-Kersee, Jackie . . . . . . Oct 92; Update
    96; Update 97; Update 98
Kerrigan, Nancy . . . . Apr 94
Kidd, Jason . . . . Sport V.9
Kiraly, Karch . . . . Sport V.4
Klug, Chris . . . . Sport V.8
Kwan, Michelle . . . . . . Sport V.3; Update 02
Lalas, Alexi . . . . Sep 94
Lee, Jeanette . . . . Apr 03
Lemieux, Mario . . . . Jul 92; Update 93
LeMond, Greg . . . . Sport V.1
Lennox, Betty . . . . Sport V.13
Leslie, Lisa . . . . Jan 04
Lewis, Carl . . . . Sep 96; Update 97
Lidstrom, Nicklas . . . . Sep 03
Lipinski, Tara . . . . Apr 98
Lobo, Rebecca . . . . Sport V.3
Lowe, Alex . . . . Sport V.4
MacArthur, Ellen . . . . Sport V.11
Madden, John . . . . Sep 97
Maddux, Greg . . . . Sport V.3
Manning, Peyton . . . . Sep 00
Mantle, Mickey . . . . Jan 96
Marino, Dan . . . . Apr 93; Update 00
Martinez, Pedro . . . . Sport V.5
Mathis, Clint . . . . Apr 03
McGrady, Tracy . . . . Sport V.11
McGwire, Mark . . . . Jan 99; Update 99
McNabb, Donovan . . . . Apr 03
McNair, Steve . . . . Sport V.11
Messier, Mark . . . . Apr 96
Milbrett, Tiffeny . . . . Sport V.10
Miller, Shannon . . . . Sep 94; Update 96
Mirra, Dave . . . . Sep 02

Moceanu, Dominique . . . . Jan 98
Montana, Joe . . . . Jan 95; Update 95
Moreno, Arturo R. . . . . Business V.1
Moseley, Jonny . . . . Sport V.8
Moss, Randy . . . . Sport V.4
Muldowney, Shirley . . . . Sport V.7
Murray, Ty . . . . Sport V.7
Nash, Steve . . . . Jan 06
Navratilova, Martina . . . . Jan 93; Update 94
Newman, Ryan . . . . Sport V.11
Ndeti, Cosmas . . . . Sep 95
Nicklaus, Jack . . . . Sport V.2
Ohno, Apolo . . . . Sport V.8
Olajuwon, Hakeem . . . . Sep 95
O'Neal, Shaquille . . . . Sep 93
Otto, Sylke . . . . Sport V.8
Pak, Se Ri . . . . Sport V.4
Palmer, Violet . . . . Sep 05
Patrick, Danica . . . . Apr 06
Patterson, Carly . . . . Sport V.12
Payton, Walter . . . . Jan 00
Pelé . . . . Sport V.1
Petty, Richard . . . . Sport V.2
Phelps, Michael . . . . Sport V.13
Pippen, Scottie . . . . Oct 92
Pippig, Uta . . . . Sport V.1
Pujols, Albert . . . . Sport V.12
Ramirez, Manny . . . . Sport V.13
Rice, Jerry . . . . Apr 93
Richardson, Dot . . . . . Sport V.2; Update 00
Riley, Dawn . . . . Sport V.4
Ripken, Cal, Jr. . . . . . . Sport V.1; Update 01
Roba, Fatuma . . . . Sport V.3
Robinson, David . . . . Sep 96
Robinson, Jackie . . . . Sport V.3
Roddick, Andy . . . . Jan 03
Rodman, Dennis . . . . Apr 96; Update 99
Rodriguez, Alex . . . . Sport V.6
Rose, Pete . . . . Jan 92
Roy, Patrick . . . . Sport V.7
Rudolph, Wilma . . . . Apr 95
Runyan, Marla . . . . Apr 02
Ryan, Nolan . . . . Oct 92; Update 93
Sakic, Joe . . . . Sport V.6
Sampras, Pete . . . . Jan 97; Update 02
Sanchez Vicario, Arantxa . . . . Sport V.1
Sanders, Barry . . . . Sep 95; Update 99
Sanders, Deion . . . . Sport V.1
Sapp, Warren . . . . Sport V.5
Schilling, Curt . . . . Sep 05
Schwikert, Tasha . . . . Sport V.7

Scurry, Briana . . . . Jan 00
Seles, Monica . . . . Jan 96
Sharapova, Maria . . . . Sep 05
Shea, Jim, Jr. . . . . Sport V.8
Shula, Don . . . . Apr 96
Singh, Vijay . . . . Sport V.13
Smith, Emmitt . . . . Sep 94
Smyers, Karen . . . . Sport V.4
Sorenstam, Annika . . . . Sport V.6
Soriano, Alfonso . . . . Sport V.10
Sosa, Sammy . . . . Jan 99; Update 99
Stewart, Kordell . . . . Sep 98
Stewart, Tony . . . . Sport V.9
Stiles, Jackie . . . . Sport V.6
Stockton, John . . . . Sport V.3
Strahan, Michael . . . . Sport V.12
Street, Picabo . . . . Sport V.3
Streeter, Tanya . . . . Sport V.11
Summitt, Pat . . . . Sport V.3
Swoopes, Sheryl . . . . Sport V.2
Taurasi, Diana . . . . Sport V.10
Thompson, Jenny . . . . Sport V.5
Urlacher, Brian . . . . Sep 04
Van Dyken, Amy . . . . Sport V.3; Update 00
Ventura, Jesse . . . . Apr 99; Update 02
Vernon, Mike . . . . Jan 98; Update 02
Vick, Michael . . . . Sport V.9
Villa, Brenda . . . . Jan 06
Wallace, Ben . . . . Jan 05
Walsh, Kerri . . . . Sport V.13
Ward, Charlie . . . . Apr 94
Warner, Kurt . . . . Sport V.4
Watley, Natasha . . . . Sport V.11
Weathersoon, Teresa . . . . Sport V.12
Webb, Alan . . . . Sep 01
Webb, Karrie . . . . Sport V.5; Update 01;
   Update 02
Weinke, Chris . . . . Apr 01
White, Reggie . . . . Jan 98
Wie, Michelle . . . . Sep 04
Williams, Serena . . . . Sport V.4; Update 00;
   Update 02
Williams, Ted . . . . Sport V.9
Williams, Venus . . . . Jan 99; Update 00;
   Update 01; Update 02
Willingham, Tyrone . . . . Sep 02
Winfield, Dave . . . . Jan 93
Woods, Tiger . . . . Sport V.1; Update 00;
   Sport V.6
Yamaguchi, Kristi . . . . Apr 92

Yao Ming . . . . Sep 03
Yelas, Jay . . . . Sport V.9
Young, Steve . . . . Jan 94; Update 00
Yzerman, Steve. . . . . Sport V.2
Zirkle, Aliy. . . . . Sport V.6
Zmeskal, Kim. . . . . Jan 94
Stachowski, Richie . . . . Science V.3
Stanford, John . . . . Sep 99
Stefani, Gwen. . . . . Sep 03
Steinem, Gloria . . . . Oct 92
Steingraber, Sandra . . . . Science V.9
Stern, Isaac. . . . . PerfArt V.1
Stewart, Jon . . . . Jan 06
Stewart, Kordell . . . . Sep 98
Stewart, Martha . . . . Business V.1
Stewart, Patrick. . . . . Jan 94
Stewart, Tony. . . . . Sport V.9
Stiles, Jackie . . . . Sport V.6
Stiles, Julia. . . . . PerfArt V.2
Stine, R.L. . . . . Apr 94
Stockman, Shawn
    see Boyz II Men. . . . . Jan 96
Stockton, John . . . . Sport V.3
Stoker, Joscelyn
    see Stone, Joss. . . . . Jan 06
Stone, Joss. . . . . Jan 06
Strahan, Michael . . . . Sport V.12
Strasser, Todd . . . . Author V.7
Street, Picabo . . . . Sport V.3
Streeter, Tanya. . . . . Sport V.11
Strug, Kerri . . . . Sep 96
Summitt, Pat. . . . . Sport V.3
Supreme Court
    Blackmun, Harry . . . . Jan 00
    Burger, Warren . . . . Sep 95
    Ginsburg, Ruth Bader . . . . Jan 94
    Marshall, Thurgood. . . . . Jan 92; Update 93
    O'Connor, Sandra Day . . . . Jul 92
    Scalia, Antonin. . . . . Jan 05
    Thomas, Clarence . . . . Jan 92
surfing
    Beachley, Layne . . . . Sport V.9
    Hamilton, Bethany . . . . Apr 05
    Hamilton, Laird . . . . Sport V.13
Suzuki, Shinichi . . . . Sep 98
Swanson, Janese . . . . Science V.4
Swedish
    Lidstrom, Nicklas . . . . Sep 03
    Lindgren, Astrid . . . . Author V.13
    Sorenstam, Annika . . . . Sport V.6

swimming
    Coughlin, Natalie. . . . . Sport V.10
    Cox, Lynne . . . . Sport V.13
    Evans, Janet . . . . Jan 95; Update 96
    Phelps, Michael . . . . Sport V.13
    Thompson, Jenny. . . . . Sport V.5
    Van Dyken, Amy . . . . Sport V.3; Update 00
Swiss
    Ammann, Simon . . . . Sport V.8
    Kübler-Ross, Elisabeth . . . . Science V.10
Swoopes, Sheryl . . . . Sport V.2
Taboo (Jamie Gomez)
    see Black Eyed Peas. . . . . Apr 06
Taiwanese
    Ho, David . . . . Science V.6
Tan, Amy. . . . . Author V.9
Tanzanian
    Nyerere, Julius Kambarage . . . WorLdr V.2;
    Update 99
Tarbox, Katie. . . . . Author V.10
Tartakovsky, Genndy . . . . Author V.11
Tartar
    Nureyev, Rudolph . . . . Apr 93
Tarter, Jill . . . . Science V.8
Tarvin, Herbert . . . . Apr 97
Taurasi, Diana . . . . Sport V.10
Taylor, Mildred D. . . . . Author V.1;
    Update 02
Taymor, Julie . . . . PerfArt V.1
teachers
    see educators
television
    Alba, Jessica. . . . . Sep 01
    Allen, Tim . . . . Apr 94; Update 99
    Alley, Kirstie . . . . Jul 92
    Amanpour, Christiane . . . . Jan 01
    Anderson, Gillian . . . . Jan 97
    Aniston, Jennifer. . . . . Apr 99
    Arnold, Roseanne. . . . . Oct 92
    Attenborough, David . . . . Science V.4
    Banks, Tyra . . . . PerfArt V.2
    Bell, Kristen . . . . Sep 05
    Bergen, Candice . . . . Sep 93
    Bialik, Mayim . . . . Jan 94
    Blanchard, Rachel. . . . . Apr 97
    Bledel, Alexis . . . . Jan 03
    Brandis, Jonathan . . . . Sep 95
    Brandy . . . . Apr 96
    Brody, Adam . . . . Sep 05
    Bryan, Zachery Ty . . . . Jan 97
    Burke, Chris. . . . . Sep 93

Burns, Ken . . . . Jan 95
Bynes, Amanda . . . . Sep 03
Cameron, Candace . . . . Apr 95
Campbell, Neve . . . . Apr 98
Candy, John . . . . Sep 94
Cantore, Jim . . . . Science V.9
Carter, Chris . . . . Author V.4
Carvey, Dana . . . . Jan 93
Chung, Connie . . . . Jan 94; Update 95; Update 96
Clarkson, Kelly . . . . Jan 03
Cosby, Bill . . . . Jan 92
Cousteau, Jacques . . . . Jan 93
Crawford, Cindy . . . . Apr 93
Crichton, Michael . . . . Author V.5
Daly, Carson . . . . Apr 00
Doherty, Shannen . . . . . Apr 92; Update 94
Duchovny, David . . . . Apr 96
Duff, Hilary . . . . Sep 02
Ellerbee, Linda . . . . Apr 94
Eve . . . . Jan 05
Fuentes, Daisy . . . . Jan 94
Garth, Jennie . . . . Apr 96
Gellar, Sarah Michelle . . . . Jan 99
Gilbert, Sara . . . . Apr 93
Goldberg, Whoopi . . . . Apr 94
Goodman, John . . . . Sep 95
Groening, Matt . . . . Jan 92
Gumbel, Bryant . . . . Apr 97
Guy, Jasmine . . . . Sep 93
Hart, Melissa Joan . . . . Jan 94
Hewitt, Jennifer Love . . . . Sep 00
Holmes, Katie . . . . Jan 00
Hunter-Gault, Charlayne . . . . Jan 00
Irwin, Steve . . . . Science V.7
Jennings, Peter . . . . Jul 92
Jones, Quincy . . . . PerfArt V.2
Kratt, Chris . . . . Science V.10
Kratt, Martin
Kutcher, Ashton . . . . Apr 04
Leno, Jay . . . . Jul 92
Letterman, David . . . . Jan 95
Lewis, Shari . . . . Jan 99
Limbaugh, Rush . . . . Sep 95; Update 02
Locklear, Heather . . . . Jan 95
López, George . . . . PerfArt V.2
Mac, Bernie . . . . PerfArt V.1
Madden, John . . . . Sep 97
McGrath, Judy . . . . Business V.1
Muniz, Frankie . . . . Jan 01
Myers, Mike . . . . PerfArt V.3

Nye, Bill . . . . Science V.2
O'Donnell, Rosie . . . . . . Apr 97; Update 02
Oleynik, Larisa . . . . Sep 96
Olsen, Ashley . . . . Sep 95
Olsen, Mary Kate . . . . Sep 95
Pauley, Jane . . . . Oct 92
Perry, Luke . . . . Jan 92
Priestley, Jason . . . . Apr 92
Probst, Jeff . . . . Jan 01
Ramos, Jorge . . . . Apr 06
Raven . . . . Apr 04
Roberts, Cokie . . . . Apr 95
Rogers, Fred . . . . PerfArt V.3
Romeo, Lil' . . . . Jan 06
Sagan, Carl . . . . Science V.1
Seinfeld, Jerry . . . . Oct 92; Update 98
Shatner, William . . . . Apr 95
Simpson, Ashlee . . . . Sep 05
Siskel, Gene . . . . Sep 99
Smith, Will . . . . Sep 94
Soren, Tabitha . . . . Jan 97
Stewart, Jon . . . . Jan 06
Stewart, Martha . . . . Business V.1
Stewart, Patrick . . . . Jan 94
Tartakovsky, Genndy . . . . Author V.11
Thiessen, Tiffani-Amber . . . . Jan 96
Thomas, Jonathan Taylor . . . . Apr 95
Trump, Donald . . . . Apr 05
Tyson, Neil deGrasse . . . . Science V.11
Vidal, Christina . . . . PerfArt V.1
Walters, Barbara . . . . Sep 94
Watson, Barry . . . . Sep 02
Wayans, Keenen Ivory . . . . Jan 93
Welling, Tom . . . . PerfArt V.3
Whedon, Joss . . . . Author V.9
White, Jaleel . . . . Jan 96
Williams, Robin . . . . Apr 92
Williamson, Kevin . . . . Author V.6
Winfrey, Oprah . . . . Apr 92; Update 00; Business V.1
Zamora, Pedro . . . . Apr 95
Teller, Edward . . . . Science V.9
tennis
Agassi, Andre . . . . Jul 92
Ashe, Arthur . . . . Sep 93
Capriati, Jennifer . . . . Sport V.6
Clijsters, Kim . . . . Apr 04
Davenport, Lindsay . . . . Sport V.5
Evert, Chris . . . . Sport V.1
Graf, Steffi . . . . Jan 92; Update 01
Hingis, Martina . . . . Sport V.2

For cumulative places of birth and birthday indexes, please see biographytoday.com.

Navratilova, Martina . . . . Jan 93; Update 94
Roddick, Andy . . . . Jan 03
Sampras, Pete . . . . Jan 97; Update 02
Sanchez Vicario, Arantxa . . . . Sport V.1
Seles, Monica . . . . Jan 96
Sharapova, Maria . . . . Sep 05
Williams, Serena . . . . Sport V.4; Update 00;
    Update 02
Williams, Venus . . . . Jan 99; Update 00;
    Update 01; Update 02
Tenzin Gyatso
   see Dalai Lama . . . . Sep 98
Teresa, Mother . . . . Apr 98
Thampy, George . . . . Sep 00
Tharp, Twyla . . . . PerfArt V.3
Thich Nhat Hahn
   see Nhat Hanh (Thich) . . . . Jan 04
Thiessen, Tiffani-Amber . . . . Jan 96
Thomas, Clarence . . . . Jan 92
Thomas, Dave . . . . Apr 96; Update 02
Thomas, Jonathan Taylor . . . . Apr 95
Thomas, Lewis . . . . Apr 94
Thompson, Jenny . . . . Sport V.5
Tibetan
   Dalai Lama . . . . Sep 98
Timberlake, Justin
   see *N Sync . . . . Jan 01
Tolan, Stephanie S. . . . . Author V.14
Tolkien, J.R.R. . . . . Jan 02
Tompkins, Douglas . . . . WorLdr V.3
Toro, Natalia . . . . Sep 99
Torvalds, Linus . . . . Science V.11
track
   Bailey, Donovan . . . . Sport V.2
   Devers, Gail . . . . Sport V.2
   Dragila, Stacy . . . . Sport V.6
   Griffith Joyner, Florence . . . . Sport V.1;
      Update 98
   Felix, Allyson . . . . Sport V.10
   Freeman, Cathy . . . . Jan 01
   Johnson, Michael . . . . Jan 97; Update 00
   Jones, Marion . . . . Sport V.5
   Joyner-Kersee, Jackie . . . . . . Oct 92; Update
      96; Update 97; Update 98
   Lewis, Carl . . . . Sep 96; Update 97
   Rudolph, Wilma . . . . Apr 95
   Runyan, Marla . . . . Apr 02
Travers, P.L. . . . . Author V.2
Tré Cool (Frank Edwin Wright III)
   see Black Eyed Peas . . . . Apr 06

triathalon
   Smyers, Karen . . . . Sport V.4
Trinidadian
   Guy, Rosa . . . . Author V.9
Trump, Donald . . . . Apr 05
Tubman, William V. S. . . . . WorLdr V.2
Tucker, Chris . . . . Jan 01
Tuttle, Merlin . . . . Apr 97
Twain, Shania . . . . Apr 99
Tyson, Neil deGrasse . . . . Science V.11
Uchida, Mitsuko . . . . Apr 99
Ugandan
   Amin, Idi . . . . WorLdr V.2
Ukrainians
   Baiul, Oksana . . . . Apr 95
   Stern, Isaac . . . . PerfArt V.1
United Nations
  – **Ambassadors to**
   Albright, Madeleine . . . . Apr 97
   Bush, George . . . . Jan 92
  – **Secretaries General**
   Annan, Kofi . . . . Jan 98; Update 01
   Boutros-Ghali, Boutros . . . . Apr 93;
      Update 98
United States
  – **Attorney General**
   Reno, Janet . . . . Sep 93; Update 98
  – **Centers for Disease Control**
   Gayle, Helene . . . . Science V.8
   Gerberding, Julie . . . . Science V.10
  – **First Ladies**
   Bush, Barbara . . . . Jan 92
   Bush, Laura . . . . Apr 03
   Clinton, Hillary Rodham . . . . Apr 93;
      Update 94; Update 95; Update 96; Update
      99; Update 00; Update 01
  – **Joint Chiefs of Staff, Chairman**
   Powell, Colin . . . . Jan 92; Update 93;
      Update 95; Update 01
  – **National Institutes of Health**
   Collins, Francis . . . . Science V.6
   Fauci, Anthony S. . . . . Science V.7
   Healy, Bernadine . . . . Science V.1;
      Update 01
  – **National Security Advisor**
   Rice, Condoleezza . . . . Apr 02
  – **Nuclear Regulatory Commission**
   Jackson, Shirley Ann . . . . Science V.2
  – **Poet Laureates**
   Collins, Billy . . . . Author V.16
   Dove, Rita . . . . Jan 94
   Pinsky, Robert . . . . Author V.7

– Presidents
    Bush, George . . . . Jan 92
    Bush, George W.. . . . . Sep 00; Update 00;
        Update 01; Update 02
    Carter, Jimmy. . . . . . . Apr 95; Update 02
    Clinton, Bill . . . . Jul 92; Update 94;
        Update 95; Update 96; Update 97; Update
        98; Update 99; Update 00; Update 01
    Nixon, Richard. . . . . Sep 94
    Reagan, Ronald . . . . Sep 04
– Secretary of Commerce
    Brown, Ron . . . . Sep 96
– Secretary of Defense
    Cheney, Dick . . . . Jan 02
**– Secretary of Housing and
Urban Development**
    Cisneros, Henry. . . . . Sep 93
– Secretary of Interior
    Babbitt, Bruce . . . . Jan 94
– Secretary of Labor
    Dole, Elizabeth Hanford . . . . Jul 92;
        Update 96; Update 99
– Secretaries of State
    Albright, Madeleine . . . . Apr 97
    Baker, James. . . . . Oct 92
– Secretary of Transportation
    Dole, Elizabeth . . . . Jul 92; Update 96;
        Update 99
– Secretary of Treasury
    Baker, James. . . . . Oct 92
– Senate Majority Leader
    Dole, Bob. . . . . Jan 96; Update 96
**– Speaker of the House of
Representatives**
    Gingrich, Newt. . . . . . . Apr 95; Update 99
– Supreme Court Justices
    Blackmun, Harry . . . . Jan 00
    Burger, Warren . . . . Sep 95
    Ginsburg, Ruth Bader . . . . Jan 94
    Marshall, Thurgood . . . Jan 92; Update 93
    O'Connor, Sandra Day. . . . . Jul 92
    Scalia, Antonin . . . . Jan 05
    Thomas, Clarence. . . . . Jan 92
– Surgeons General
    Carmona, Richard . . . . Science V.8
    Novello, Antonia . . . . . Apr 92; Update 93
    Satcher, David . . . . Sep 98
– Vice-Presidents
    Bush, George . . . . Jan 92
    Cheney, Dick . . . . Jan 02

Gore, Al . . . . Jan 93; Update 96;
    Update 97; Update 98; Update 99; Up-
    date 00; Update 01
Nixon, Richard. . . . . Sep 94
Urlacher, Brian . . . . Sep 04
Usher. . . . . PerfArt V.1
Van Allsburg, Chris . . . . Apr 92
Van Draanen, Wendelin. . . . . . Author V.11
Van Dyken, Amy. . . . . Sport V.3; Update 00
Van Meter, Vicki . . . . Jan 95
Vasan, Nina . . . . Science V.7
Vega, Alexa . . . . Jan 04
Ventura, Jesse. . . . . Apr 99; Update 02
Vernon, Mike. . . . . Jan 98; Update 02
veterinarians
    Herriot, James . . . . Author V.1
    Spelman, Lucy . . . . Science V.6
Vice-Presidents
    Bush, George . . . . Jan 92
    Cheney, Dick . . . . Jan 02
    Gore, Al . . . . Jan 93; Update 96;
        Update 97; Update 98; Update 99; Update
        00; Update 01
    Nixon, Richard . . . . Sep 94
Vick, Michael. . . . . Sport V.9
Vidal, Christina . . . . PerfArt V.1
Vietnamese
    Nhat Hanh (Thich) . . . . Jan 04
Villa, Brenda . . . . Jan 06
Villa-Komaroff, Lydia . . . . Science V.6
Vincent, Mark
    see Diesel, Vin. . . . . Jan 03
Voigt, Cynthia . . . . Oct 92
volleyball
    Kiraly, Karch. . . . . Sport V.4
    Walsh, Kerri . . . . Sport V.13
Vonnegut, Kurt, Jr. . . . . Author V.1
Wa, Ka Hsaw
    see Ka Hsaw Wa. . . . . WorLdr V.3
Wadhwa, Meenakshi . . . . Science V.11
wakeboarder
    Friday, Dallas . . . . Sport V.10
Wallace, Ben . . . . Jan 05
Walsh, Kerri. . . . . Sport V.13
Walters, Barbara. . . . . Sep 94
Wang, An. . . . . Science V.2
Ward, Charlie . . . . Apr 94
Ward, Lloyd D. . . . . Jan 01
Warhol, Andy. . . . . Artist V.1
Warner, Kurt. . . . . Sport V.4
Warrick, Earl. . . . . Science V.8
Washington, Denzel . . . . Jan 93; Update 02

water polo
Villa, Brenda . . . . Jan 06
Watley, Natasha. . . . . Sport V.11
Watson, Barry . . . . Sep 02
Watson, Emma . . . . Apr 03
Watson, James D.. . . . . Science V.1
Watson, Paul . . . . WorLdr V.1
Watterson, Bill. . . . . Jan 92
Wayans, Keenen Ivory . . . . Jan 93
Weatherspoon, Teresa . . . . Sport V.12
Webb, Alan . . . . Sep 01
Webb, Karrie . . . . Sport V.5; Update 01;
Update 02
Weinke, Chris. . . . . Apr 01
Welling, Tom . . . . PerfArt V.3
Werbach, Adam . . . . WorLdr V.1
Whedon, Joss . . . . Author V.9
White, E.B. . . . . Author V.1
White, Jaleel. Jan 96
White, Reggie . . . . Jan 98
White, Ruth . . . . Author V.11
Whitestone, Heather . . . . Apr 95; Update 02
Whitman, Meg . . . . Sep 03
Whitson, Peggy . . . . Science V.9
Wie, Michelle . . . . Sep 04
Wilder, Laura Ingalls. . . . . Author V.3
WilderBrathwaite, Gloria . . . . . Science V.7
Wiles, Deborah. . . . . Author V.18
will.i.am (William Adams)
see Black Eyed Peas. . . . . Apr 06
Williams, Garth . . . . Author V.2
Williams, Lori Aurelia. . . . . . . Author V.16
Williams, Michelle
see Destiny's Child . . . . Apr 01
Williams, Robin. . . . . Apr 92
Williams, Serena . . . . Sport V.4; Update 00;
Update 02
Williams, Ted. . . . . Sport V.9
Williams, Venus. . . . . Jan 99; Update 00;
Update 01; Update 02
Williamson, Kevin. . . . . Author V.6
Willingham, Tyrone . . . . Sep 02
Wilson, August. . . . . Author V.4
Wilson, Edward O. . . . . Science V.8
Wilson, Mara . . . . Jan 97
Winans, CeCe. . . . . Apr 00
Winfield, Dave . . . . Jan 93
Winfrey, Oprah . . . . Apr 92; Update 00;
Business V.1
Winslet, Kate . . . . Sep 98
Witherspoon, Reese . . . . Apr 03

Wojtyla, Karol Josef
see John Paul II . . . . Oct 92; Update 94;
Update 95; Sep 05
Wolf, Hazel. . . . . WorLdr V.3
Wolff, Virginia Euwer . . . . Author V.13
Wood, Elijah . . . . Apr 02
Woods, Tiger. . . . . Sport V.1; Update 00;
Sport V.6
Woodson, Jacqueline . . . . Author V.7;
Update 01
Woo-Ping, Yuen
see Yuen Wo-Ping . . . . PerfArt V.3
Wo-Ping, Yuen
see Yuen Wo-Ping . . . . PerfArt V.3
World Wide Web
see Internet
Wortis, Avi
see Avi . . . . Jan 93
Wozniak, Steve . . . . Science V.5
Wrede, Patricia C.. . . . . Author V.7
wrestling
Hogan, Hulk . . . . Apr 92
Ventura, Jesse . . . . Apr 99; Update 02
Wright, Frank Edwin III (Tré Cool)
see Green Day . . . . Apr 06
Wright, Frank Lloyd. . . . . Artist V.1
Wright, Richard . . . . Author V.5
Wright, Will . . . . Apr 04
Yamaguchi, Kristi . . . . Apr 92
Yao Ming . . . . Sep 03
Yelas, Jay. . . . . Sport V.9
Yeltsin, Boris . . . . Apr 92; Update 93;
Update 95; Update 96; Update 98; Update 00
Yep, Laurence . . . . Author V.5
Yolen, Jane. . . . . Author V.7
Young, Steve . . . . Jan 94; Update 00
Yuen Wo-Ping. . . . . PerfArt V.3
Yzerman, Steve . . . . Sport V.2
Zairian
Mobutu Sese Seko . . . . WorLdr V.2;
Update 97
Zambian
Kaunda, Kenneth . . . . WorLdr V.2
Zamora, Pedro . . . . Apr 95
Zimbabwean
Mugabe, Robert . . . . WorLdr V.2
Zindel, Paul . . . . Author V.1; Update 02
Zirkle, Aliy . . . . Sport V.6
Zmeskal, Kim . . . . Jan 94

Biography Today

General Series

Biography Today **General Series** includes a unique combination of current biographical profiles that teachers and librarians — and the readers themselves — tell us are most appealing. The **General Series** is available as a 3-issue subscription; hardcover annual cumulation; or subscription plus cumulation.

Within the **General Series**, your readers will find a variety of sketches about:

- Authors
- Musicians
- Political leaders
- Sports figures
- Movie actresses & actors
- Cartoonists
- Scientists
- Astronauts
- TV personalities
- and the movers & shakers in many other fields!

"Biography Today will be useful in elementary and middle school libraries and in public library children's collections where there is a need for biographies of current personalities. High schools serving reluctant readers may also want to consider a subscription."
— *Booklist,* American Library Association

"Highly recommended for the young adult audience. Readers will delight in the accessible, energetic, tell-all style; teachers, librarians, and parents will welcome the clever format [and] intelligent and informative text. It should prove especially useful in motivating 'reluctant' readers or literate nonreaders."
— *MultiCultural Review*

"Written in a friendly, almost chatty tone, the profiles offer quick, objective information. While coverage of current figures makes *Biography Today* a useful reference tool, an appealing format and wide scope make it a fun resource to browse." — *School Library Journal*

"The best source for current information at a level kids can understand."
— Kelly Bryant, School Librarian, Carlton, OR

"Easy for kids to read. We love it! Don't want to be without it."
— Lynn McWhirter, School Librarian, Rockford, IL

ONE-YEAR SUBSCRIPTION
- 3 softcover issues, 6" x 9"
- Published in January, April, and September
- 1-year subscription, list price $62. **School and library price $60**
- 150 pages per issue
- 10 profiles per issue
- Contact sources for additional information
- Cumulative Names Index

HARDBOUND ANNUAL CUMULATION
- Sturdy 6" x 9" hardbound volume
- Published in December
- List price $69. **School and library price $62 per volume**
- 450 pages per volume
- 30 profiles — includes all profiles found in softcover issues for that calendar year
- Cumulative General Index

SUBSCRIPTION AND CUMULATION COMBINATION
- $99 for 3 softcover issues plus the hardbound volume

For Cumulative General, Places of Birth, and Birthday Indexes, please see www.biographytoday.com.

Biography Today

Subject Series

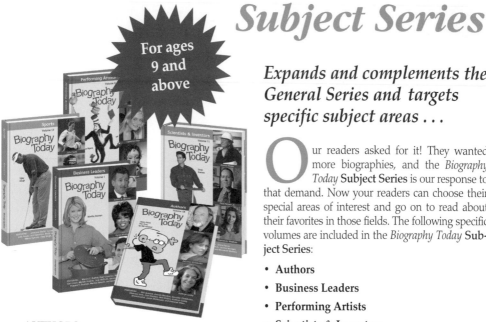

For ages 9 and above

Expands and complements the General Series and targets specific subject areas . . .

Our readers asked for it! They wanted more biographies, and the *Biography Today* **Subject Series** is our response to that demand. Now your readers can choose their special areas of interest and go on to read about their favorites in those fields. The following specific volumes are included in the *Biography Today* **Subject Series**:

- **Authors**
- **Business Leaders**
- **Performing Artists**
- **Scientists & Inventors**
- **Sports**

FEATURES AND FORMAT

- Sturdy 6" x 9" hardbound volumes
- Individual volumes, list price $44 each. **School and library price $39 each**
- 200 pages per volume
- 10 profiles per volume — targets individuals within a specific subject area
- Contact sources for additional information
- Cumulative General Index

For Cumulative General, Places of Birth, and Birthday Indexes, please see www.biographytoday.com.

NOTE: There is *no duplication of entries* between the **General Series** of *Biography Today* and the **Subject Series**.

AUTHORS

"A useful tool for children's assignment needs." — *School Library Journal*

"The prose is workmanlike: report writers will find enough detail to begin sound investigations, and browsers are likely to find someone of interest." — *School Library Journal*

SCIENTISTS & INVENTORS

"The articles are readable, attractively laid out, and touch on important points that will suit assignment needs. Browsers will note the clear writing and interesting details." — *School Library Journal*

"The book is excellent for demonstrating that scientists are real people with widely diverse backgrounds and personal interests. The biographies are fascinating to read." — *The Science Teacher*

SPORTS

"This series should become a standard resource in libraries that serve intermediate students." — *School Library Journal*

Order Annual Sets of *Biography Today* and Save Up to 20% Off the Regular Price!

Now, you can save time and money by purchasing *Biography Today* in Annual Sets! Save up to 20% off the regular price and get every single biography we publish in a year. Billed upon publication of the first volume, subsequent volumes are shipped throughout the year upon publication. Keep your *Biography Today* library current and complete with Annual Sets!

Place a standing order for annual sets and receive an additional 10% off!

Regular price $239
2006 or 2005 Annual Set $192
You Save $47

Biography Today 2006 Annual Set

7 volumes. 0-7808-0940-8. Annual set, $192. Includes:

2006 subscription (3 softcover issues);
2006 Hardbound Annual; Authors, Vol. 18;
Scientists & Inventors, Vol. 11; Sports, Vol. 14

Biography Today 2005 Annual Set

7 volumes. 0-7808-0782-0. Annual set, $192. Includes:

2005 subscription (3 softcover issues);
2005 Hardbound Annual; Authors, Vol. 17;
Scientists & Inventors, Vol. 10; Sports, Vol. 13

Regular price $335
2004 or 2003 Annual Set $268
You Save $67

Biography Today 2004 Annual Set

8 volumes. 0-7808-0731-6. Annual set, $268. Includes:

2004 Hardbound Annual; Authors, Vols. 15 and 16;
Business Leaders, Vol. 1; Performing Artists, Vol. 3;
Scientists & Inventors, Vol. 9; Sports, Vols. 11 and 12

Biography Today 2003 Annual Set

8 volumes. 0-7808-0730-8. Annual set, $268. Includes:

2003 Hardbound Annual; Authors, Vols. 13 and 14;
Performing Artists, Vols. 1 and 2;
Scientists & Inventors, Vol. 8; Sports, Vols. 9 and 10

Regular price $297
2002 Annual Set $237
You Save $60

Biography Today 2002 Annual Set

7 volumes. 0-7808-0729-4. Annual set, $237. Includes:

2002 Hardbound Annual; Authors, Vols. 11 and 12;
Scientists & Inventors, Vols. 6 and 7; Sports, Vols. 7 and 8